THE COMPLETE BRAIN WORKOUT

THE COMPLETE BRAIN WORKOUT

500 NEW PUZZLES TO EXERCISE YOUR BRAIN & MAXIMIZE YOUR MEMORY

MARCEL DANESI, Ph.D.

University of Toronto

THE COMPLETE BRAIN WORKOUT

ISBN-13: 978-0-373-89308-9

© 2015 by Marcel Danesi

Library of Congress Cataloging-in-Publication Data on file with the publisher.

www.Harlequin.com

Printed in China.

CONTENTS

INTRODUCTION

Who in the world am I? Ah, that's the great puzzle.

(LEWIS CARROLL, 1832–1898)

IN THE PAST FEW YEARS, neuroscience has provided a truly remarkable understanding of how the human brain works. Especially fascinating is the work on how certain kinds of activities lead to a "rewiring" of the brain. Puzzles seem to fall into this category.

This book will hopefully help stimulate the brain in specific ways. It constitutes a follow-up to my previous two books, *Total Brain Workout* and *Extreme Brain Workout,* concentrating on how puzzles can—at least in theory—stimulate certain areas of the brain. Puzzles are "brain foods" that boost brain function and support positive neuroplasticity (brainpower). If you are a newcomer to many of these puzzles, there is no need to worry. Each type of puzzle is explained fully beforehand. Responding to readers' input, I have created more of the same kinds of puzzles you found to be the most useful or interesting (riddles, anagrams, word searches, liar puzzles and so on). But I have also added other kinds of puzzles that I believe will help stimulate brain health. So, you will be getting more of the same—with a few twists and turns here and there—as well as many new kinds of puzzles.

Do puzzles contribute to brain health? Scientific answers to this question tend to be highly positive. As a researcher myself, I have written about this topic on my blog for *Psychology Today* and have maintained a cautiously skeptical stance on the issue. But I am shedding that skepticism. The research that is accumulating is rather convincing. The gist of the findings can be expressed with the dictum that "Puzzles are to brain health what physical exercise is to body health." Given the ancient origins of most puzzle genres, it is likely that this has always been the case. Puzzles have captured the fancy of many famous people, including Charlemagne, the founder of the Holy Roman Empire; Edgar Allan Poe, the famous American writer; Lewis Carroll, known for his two great children's books, *Alice's Adventures in Wonderland* and *Through the Looking-Glass*; and Benjamin Franklin, the American statesman and entrepreneur. Carroll is one of the greatest puzzle makers of all time. These people certainly had a lot of brainpower.

WHAT THE RESEARCH SAYS

Studies investigating the relationship between puzzles and IQ have shown that the two do not always correlate. Puzzles can be solved by all kinds of individuals, no matter what their IQs are. Some people are simply better at it than others. While this is true of anything in life, this is actually very good news. Simply put, you do not need a high IQ to solve the different kinds of puzzles in this book—all you need is perseverance.

Perhaps the most relevant finding of all the research is that the positive effects of puzzles in later life (from the late forties to the eighties and beyond) are independent of education, gender, ethnicity or social background. A few years ago, researchers from the Albert Einstein College of Medicine in New York found that people from all different walks and stages of life who performed a mental exercise twice a day could delay the rapid memory loss associated with dementia for more than a year. Keeping the brain active with mental hobbies such as crosswords, reading, writing and playing card games can postpone the start of dementia-related symptoms. No wonder, then, that puzzles stand out on the Mayo Clinic's website, which lists a set of steps that anyone can follow in order to keep the brain fit.

Research has also linked brain shrinkage to Alzheimer's disease. New studies show that physical exercise combined with puzzles of all kinds constitute a powerful strategy for preventing such shrinkage. A recent study in the *Archives of Neurology* claims to have found a link between playing games such as sudoku and decreased levels of a protein thought to cause Alzheimer's disease. Such games seem to help considerably.

The medical community is not sure why puzzles benefit the brain, but one theory suggests that they may keep brain cells healthy and less prone to disease or damage. Another theory is that puzzles may help build up what neurologists call "cognitive reserve," or the brain's ability to replace lost brain cells with new ones.

WHAT TO DO

When looked at cumulatively, the research is unequivocal—do all kinds of puzzles, even if you prefer one genre to the others, in order to keep your brain healthy. The purpose of this book is to get you to do exactly that.

Each chapter is organized around a specific brain function: memory, perception, cognition and so on. There are ten chapters consisting of fifty puzzles each, for a total of five hundred puzzles. You can actually read this book as an exposition on the brain and puzzles as you engage with the subject matter (the puzzles themselves) along the way.

Puzzles are fun to do…when you know how to do them. So each chapter shows you exactly how to solve a specific type of puzzle. If the research is correct, then we should all be doing puzzles *systematically*. Going on the internet and getting different types of puzzles to solve will be only partially beneficial (in my opinion, of course). However, organizing them into a puzzle-solving system, with lots of anecdotes and fun informational tidbits is more beneficial for preserving and increasing brain health.

If you are using this book for increasing your brainpower, I would suggest that you start at the beginning and work progressively through the book, right to the end. If you are using this book simply to have fun solving puzzles, then the order isn't as relevant. In either case, there is enough material here for one and all.

1

MEMORY

Memory is the diary that we all carry about with us.
(OSCAR WILDE, 1854–1900)

IF THE BRAIN STORED NOTHING FROM THE PAST, we would be unable to learn anything new. All our experiences would be lost as soon as they ended, and each new situation would be totally unfamiliar. Without memory, we would be living in a *Groundhog Day* world, repeatedly having the same experiences as if they occurred for the first time. Memory gives continuity to life, literally making it possible for us to know who we are.

How memory works in the human brain remains largely a mystery. One thing is for certain though—the weakening of memory starts early in life. According to some neuroscientists, such loss starts as early as puberty. In our later years, the loss may become severe and in some cases, such as in Alzheimer's disease, even tragic.

WORD PUZZLES AND MEMORY

A study published in 2000 in the journal *Psychology of Aging* found that older people who solved crossword puzzles regularly were able to stave off many of the negative effects of age on memory. This type of study has been repeated over and over since the turn of the millennium with the same pattern of findings. Simply put, puzzles seem to help counter or at least reduce the risk of severe memory loss.

The fear of Alzheimer's is a major incentive for such research. In study after study, older adults (from their sixties on) who engaged in mentally stimulating activities throughout their lives showed fewer deposits of beta-amyloid, the hallmark protein of Alzheimer's. The findings apply to all individuals, regardless of their gender, years of education or occupation. Moreover, the research strongly indicates that one should start doing puzzles early, not wait till later in life and use them as a type of "magic pill." While therapy with puzzles can help improve memory in the elderly, the evidence suggests that optimal benefits come from a lifetime of puzzle solving.

The brain has between 10 billion and 100 billion neurons. After a person reaches about twenty years of age, some neurons die each day. Over a lifetime, these daily losses add up to around 10 percent of a person's neurons. Scientists have found that adults can, to greater or lesser degrees, grow new neurons in the hippocampus, a portion of the brain associated with learning and memory, through the regular use of puzzle and game-playing activities, which activate neurons in this portion of the brain. Puzzles are not a magic pill, but they seem to have the capacity to boost memory retention and to delay severe memory loss in some people.

OBJECTIVES OF THIS CHAPTER

This chapter contains fifty puzzles aiming to build or reinforce memory of words, their meanings and their uses. The puzzles chosen for the goal are classics: acrostics, word squares, odd-one-out puzzles, jumbles and crosswords. These should get your brain to remember words or to guess them by inference.

ACROSTICS

WHAT IS AN ACROSTIC?

The word *acrostic* derives from the Greek term *akrostikhis*, which is a combination of two words: *akron*, or "head," and *stikhos*, which means "line of verse." Originally, it meant "the line at the head of a verse," indicating that in addition to the words in the horizontal rows, an acrostic poem had a vertical row hiding a word that was formed with the letters at the "head" of each line.

HOW TO SOLVE ACROSTICS

Acrostics are solved like crosswords. The clues refer to the words that fit into the horizontal lines of empty cells. The kind of acrostic you will be solving here contains the hidden word in the vertical column outlined in bold. The number of the clue corresponds to the number of the horizontal line.

Let's go through a very simple acrostic. The theme is family and relatives, and the word hidden in the bold column refers to a female relative.

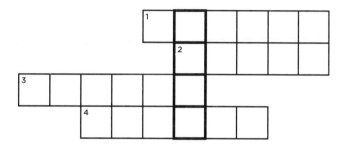

CLUES

1. Male parent
2. Your mother's or father's brother
3. The son or daughter of your aunt or uncle
4. Female sibling

The answer to (1) is *FATHER*, to (2) is *UNCLE*, to (3) is *COUSIN* and to (4) is *SISTER*. Now, simply insert these answers in the corresponding horizontal lines:

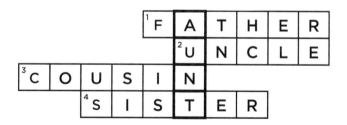

As you can now read, the hidden word in the vertical column in bold is *aunt*. That's all there is to it. Enjoy exercising your memory with the following ten acrostics.

PUZZLES

1 **Theme: The seasons or the year.** The clues refer to some aspect of the seasons or the year. The column in bold contains the word for a holiday that occurs during winter.

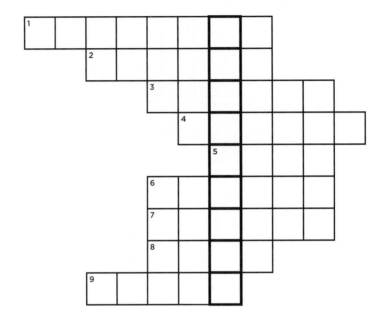

CLUES

1. Time of the year when the sun reaches either its highest or lowest point in the noon sky
2. There are twelve of these in a year
3. The season that comes before summer
4. The coldest season of the year
5. It falls mainly in winter
6. The season when the leaves fall
7. The hottest season of the year
8. A year with 366 days
9. There are fifty-two of these in a year

2 **Theme: Love and romance.** The clues refer to some aspect of love and romance. The column in bold contains the word referring to the marriage ceremony.

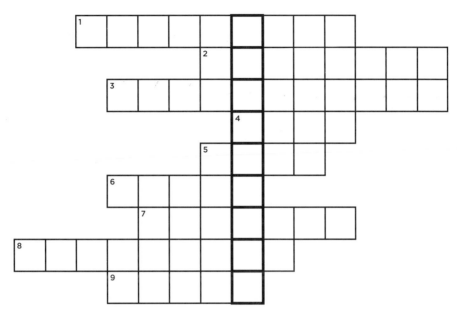

CLUES

1. Post-marriage vacation
2. As a famous song says, love and marriage go together like a horse and this
3. An intense but short-lived romantic passion
4. Worn on a finger as a sign of love and fidelity
5. Romantic act that involves the lips
6. The bride's companion
7. The dissolution of marriage
8. Card given to a loved one on February 14
9. Wed

3 **Theme: Sports.** The clues refer to different types of sports. The column in bold contains the word referring to an international sporting event, which is held alternately in summer and winter every two years.

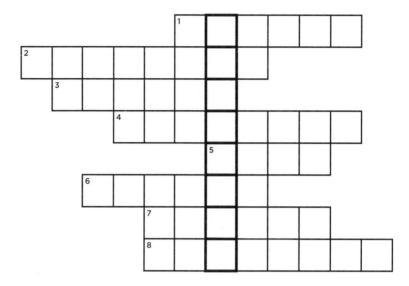

CLUES

1. Pugilism
2. Popular sport played on a field marked out as a gridiron
3. In both the ice and field versions of this sport, hooked sticks are used
4. Water sport whereby competitors propel themselves through the water using the limbs
5. Sport resembling field hockey that is played on horseback with a mallet
6. Sport played with a ball and racket on a court with a net stretched across it
7. Game played with a large round ball that can be touched with the hands only by the goalkeepers during play
8. Sport played in nine innings with no preset time limit

> The American writer Ralph Waldo Emerson (1803–1882) once wrote that "A character is like an acrostic or Alexandrian stanza; read it forward, backward or across, it still spells the same thing."

4 **Theme: The digital universe.** The clues refer to various aspects of the digital universe. The column in bold contains the word referring to the space in which communication over computer networks occurs.

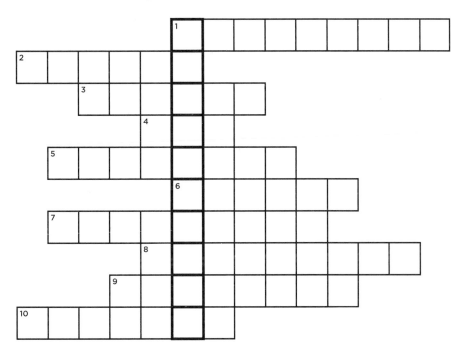

CLUES

1. Electronic machines that we use especially for word processing and searching the internet
2. Part of a computer that stores information and program instructions
3. Virtual village that links the world through telecommunications
4. Common abbreviation for the World Wide Web
5. System of interconnected computer networks using standardized communication protocols
6. Where information on a computer is displayed
7. Handheld wireless phone with access to a radio system for wide area usage
8. It orbits the earth, making global telecommunications possible
9. A common social networking medium that originated at Harvard University
10. A social networking medium that disseminates Tweets

5 **Theme: Vehicles.** The clues refer to various kinds of vehicles. The column in bold contains the name of a very expensive Italian car.

CLUES

1. A road vehicle with four wheels powered by a combustion engine or electric motor
2. A powered flying vehicle with fixed wings
3. A vessel larger than a boat
4. A vehicle with two wheels propelled by pedals
5. It travels on tracks
6. Underground train or railroad
7. A vehicle with two wheels powered by a motor
8. Aircraft with overhead rotors

6 **Theme: Happiness.** The clues refer to various forms or manifestations of happiness. The column in bold contains a word that refers to a feeling of intense happiness.

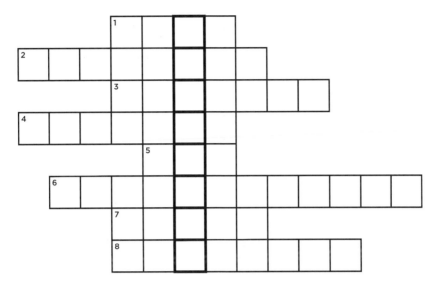

CLUES

1. Elation
2. Enjoyment or satisfaction
3. Intense pleasure
4. Great pleasure
5. Equivalent to French joie
6. Optimistic or jolly happiness
7. Perfect or heavenly happiness
8. Contentment

> **Acrostics were common in medieval writings. They were usually intended to draw attention to the name of a saint or an aristocrat.**

7 **Theme: Literature.** The clues refer to genres of literature or to some aspect of literary writing. The column in bold contains the name of one of the greatest playwrights of all time.

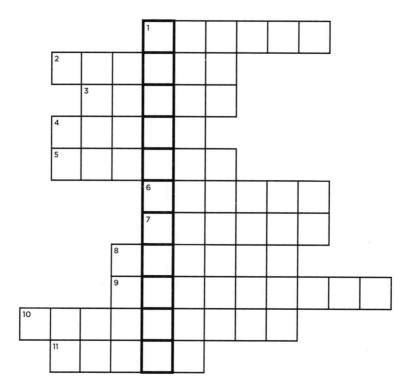

CLUES

1. A poem with a formal rhyme scheme, traditionally of fourteen lines
2. Popular genre of eighteenth- and ninteenth-century novel characterized by mystery, horror and a dark atmosphere
3. A serious or engaging genre of theater
4. A Japanese poem of seventeen syllables
5. A humorous genre of theater
6. A literary genre used to ridicule, expose or criticize something or someone
7. Genre of literature for which Emily Dickinson is famous
8. A written account of one's memory of certain events or individuals
9. Technical name for story
10. Account of a person's life written by someone else
11. A long-form fictitious prose narrative

8 **Theme: Bodies of water.** The clues refer to bodies of water. The column in bold contains the name of a sea.

CLUES

1. Type of bog or marsh
2. The Atlantic or Pacific
3. Small body of still water
4. Small arm of a river, lake or sea
5. Small mountain lake, or the name of a French river
6. Minor river tributary
7. It flows to the sea or into a lake
8. Small narrow river
9. Large body of water surrounded by land
10. Stretch of water linking two larger bodies of water
11. The Baltic or Caspian
12. Broad inlet of the sea where the land curves inward
13. Stretch of salt water separated from the sea by a reef, or a small freshwater lake near a larger lake

9 **Theme: Fruit.** The clues refer to types of fruit. The column in bold contains the technical word referring to the growing and cultivation of fruit.

CLUES

1. In some legends it is called the golden fruit
2. Round juicy citrus fruit with a tough rind; its name is also a basic color term
3. Yellow citrus fruit with thick skin
4. Soft juicy fruit resembling a small peach
5. Small red acidic berry used in cooking
6. Large round yellow citrus fruit with a juicy pulp
7. Small oval fleshy fruit that is usually purple in color
8. Glossy red pulpy fruit that is eaten as a vegetable or used to make sauce for pasta
9. Large oval fruit consisting of a hard shell that grows inside a woody husk
10. Soft red fruit with a seedy surface
11. A yellowish, brownish, greenish fruit that is narrow at the stalk and wider toward the base

10 **Theme: Gardens.** The clues refer to what you will find in typical gardens. The column in bold contains the technical word referring to the art and practice of gardening.

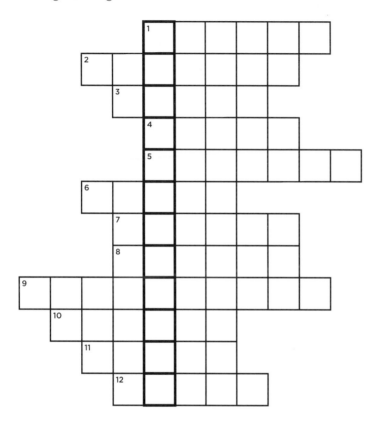

CLUES

1. Fences formed by closely growing bushes or shrubs
2. Roses and petunias
3. This is always greener on the other side
4. Money doesn't grow on these
5. Ants and termites
6. Stones used to decorate parts of a garden
7. Shrubs with stems of moderate length
8. Trees, shrubs, flowers, herbs and mosses
9. Grown and used as food
10. Woody plants smaller than a tree with several main stems
11. Plants that are often used in food, medicine and cosmetics
12. Unwanted wild plants

There is an acrostic puzzle in the final part of Vladimir Nabokov's short story "The Vane Sisters." The acrostic contains a message from beyond.

WORD SQUARES

WHAT IS A WORD SQUARE?

Word squares are exactly what the term says—words whose letters cross within a square grid. For example, in the word square below, the words *KISS*, *IOTA* (a very small amount), *STEM* and *SAME* cross as follows: the word *KISS* is in the top row and left-most column; *IOTA* is in the second row from the top and the second column from the left; *STEM* is in the third row from the top and the third column from the left; and *SAME* is in the bottom row and in the right-most column. Each word, as you can see, occurs in a row and corresponding column, with one of its letters in a row crossing the same letter in a column:

K	I	S	S
I	O	T	A
S	T	E	M
S	A	M	E

Word squares are a kind of "word sudoku," getting your brain to access its semantic memory system in tandem with logical reasoning processes.

HOW TO SOLVE WORD SQUARES

In this section, you will find two kinds of word squares: (1) those with clues to help you identify the words and (2) those with letter clues only. Let's go through each type with simple three-by-three squares.

You are given three clues that correspond to the three words inserted in the rows and columns. Three clues mean that there are three rows and columns and that the answers are three-letter words; four clues means that there are four rows and columns and that the answers are four-letter words; and so on.

CLUES

1. A wager
2. Period of historical time
3. Shade of skin after exposure to the sun

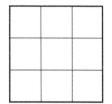

The answer to clue (1) is *BET*. So we insert this word in the top row and repeat it in the left-most column, as shown below. The answer to (2) is *ERA*. We now insert this word into the second row from the top and repeat it in the middle column. The answer to (3) is *TAN*, which we insert into both the bottom row and the right-most column. As you can see, the words now cross perfectly to form a square:

B	E	T
E	R	A
T	A	N

Now take a look at the puzzle below. You are given letters rather than clues, in order to complete the square. Pure verbal logic is required in this case:

S		
	N	
	E	R

Look at the middle column. There are two letters: *N* and *E*. The only logical choice for an English word in the column is *ONE*. By the way, abbreviations and acronyms are not allowed—only complete words. So let's put the letter *O* in the grid and then complete the insertion of *ONE* in the middle column and the second row:

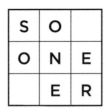

Now, we have several choices to complete the top row and left-most column: *SOB, SOD, SON, SOP, SOW* and *SOY*. We have to choose the one whose final letter can also be used to make a word in the right-most column and corresponding bottom row. A little trial and error will show that the only word that fits is *SOP*, which produces *PER* in the right-most column. All other possibilities do not produce a legitimate word. This allows us to complete the word square as follows:

S	O	P
O	N	E
P	E	R

That's all there is to it. The first set of five word squares below are type-1 puzzles (with clues) and the last five are type-2 puzzles (with a few letters as clues). For each set, you will find two three-by-three squares, two four-by-four squares and one five-by-five square.

> A word square is also called a Latin Square, because originally the Latin language was used in the creation of the squares.

PUZZLES

For puzzles 11–15, you are given clues.

 CLUES

1. Epoch
2. A common rodent
3. Past tense of eat

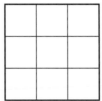

 CLUES

1. Summit, pinnacle
2. Lubricate
3. Work at a trade or occupation

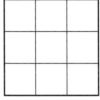

13 **CLUES**

1. The season when the leaves change color
2. Region or district
3. Thin and very slender
4. Division of a road, especially a highway

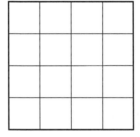

14 **CLUES**

1. Additional
2. Not closed
3. Recite
4. Finishes

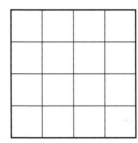

CLUES

1. Pieces, portions
2. A Hawaiian greeting
3. It is found on the top of a helicopter
4. Plural of that
5. A traditional garment worn by women from or in the Indian subcontinent (alternative spelling)

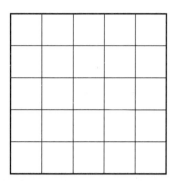

For puzzles 16–20, you are given only letter clues. You will have to reconstruct each word square using logic and verbal inference. Remember—no abbreviations or acronyms allowed. Good luck!

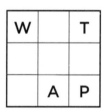

One of the earliest examples of a word square dates from the second or third century CE. It is an incredible thirty-nine-by-thirty-nine square array of Greek letters, carved in alabaster, attributed to the Egyptian sculptor Moschion. The square contains the phrase "Moschion to Osiris, for the treatment which cured his foot," which is repeated over and over. The square is clearly a tribute from Moschion to the healing god Osiris.

18

W	A		L
	R		
		A	
		D	S

19

M	A		
	I	S	E
			L

An important word square from a historical standpoint is the *Sator Acrostic*, found in the Roman city of Cirencester in England and also on a column in Pompeii. It is a five-by-five word square that still defies interpretation. The word *sator* (whatever it means) is found in the top row and left-most column.

20 This is a tough one! You may need to do a lot of trial and error.

P		C	K	
	A	N		E
	N	O		K
	E			S

ODD-ONE-OUT PUZZLES

WHAT IS AN ODD-ONE-OUT PUZZLE?

If you have ever taken an IQ test, then you are already familiar with the principle underlying odd-one-out puzzles. You will have to find the word that does not belong in a set of four words.

For example, in the list below, the word *GRASS*, unlike the other three words, does not refer to a color. So, logically, it is the odd one out:

BLUE
WHITE
GRASS
YELLOW

Nothing is known about the origin of these puzzles, other than they are commonly found on IQ tests of all kinds and sometimes used to assess candidates for job positions.

HOW TO SOLVE ODD-ONE-OUT PUZZLES

You will find two types of odd-one-out puzzles below: (1) those that involve recognizing the meanings or functions of individual words, like the example above, and (2) puzzles that involve recognizing some aspect of the physical makeup of the given words.

We have already discussed type one above. The only additional thing to note is that the odd one out could be a word that functions grammatically in a different way from the others and not just carry a different meaning or connotation. For example, in the puzzle below, the first word is a verb and the other three are nouns. So, the first word—*WENT*—is the odd one out:

WENT
GOAL
BRAVERY
FRIENDSHIP

Below is an example of type two:

GREENER
GREAT
GAVE
BELOW

Note that the first three words start with the letter *G*, but the last one does not. So *BELOW* is the odd one out. Anything goes in this case. Moreover, you will not be told what to look for in the puzzle, so be ready.

PUZZLES

For all the puzzles in this section, identify the odd one out in the list of four words.

21
ROSE
FLOUR
TULIP
ORCHID

22
MICE
HORSES
GAMES
LADY

23
ROCK
WATER
STONE
PEBBLE

24
TABLE
TOY
RUN
GOT

> The first intelligence test for standardized use was devised in 1905 by the French psychologist Alfred Binet (1857–1911) and his colleague Théodore Simon (1872–1961). Binet's goal was to make sure that no child would be denied instruction in the Paris school system, regardless of the socioeconomic class from which the child came.

25
CIRCLE
TOOL
LINE
SQUARE

26
BASIS
HYPOTHESIS
CRISIS
MASSES

27 THING
BEAUTIFUL
INTELLIGENT
NEW

28 DEEM
SPOON
FORK
AARDVARK

29 BOLD
BALL
CHATTER
WINNER

30 HEAD
TOE
FINGER
JACKET

JUMBLES

WHAT IS A JUMBLE?

Jumbles are words whose letters are scrambled up. The idea is to unscramble the letters to reconstruct the original words. For example, *MILES* is one jumble (among others) of the word *SMILE*.

There are various versions of jumble puzzles, including one in which several words are given, with a specific letter within each one marked in some way so that they create another word. This is the type of jumble that will be used below.

HOW TO SOLVE JUMBLES

First, you will be given a set of jumbled words, which you will then unscramble by putting each letter of each reconstructed word into its appropriate cell. Notice that there are also shaded cells:

GLNFOIG

CADR-PALYIGN

AGMLBING

HCADRAES

QSUAHS

The answers to the jumbles are given below. Now, simply put the letters in the shaded cells together *(G, A, M, E and S)* and you will get the word *GAMES*:

GLNFOIG	G	O	L	F	I	N	G				
CADR-PALYIGN	C	A	R	D	–	P	L	A	Y	I	N	G
AGMLBING	G	A	M	B	L	I	N	G				
HCADRAES	C	H	A	R	A	D	E	S				
QSUAHS	S	Q	U	A	S	H						

Note that each unscrambled jumble *(GOLFING, CARD-PLAYING, GAMBLING, CHARADES, SQUASH)* refers to a game of some kind.

PUZZLES

31
IIKSNG
INGP-ONPG
WORGNI
BUGYR
NISNET
COSREC

32
ROTCA
RECDIROT
NIOTMAANI
VIMOSE
LIMF
OASSCR

33
CARSLET
DIGOIN
IOLVET
CRMISNO
RAZEU
LESETCE

34

HATHEEC

NIOL

GETIR

SOOME

RANGTANUO

PHAELENT

AKENS

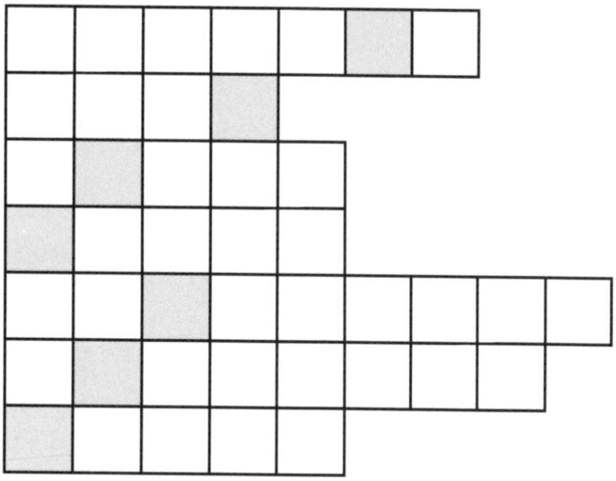

35

ERATH

ININETEST

DIBMANLE

THODYRI

SLISONTR

CLESUMS

NXYRAL

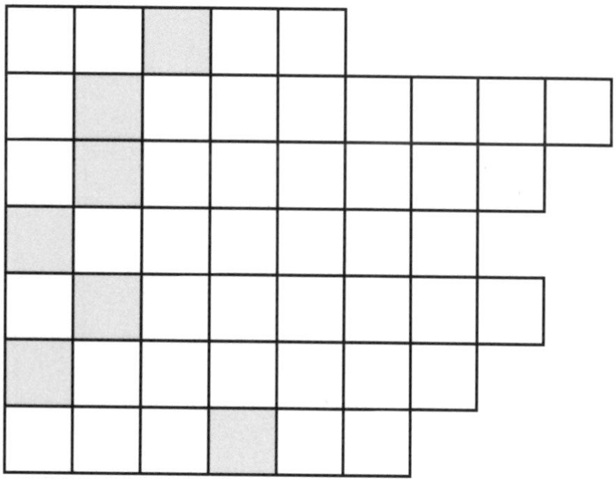

36

COMEIN

LARDOL

CURERNYC

RUEO

ENY

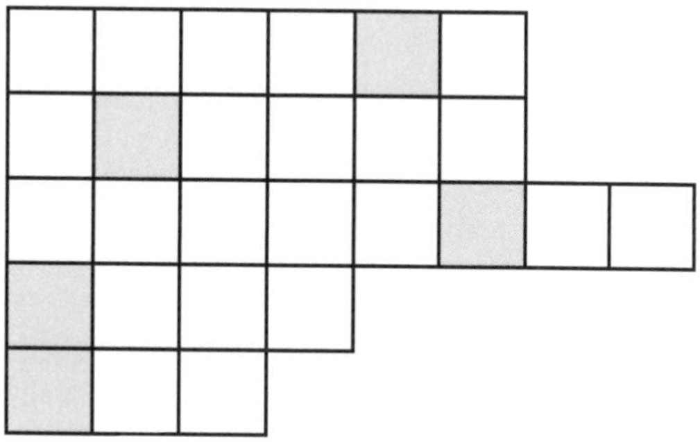

37

SEIDCAN

FFLWAES

RAMELCA

AKEC

FFTEEO

NOBNOBS

38

AMOST

NORTECLE

RAVGITY

RGYNEE

QUNTAA

OLEUCLEM

ATIRELVIYT

39

RAIPORTRUET

AADDSMI

MISBUC

APENALDSC

TABSCART

HIARCOCURSO

DERMONIMS

THICGO

40

VELANOL

ICTFNIO

TRYPOE

MANOREC

RAMAD

LABEF

RRANAVETI

UTAHOR

SOREP

YSYMTER

CROSSWORDS

WHAT IS A CROSSWORD?

Most people know what a crossword is, even if they have never done one. A crossword consists of vertical and horizontal clues that correspond to the rows and columns that make up the puzzle. The idea is to complete the entire grid with the appropriate letters or words. The inventor of the crossword puzzle was the British-born inventor Arthur Wynne (1871–1945). He created his first puzzle for the Fun section of the December 21, 1913, edition of the *New York World*. He titled it "Word-Cross." It appeared in print as "Cross-Word" because of a typesetting error. That erroneous name stuck, and Wynne's puzzle has been called a crossword ever since.

At first many people viewed the crossword puzzle with alarm, expecting it to be a short-lived fad. In 1924, the *New York Times* complained that the puzzle was a "sinful waste in the utterly futile finding of words the letters of which will fit into a prearranged pattern, more or less complex." History has proven this stance to be wrong. According to Will Shortz, editor of the *New York Times* crossword puzzle, as many as 50 million people solve crosswords just in America.

Crosswords facilitate what neuroscientists call brain fluency. All the puzzles in this chapter enable this process, too, but crosswords seem to be particularly effective at it.

HOW TO SOLVE CROSSWORDS

Like acrostics, crosswords are solved by filling in the cells horizontally and vertically according to the corresponding clues. Let's take a very simple crossword puzzle, just in case you have never done a puzzle of this type.

ACROSS

1. The color of the sky
5. The color of grass
10. The "love" flower
11. A red cosmetic for coloring the lips or cheeks
12. Order of St. Augustine
13. An article
14. A personal pronoun
15. Utter
17. The color of blood
20. No returns
21. Overtime
22. Much ... about nothing

DOWN

1. The color of chestnuts
2. Opposite of winner
3. United States of America
4. Electrical engineer
5. The color of hair as we age
6. Movie director Howard's first name
7. European Union
8. For example
9. Northeast
15. Thus
16. On, by
17. Egyptian sun god
18. Common male name, abbreviated
19. Perform, make

The answer to clue 1 across is *BLUE*. We insert this in the horizontal row of cells starting with the superscript number 1. Now, let's choose clue 1 down. The answer is *BROWN*. We insert this in the vertical column of cells starting with superscript 1. We continue this way until we complete the whole grid. The answer is shown below. Notice that some of the clues refer to abbreviations. For example, the answer to 12 across (Order of St. Augustine) is the abbreviation OSA:

1 B	2 L	3 U	4 E		5 G	6 R	7 E	8 E	9 N
10 R	O	S	E		11 R	O	U	G	E
12 O	S	A			13 A	N			
14 W	E		15 S	16 A	Y		17 R	18 E	19 D
20 N	R		21 O	T			22 A	D	O

That's all there is to it. We will start with small grids in the early puzzles, increasing them gradually in size and difficulty.

PUZZLES

41

1	2	3	4
5			
■		6	
■		7	

ACROSS

1. Hit, strike
5. Too
6. Opposite of out
7. While

DOWN

1. A university degree
2. ... Dorado
3. The largest continent
4. Lots and lots

42

ACROSS

1. Out-of-home lodging
6. Makes
7. New Testament
8. Doctor of Divinity
9. Long-handled gardening tool
11. Cheerless

DOWN

1. A female bird
2. Pledges
3. Transitive
4. Finished
5. Drug made famous by the hippies
10. Osteoarthritis

Some historians believe that the forerunner of the crossword can be traced to an Italian magazine called *Il Secolo Illustrato della Domenica* (*The Illustrated World of Sunday*), published in 1890. The inventor was a man named Giuseppe Airoldi.

43

ACROSS

1. Covetous jealousy
5. Television
7. Fibber
8. Alcoholics Anonymous
9. Sick
10. Barrel
11. Inuit dwelling built with snow
14. Benefactor

DOWN

1. Biblical Hebrew name
2. Nothing
3. Legitimate
4. Year
5. Forbidden
6. Courage
12. Leave
13. Symbol for natural logarithm

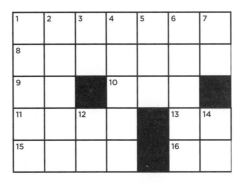

ACROSS

1. Atmospheric conditions
8. They are used to keep ships in place
9. Identification
10. I owe you
11. An urban area
13. The ratio of the circumference of a circle to its diameter
15. Large gulp
16. Common preposition

DOWN

1. Stays
2. Provide something valuable
3. Type of electrical current
4. Object
5. Sound made by an owl
6. Explode
7. Right side
12. Wisconsin
14. A satellite of Jupiter

The first crossword puzzle editor of the *New York Times* was American journalist Margaret Petherbridge Farrar (1897–1984), who edited the puzzles from 1942 to 1968. She helped make the crossword puzzle into the popular recreation it is today.

ACROSS

1. Attempt
4. A common conjunction
6. The listening organ
7. Warrant officer
8. North Dakota
9. Egg-shaped
11. The evening meal
13. The father of geometry
14. Republic of Serbia
15. "Crossed fingers" in internet slang, or Yes/No

DOWN

1. Caring
2. A circle measure
3. Year
4. Prize
5. A musical note
9. Merely
10. A blood vessel
12. North Carolina

Broadway composer Stephen Sondheim had a brief career as a puzzle maker in 1968 and 1969, creating cryptic crosswords for *New York* magazine.

46

ACROSS

1. Slow romantic song
7. Having large numbers or quantities
8. The baseball pitcher's terrain
9. Opposite of yes
11. By way of
12. A common preposition
13. Energy-efficiency ratio
14. Past tense of eat

DOWN

1. Loud hammering noise or thud
2. Over
3. A colloquial version of Louis
4. Relating to the moon
5. A common conjunction
6. Doctor of Divinity
9. A negative adverb
10. A natural mineral
12. A musical note

47

ACROSS

1. Triumph
8. Unfriendliness, coldness
11. Chilled over ice cubes
12. Stand out
14. Guided
15. A personal pronoun
16. A common conjunction
17. Internet code for Republic of Serbia
18. It follows "either"
19. Road

DOWN

1. Travel by water
2. Stomach sore often caused by stress
3. Male and female students together
4. A saltwater edible fish
5. The word for, or name of, the letter *F*
6. Scorn
7. Biological gender
9. Mark left by a wound
10. Mail, transmit
13. Lethal dose
15. Modus operandi

1	2	3	4	5		6	7	8	9
10						11			
12					13				
	14				15				16
						17			

ACROSS

1. Opposite of falsehood
6. Affection
10. Wash
11. By word of mouth
12. An electronics brand
13. Used to wash or clean oneself
14. Extremely hazardous substance
15. Space under the roof
17. Electronic data interchange

DOWN

1. To be announced
2. Tool used to gather fallen leaves
3. A western American state
4. A demonstrative word
5. The counterpart of she
6. Burglarize
7. Give a sermon
8. Insipid
9. ... Niño
13. Salvation Army
16. Channel Islands

The 2006 movie *Wordplay,* directed by Patrick Creadon, features Will Shortz, the current *New York Times* puzzle editor. Shortz founded an annual crossword tournament in 1978. The movie brings out the enthusiasm that the annual competition generates in people from all walks of life, along with the camaraderie that crossword aficionados establish among themselves.

49

	1	2	3	4	5	6		7	8	9	10	11	12	13
	14							15						
	16											17		
	18				19	20	21	22		23	24			
	25				26					27			28	29
	30				31					32				

ACROSS

1. Complies with
7. Extraordinary, unusual
14. Ecclesiastical laws
15. Odd
16. Grown-up
17. You sleep in it
18. Center for Defense Information
19. Cord
23. Chief executive officer
25. Institution of Engineering and Technology
26. Region
27. Collection
30. Symbol for argon
31. A fruit
32. Passionate Latin American dance

DOWN

1. A type of tree
2. Informal for worse
3. An aboriginal people
4. Department of Labor
5. Snare
6. More than one *S*
7. Secret Service
8. Symbol for platinum
9. Emergency room
10. Symbol for calcium
11. Inherited or possessed from birth
12. Length of time you have lived
13. Past tense of lead
20. Mineral used to make metals
21. It grows in a pod
22. The hearing organ
23. Feline pet
24. Period of time
28. Symbol for silver
29. Greeting used to get attention

ACROSS

1. Friendly
9. A preposition
11. Ancient Mesopotamian city
13. Capital of country music
15. Turns over
17. Tennessee
18. Angola (country code)
19. The unit digit
21. Attention-grabbing greeting
22. Opposite of out
23. Musical work
25. Teaching assistant
27. Back
30. For each
31. Cleansing substance
33. Form of the verb to be
34. Part of the foot
36. Flow out rapidly and abundantly
38. Extended play (phonograph record)
40. A preposition
41. A female first name
42. "Your problem" in internet slang
43. Symbol for xenon

DOWN

1. A "social" insect
2. Opposite of woman
3. A form of the verb to be
4. You sit on it
5. An English river
6. Bisexual
7. Cool J's initials
8. Secretly get married by running away
9. A preposition
10. Birds do this
11. Opposite of down
12. Right side
14. Vitality
16. Trifling amount
20. Symbol for erbium
23. Unlocked
24. Donkey
26. The highest point
27. Strike something with a quick blow
28. Before in time (literary, archaic)
29. ... Lingus
32. An exclamation
34. Symbol for tantalum
35. Not off
37. Not down
39. Physical education

2

PERCEPTION

There is no truth. There is only perception.

(GUSTAVE FLAUBERT, 1821–1880)

A LARGE PORTION OF THOUGHT involves mental imagery, which can be described as the ability to visualize things with one's mind. The production of imagery is how the brain makes sense of pattern and then stores it in memory. Visual puzzles are particularly adept at engaging the imagery system (the visual images collectively generated by the brain). Research has shown, in fact, that visual activities of all kinds stimulate crucial centers in the right hemisphere of the brain. When this occurs, "whole brain" thinking and broader problem-solving skills are activated.

VISUAL PUZZLES AND PERCEPTION

The right hemisphere is sometimes called the "visual hemisphere" because it is designed to process incoming visual information and make sense of it. For this purpose, this area of the brain contains special cell structures that detect or recognize visual patterns and thus allow us to think imaginatively about how they fit together.

Our sense organs translate the incoming information into nerve impulses, and these impulses then go to the brain. Through perception mechanisms, the impulses are converted to images of objects, events, people and other aspects of the world. Evidence suggests that early experience with visual puzzles, such as locating Xs on treasure maps, is important for keeping perception fine-tuned throughout a person's life.

OBJECTIVES OF THIS CHAPTER

This chapter contains fifty puzzles that are designed to activate visual perception. The types of puzzles here include recognizing figures in a layout, solving stick puzzles and solving a version of a maze puzzle—all of which will increase your puzzle power (and brainpower).

FIGURE COUNTING PUZZLES: CIRCLES

WHAT IS A FIGURE COUNTING PUZZLE?

A figure counting puzzle is exactly what its name implies—a puzzle in which you count a number of figures. The goal is to determine how many figures (circles, squares and rectangles, and triangles) occur in a layout. A figure can be composed of smaller constituent figures.

HOW TO SOLVE CIRCLE COUNTING PUZZLES

In this type of figure counting puzzle, you have to detect the number of separate (full) circles in the layout of overlapping and enclosed figures. How many distinct (separate and complete) circles do you see in the layout below?

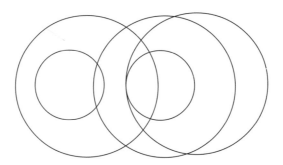

The answer is five.

There isn't a step-by-step method for solving this type of puzzle. Instead, you will have to look carefully at the figures in the layout to determine the answer. One trick that might help, though, is tracing the full circumference of each circle you see until that particular circle is bolder than the others. For example, in the layout above, one of the circles can be bolded as follows:

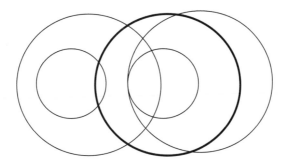

We can then do the same to another one we spot:

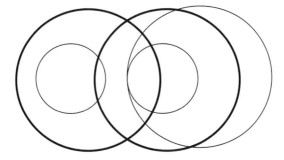

As you can see, it is now easier to identify the remaining circles.

To sharpen your visual perception, we will start off with very simple puzzles, gradually making them more complex.

51 How many distinct circles are there in the layout below?

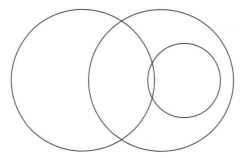

52 How many distinct circles are there in the layout below?

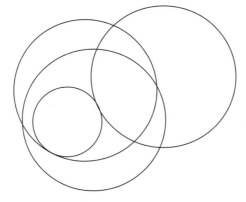

Dementia results when brain tissues and structures deteriorate and the functions housed in those areas are lost. Solving perception puzzles puts cells to work and subsequently gives the brain a workout. This type of mental activity slows down the onset of dementia by keeping more parts of the brain active and in shape longer.

53 How many distinct circles are there in the layout below?

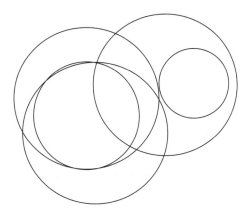

54 How many distinct circles are there in the layout below?

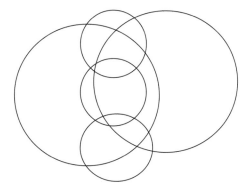

55 How many distinct circles are there in the layout below?

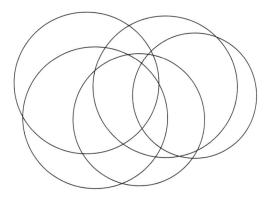

56 How many distinct circles are there in the layout below?

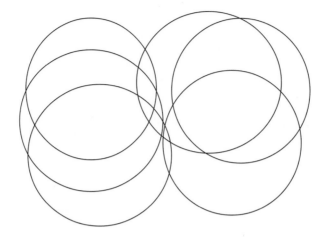

57 How many distinct circles are there in the layout below?

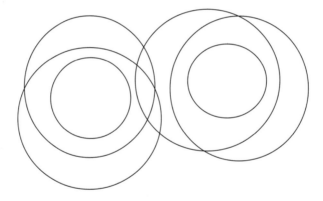

58 How many distinct circles are there in the layout below?

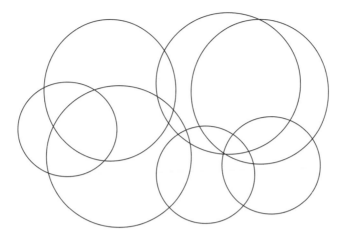

59 How many distinct circles are there in the layout below?

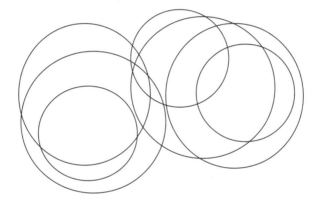

Research shows that cognitive therapy with puzzles can help improve memory and enhance visual perception in the elderly, but it has also shown that the lifelong practice of solving puzzles is more beneficial than picking up the habit in one's later years.

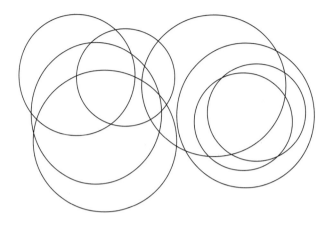

FIGURE COUNTING PUZZLES: SQUARES AND RECTANGLES

COUNTING FOUR-SIDED FIGURES

Like circular figure counting, this kind of puzzle involves determining how many complete four-sided figures (squares and rectangles) there are in a layout.

HOW TO SOLVE FOUR-SIDED FIGURE COUNTING PUZZLES

Let's go through the typical four-sided figure counting puzzle. How many squares and rectangles are there in the following figure? Note that a square or rectangle can be composed of multiple smaller constituent squares and rectangles.

An effective solution method is to assign a number to each individual square and rectangle you see within the larger shape. In the example below, there are a total of nine. Then, using the number of each individual shape to keep track of your combinations, start visually combining individual segments together to create larger shapes, much like a LEGO set.

There are twenty-six complete four-sided figures. Here is how they are composed:

1.	1		**14.**	3+8+9
2.	1+2+4+5		**15.**	4
3.	1+2+3+4+5		**16.**	4+5
4.	1+2+4+5+6+7		**17.**	4+6
5.	1+2+3+4+5+6+7+8+9		**18.**	5
6.	1+4		**19.**	6
7.	1+4+6		**20.**	6+7
8.	2+5		**21.**	6+7+8+9
9.	2+3+5		**22.**	7
10.	2+5+7		**23.**	7+8+9
11.	2+3+5+7+8+9		**24.**	8
12.	3		**25.**	8+9
13.	3+8		**26.**	9

If you are having problems understanding this method of solution, consider, for example, 12, 13 and 14 in the solution, which are identified above, and you will see that segment 3 can stand on its own as a four-sided figure. Add segment 8 to it and, like blocks in a LEGO set, they make up a four-sided figure together. Similarly, if you take segments 3, 8 and 9 and join them together, another four-sided figure appears.

PUZZLES

61 Altogether, how many squares and rectangles are there in the figure below? Note that a square or rectangle can be composed of smaller constituent squares and rectangles.

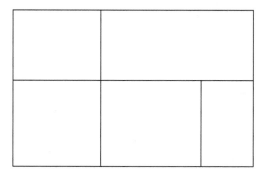

62 Altogether, how many squares and rectangles are there in the figure below? Note that a square or rectangle can be composed of smaller constituent squares and rectangles.

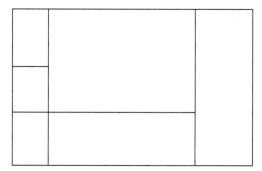

63 Altogether, how many squares and rectangles are there in the figure below? Note that a square or rectangle can be composed of smaller constituent squares and rectangles.

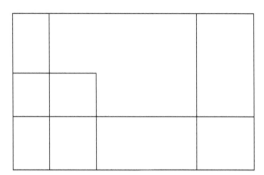

The brain needs many different kinds of stimuli in order to keep functioning properly. A certain puzzle genre by itself, such as figure counting puzzles, can be only a small part of the overall "input software" the brain might need to fend off or delay serious deterioration. Engaging with music, reading and other pleasurable activities will help immensely.

64 Altogether, how many squares and rectangles are there in the figure below? Note that a square or rectangle can be composed of smaller constituent squares and rectangles.

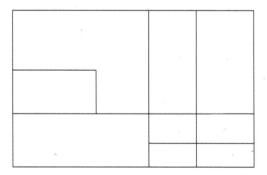

65 Altogether, how many squares and rectangles are there in the figure below? Note that a square or rectangle can be composed of smaller constituent squares and rectangles.

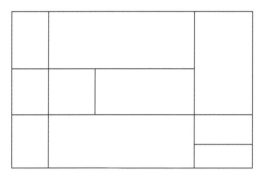

66 Altogether, how many squares and rectangles are there in the figure below? Note that a square or rectangle can be composed of smaller constituent squares and rectangles.

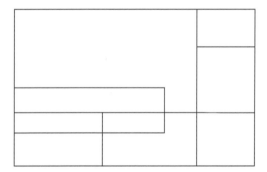

Jigsaw puzzles and figure counting puzzles are based on the same principle: they require the mind to perceive shapes and how they fit together. Thus, figure counting is a form of "mental jigsaw." There is strong evidence that doing jigsaw puzzles improves hand-eye coordination and enhances logical reasoning.

67 Altogether, how many squares and rectangles are there in the figure below? Note that a square or rectangle can be composed of smaller constituent squares and rectangles.

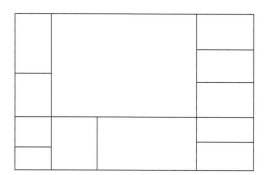

68 Altogether, how many squares and rectangles are there in the figure below? Note that a square or rectangle can be composed of smaller constituent squares and rectangles.

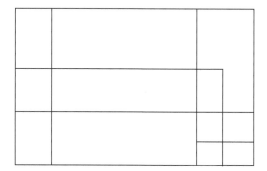

Jigsaw puzzles became a craze the instant they were commercialized around 1767 by mapmaker John Spilsbury. He wanted children to become familiar with the shapes that made up maps.

69 Altogether, how many squares and rectangles are there in the figure below? Note that a square or rectangle can be composed of smaller constituent squares and rectangles.

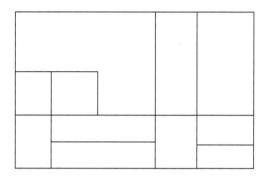

70 Altogether, how many squares and rectangles are there in the figure below? Note that a square or rectangle can be composed of smaller constituent squares and rectangles.

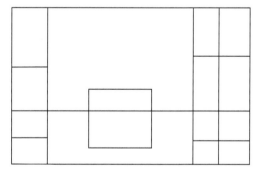

FIGURE COUNTING PUZZLES: TRIANGLES

COUNTING TRIANGULAR FIGURES

Like the previous two puzzle types, this kind of puzzle involves determining how many complete triangles there are in a layout.

HOW TO SOLVE TRIANGLE COUNTING PUZZLES

Let's go through one typical puzzle. How many triangles are there in the figure below? Note that a triangle can be composed of smaller constituent shapes:

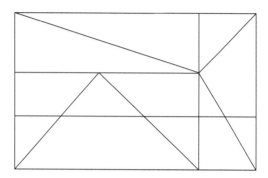

As in the case of the four-sided figure counting puzzle, an effective solution method is to number the various segments as shown:

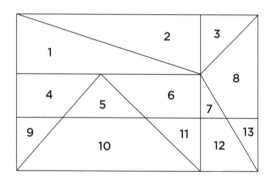

The answer is fourteen. The solution is below:

1.	1		**8.**	6+11
2.	2		**9.**	7
3.	2+3		**10.**	7+12
4.	3		**11.**	8+13
5.	4+9		**12.**	9
6.	5		**13.**	11
7.	5+10		**14.**	13

As with the four-sided figure puzzles, first start by numbering the individual, standalone shapes. Then see if there are larger triangles formed when smaller shapes are combined. Needless to say, some of the numbered shapes are not involved in the solution.

PUZZLES

71 Altogether, how many triangles are there in the figure below? Note that a triangle can be composed of smaller constituent shapes.

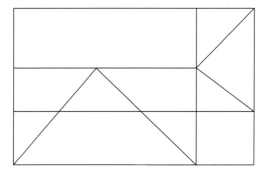

72 Altogether, how many triangles are there in the figure below? Note that a triangle can be composed of smaller constituent shapes.

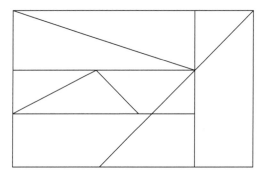

73 Altogether, how many triangles are there in the figure below? Note that a triangle can be composed of smaller constituent shapes.

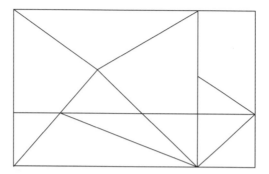

Jigsaw puzzles take their name from the jigsaw tool that was originally used to cut the individual puzzle pieces from the sheets of wood on which they were drawn.

74 Altogether, how many triangles are there in the figure below? Note that a triangle can be composed of smaller constituent shapes.

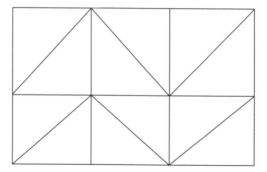

75 Altogether, how many triangles are there in the figure below? Note that a triangle can be composed of smaller constituent shapes.

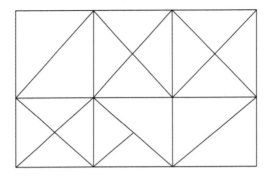

76 Altogether, how many triangles are there in the figure below? Note that a triangle can be composed of smaller constituent shapes.

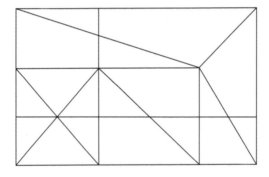

One of the largest jigsaw puzzles in existence weighs over 40 pounds and consists of 32,000 pieces.

77 Altogether, how many triangles are there in the figure below? Note that a triangle can be composed of smaller constituent shapes.

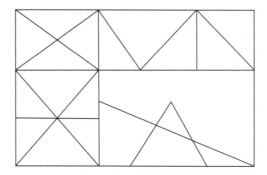

78 Altogether, how many triangles are there in the figure below? Note that a triangle can be composed of smaller constituent shapes.

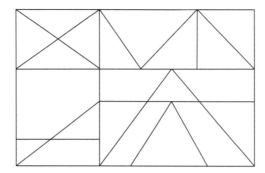

79 Altogether, how many triangles are there in the figure below? Note that a triangle can be composed of smaller constituent shapes.

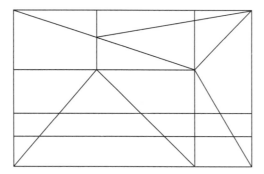

80 Altogether, how many triangles are there in the figure below? Note that a triangle can be composed of smaller constituent shapes.

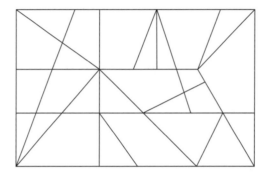

ARITHMETICAL STICK PUZZLES

WHAT IS A STICK PUZZLE?

The ancient geometers constructed figures from other figures in order to study general geometrical principles. They also invented puzzles and games that involved making new figures or showing a relationship among given figures. One of these games was Archimedes's *loculus*—a fourteen-piece puzzle forming a square, much like a jigsaw puzzle. By rearranging the pieces, one could make a host of other figures. An online version of the game, with instructions in Latin, can be found on the *Bibliotheca Augustana* website:

www.hs-augsburg.de/~harsch/graeca/Chronologia/S_ante03/Archimedes/arc_ost4.html

Stick puzzles are based on the principle of rearrangement. They require you to move and rearrange the sticks into different figures in order to solve the puzzle.

HOW TO SOLVE ARITHMETICAL STICK PUZZLES

Arithmetical stick puzzles will ask you to rearrange certain upright sticks in order to get some arithmetical result. The puzzles constitute "visual arithmetic." Here is a simple example.

Rearrange the following four upright sticks to form an expression that stands for the quantity two:

As you can see, you will really have to use your brain's imagery system together with your knowledge of arithmetic. The solution is to form a plus sign with the two middle sticks. The result is 1 + 1, which, of course, equals two:

In solving the puzzles below, you might want to have real sticks—like matchsticks—handy.

PUZZLES

81 Rearrange the following three sticks to form an arithmetical expression that equals zero.

82 Rearrange the following four sticks to form an arithmetical expression that equals ten.

83 Rearrange the following four sticks to form an expression that equals one.

At the turn of the twentieth century, the jigsaw puzzle became so popular in the United States that in 1909 Parker Brothers, the company behind the famed board game Monopoly, devoted an entire section of its factory to producing jigsaw puzzles.

84 Rearrange the following five sticks to form an arithmetical expression that equals 110.

85 Rearrange the following five sticks to form an arithmetical expression that equals eleven.

86 Rearrange the following six sticks to form an arithmetical expression that equals twenty-two.

87 Rearrange the following seven sticks to form an expression that equals two.

The tangram is a fascinating assembly puzzle. It consists of a square cut into five triangles, a smaller square, and a parallelogram. The ultimate goal—and challenge—is to reassemble the different pieces into specific figures. As simple as it may seem, the tangram is one of the most challenging, yet rewarding, puzzles around.

88 Rearrange the following seven sticks to form an arithmetical expression that equals zero.

89 Rearrange the following eight sticks to form an arithmetical expression that equals twelve.

> The tangram puzzle has been adopted by artists and designers. Italian Massimo Morozzi used it as the basis for a modernistic and popular table design he created in the 1980s.

90 Rearrange the following ten sticks to form an arithmetical expression that results in one.

NUMBER MAZES

WHAT IS A MAZE PUZZLE?

Mazes are among the most popular types of puzzles we give to children. These often come in the form of treasure maps with an X indicating the buried treasure. The origins of this type of puzzle can be traced to the legendary ancient labyrinths, which were made from a collection of multiple confusing passageways. According to Greek legend, the first labyrinth was built by Daedalus, the skilled Athenian inventor, for King Minos of Crete, who wanted to use the labyrinth as a prison for the Minotaur.

Like all visual puzzles, mazes activate the areas of the brain associated with visual perception and also enhance the brain's ability to make significant decisions at critical points in a problem;

mazes are based on the principle of deciding which path to take according to the situation. In the case of number mazes, a logical arithmetical dimension is added to the neural mix.

HOW TO SOLVE NUMBER MAZE PUZZLES

Anything can be a maze if it consists of some pattern in a path that leads from one point to another. In the puzzles below, the path is arithmetical. That is, you have to follow a number that leads from the top of the maze to the bottom according to a given sum.

Let's go through a typical number maze. You are shown the initial and end numbers in the path, indicated by the shaded numbers at the top and the bottom of the puzzle. For this particular puzzle, the sum of the numbers in the single, unbroken path you take between the 1 and 3 must add up to twenty-three.

The solution path is shown below:

6	1	1	3	4	5
7	2	0	1	0	6
7	8	3	9	8	2
3	4	4	0	5	6
7	8	9	1	2	7
0	9	8	2	2	2
4	5	7	8	2	9
4	5	7	8	1	9
1	0	3	6	1	5
5	6	7	5	1	9
8	9	7	6	3	5

As you can see, the solution path is made up of the number sequence 1+2+0+3+4+0+1+2+2+2+1+1+1+3 = 23. Notice that the sum includes the starting and ending numbers. And note that you cannot skip over or around numbers. Challenging, isn't it? But it is worth the brain effort to solve the ten puzzles below. Good luck!

PUZZLES

91 **Find the path from the shaded 0 to the shaded 6.** The path is made up of numbers that add up to twenty-six.

0	9	8	2
0	5	1	1
4	4	1	0
1	0	3	6

92 **Find the path through the maze from the shaded 1 to the shaded 3.** The path is made up of numbers that add up to fourteen.

6	1	1	3	4
7	2	0	1	0
1	0	3	9	8
1	1	3	5	1
6	0	3	2	3

93 **Find the path through the maze from the shaded 2 to the shaded 7.** The path is made up of numbers that add up to fifteen.

1	1	2	3	4
4	2	0	1	6
7	1	0	3	2
1	0	3	6	2
8	9	7	5	1

94 Find the path through the maze from the shaded 4 to the shaded 8. The path is made up of numbers that add up to eighteen.

6	1	3	4	5
7	0	1	0	6
0	8	2	2	2
1	3	6	1	1
8	0	0	3	5

95 Find the path through the maze from the shaded 4 to the shaded 8. The path is made up of numbers that add up to sixteen.

9	1	1	0	4	5
7	0	0	2	0	1
0	2	3	9	8	2
3	0	4	0	5	3
1	0	3	0	1	5
8	0	7	2	3	0

96 **Find the path through the maze from the shaded 1 to the shaded 5.** The path is made up of numbers that add up to fourteen.

6	1	1	3	1	1
7	2	0	1	0	0
4	5	7	0	9	3
1	0	3	0	1	5
5	6	1	1	1	1
8	9	0	1	9	5

97 **Find the path through the maze from the shaded 6 to the shaded 0.** The path is made up of numbers that add up to ten.

1	6	1	0	1	5
4	5	0	8	2	9
4	5	0	8	1	1
1	0	1	0	1	5
5	6	7	0	9	1
0	0	1	1	3	5

Maze video games came into circulation in the 1980s and are still somewhat popular today. The playing field is in the form of a maze, and players must successfully navigate it within a given time frame in order to escape monsters, enemies and other dangers.

98 Find the path through the maze from the shaded 5 to the shaded 1. The path is made up of numbers that add up to twenty.

5	1	1	3	4	0	5
7	2	0	1	0	3	6
7	8	3	3	8	1	2
3	4	4	0	5	1	6
7	8	9	1	2	0	7
0	9	8	2	9	2	9
8	9	7	6	3	1	5

99 Find the path through the maze from the shaded 1 to the shaded 1. The path is made up of numbers that add up to fifteen.

6	1	1	3	4	0	7	5
7	2	0	1	0	3	7	6
7	8	3	9	9	1	0	2
3	4	1	0	5	0	1	6
7	8	9	1	2	1	8	7
1	0	3	6	1	1	6	5
5	6	7	5	1	2	0	9
8	9	7	6	3	3	1	5

Puzzle mazes are popular with children, but they also have a scientific use. Psychologists use them for experiments designed to study perception, mental imagery and learning.

100 **Find the path through the maze from the shaded 7 to the shaded 2.** The path is made up of numbers that add up to seventeen.

7	1	1	3	0	1	7	8	4	5
7	2	0	1	0	1	2	4	0	6
7	8	3	9	1	0	0	5	8	2
3	4	4	0	1	1	2	0	5	6
7	8	9	1	0	8	3	0	2	7
0	9	8	2	0	1	2	0	2	2
4	5	7	8	1	0	0	1	2	9
4	5	7	8	0	1	1	1	1	9
1	0	3	6	4	1	0	1	1	5
8	9	7	6	0	9	2	3	3	5

COGNITION

Intuitive cognition of a thing is cognition that enables us
to know whether the thing exists or does not exist.
(WILLIAM OF OCCAM, C. 1287–1347)

COGNITION IS THE FACULTY WE USE TO DECIPHER INFORMATION, apply knowledge and process thoughts and ideas. The concept of cognition is closely related to the concepts of mind and intelligence. Fundamentally, all types of puzzles activate the synapses that control basic cognitive processes, but all puzzles also involve the imagination. This combination of the brain's cognitive and creative functions was called the brain's "bi-part soul" by none other than Edgar Allan Poe.

PUZZLES AND COGNITION

Cognition is essentially awareness, which is the ability to understand what something is all about at a conscious level. All aspects of cognition are activated by doing puzzles since you have to know what you are doing and how to do it in order to solve a puzzle. Research has shown that individuals who engage in cognitive activities, such as crosswords and logic games, during youth and midlife, show a reduced risk of all kinds of brain pathologies later in life. Individuals with mentally stimulating lifestyles also show less buildup of corrosive plaques in their brain.

OBJECTIVES OF THIS CHAPTER

This chapter contains fifty puzzles that are designed to stimulate various aspects of your cognitive abilities, such as applying your knowledge of basic English grammar and spelling or of basic arithmetic. You will also find a touch of mystery in this chapter, since most of the puzzles involve deciphering hidden messages. Cryptograms are thus featured here.

ARITHMETICAL PATTERN PUZZLES

WHAT IS AN ARITHMETICAL PATTERN PUZZLE?

The word *arithmetic* comes from Greek *arithmētikē*, which combines two words, *arithmos*, which means "number," and *technē*, or "art, skill." Arithmetic coincided with the advent of pictographic writing. Sumerian and Babylonian cuneiform, written on baked-clay tablets from about 5,000 years ago, show that even the earliest civilizations had sophisticated number systems and symbols for carrying out common practical activities.

Arithmetical pattern puzzles focus on the patterns and relationships between numbers that characterize the basic operations of arithmetic—adding, subtracting, multiplying, dividing, squaring, roots, fractions and so on. In this case, you will have to figure out which symbols need to be used in order to connect numbers arithmetically.

HOW TO SOLVE ARITHMETICAL PATTERN PUZZLES

Let's go through two simple examples. For each puzzle, you are given a set of numbers. The idea is to insert basic mathematical symbols (+, -, ×, ÷ and so on) to create an equation that connects the numbers logically. Note: you cannot insert numbers other than the ones given to you—just the arithmetical operation symbols. And you have to use all the given numbers in the solution.

    1. 3, 3, 9   **2.** 4, 16

As you can see below, the answers are:

    1. $3 \times 3 = 9$ or   **2.** $\sqrt{16} = 4$
        $9 \div 3 = 3$

Insert mathematical symbols to create an equation that connects the numbers logically. The principle behind solving this type of puzzle is simple; however, finding a solution requires plenty of cognitive effort and involves remembering the rules of elementary arithmetic and detecting patterns.

PUZZLES

101 2, 2, 0

102 5, 1, 4, 20

103 9, 3, 1

"I know that two and two make four and should be glad to prove it too if I could—though I must say if by any sort of process I could convert 2 and 2 into five it would give me much greater pleasure." (Lord Byron, 1788–1824).

104 2, 2, 16

105 3, 2, 7, 2

106 36, 6, 5, 1

All problems in arithmetic involve counting, grouping and comparing. Arithmetical pattern puzzles are designed to help you grasp and apply those cognitive processes.

107 7, 49, 9, 2

108 5, 5, 23, 2

109 7, 7, 7, 42, 1

110 1, 2, 3, 4, 5

HIDDEN MESSAGE PUZZLES

WHAT IS A HIDDEN MESSAGE PUZZLE?

Secret codes have been around since the dawn of history, so it is safe to say they have always fascinated us. The goal of a secret code is to transform a message written in plain language into text that hides the original message. The puzzles with this focus are called cryptograms, and you will have the opportunity to solve some later in this chapter.

HOW TO SOLVE HIDDEN MESSAGE PUZZLES

Hidden message puzzles are actually straightforward; you must find a phrase (a proverb, a saying or the like) that has been broken up and hidden within an array of letters. The idea is to sift the message out.

There is a saying hidden among the letters below. The words of the answer phrase are randomly placed throughout. Note that there may be the odd extraneous word spelled out in the aray. It is there to confuse you a little. The words of the saying can be read from left to right, and there are six words total. Once you have found the words, join them together to get the saying.

W	R	X	N	D	A	L	L	N	E	R	C	B
H	X	T	N	E	Z	O	F	B	T	H	X	R
X	S	X	H	X	B	M	M	N	X	S	P	E
N	R	O	T	H	R	R	T	P	M	N	N	H
M	S	C	D	C	E	D	W	E	L	L	R	K
E	I	S	T	E	L	G	N	W	R	N	C	W
C	R	D	S	P	L	S	V	H	S	B	X	L
T	W	X	Y	H	T	H	A	T	R	N	D	X
C	X	C	S	L	L	D	H	C	C	G	S	Y
E	N	D	S	U	T	H	R	H	S	H	L	X
X	Y	W	X	Z	X	M	X	W	E	L	L	Z

The words (shaded below) are: *ALL, WELL, IS, THAT, ENDS, WELL.*

W	R	X	N	D	A	L	L	N	E	R	C	B
H	X	T	N	E	Z	O	F	B	T	H	X	R
X	S	X	H	X	B	M	M	N	X	S	P	E
N	R	O	T	H	R	R	T	P	M	N	N	H
M	S	C	D	C	E	D	W	E	L	L	R	K
E	I	S	T	E	L	G	N	W	R	N	C	W
C	R	D	S	P	L	S	V	H	S	B	X	L
T	W	X	Y	H	T	H	A	T	R	N	D	X
C	X	C	S	L	L	D	H	C	C	G	S	Y
E	N	D	S	U	T	H	R	H	S	H	L	X
X	Y	W	X	Z	X	M	X	W	E	L	L	Z

Putting these together logically produces the saying *All is well that ends well.* In puzzles 111–116, you will be told whether the words go from left to right or from the top down. These are the only two directions that are used in the puzzles. Also, in the earlier puzzles, you will be told how many words there are. Note, too, that American English spelling will be used.

111 Direction of words: left to right. Number of words: four

W	R	X	N	D	A	L	K	R	E	R	C	B
H	X	T	Z	E	Z	N	F	B	T	H	X	R
X	S	X	H	X	Z	B	M	Q	X	S	P	E
N	R	L	E	T	R	R	T	P	M	N	N	H
M	S	C	D	Z	E	J	W	Q	L	L	R	Q
E	Z	S	T	E	R	G	Z	W	R	N	C	W
Y	O	U	R	Z	L	S	Z	H	S	B	Z	Z
T	J	H	Y	H	A	I	R	T	J	N	D	J
C	X	C	S	L	L	V	H	C	C	G	S	Y
E	Q	D	S	U	T	H	R	H	S	H	L	X
H	Y	W	D	O	W	N	X	W	Q	L	L	S

In the fifth century BCE, Spartan soldiers communicated with their field generals during battle by concealing messages across a strip of parchment which was wrapped spirally around a staff called a *scytale.* The message became unreadable when the parchment was unwound. Only the generals could read it because they had a matching staff around which they could rewrap the parchment to reveal the message.

112 **Direction of words: left to right.** Number of words: five

R	R	X	N	D	J	L	L	R	E	R	C	B
H	G	O	Q	E	Z	T	H	E	T	H	X	R
X	S	X	H	X	U	B	M	Q	S	S	P	E
N	R	O	T	Z	R	R	T	P	M	N	N	H
M	S	C	D	C	E	D	W	H	O	L	E	O
E	Q	S	T	E	R	G	Z	W	R	N	C	Q
C	R	D	S	L	L	S	U	H	S	B	Z	E
T	W	H	Z	H	T	H	J	T	R	N	D	J
C	J	C	S	L	B	D	H	C	C	G	S	Y
E	N	I	N	E	N	H	R	Y	A	R	D	S
X	Y	W	X	J	X	O	X	Q	E	Z	L	S

113 **Direction of words: top to bottom.** Number of words: five

T	R	X	N	D	X	T	L	R	E	R	C	M
H	X	B	H	B	Z	H	F	B	T	H	X	R
X	S	L	H	I	U	I	M	J	X	S	P	E
N	K	O	T	S	R	C	T	P	M	N	N	H
M	S	O	K	B	K	K	Z	K	L	L	W	Z
L	B	D	T	E	R	E	O	W	R	N	A	W
C	R	K	S	L	L	R	B	T	S	B	T	E
T	T	H	Y	H	T	H	Z	H	R	N	E	Z
C	Z	C	S	L	T	D	H	A	Q	G	R	Y
T	N	T	S	U	T	H	R	N	S	H	L	X
T	Q	W	T	A	Q	K	T	W	Z	T	L	S

Direction of words: top to bottom. Number of words: eight

C	R	I	J	D	A	K	L	R	J	R	C	B
A	X	N	H	J	Z	O	F	B	T	H	X	R
X	S	X	H	X	F	B	M	L	X	S	P	E
F	R	O	J	H	R	R	T	P	I	Q	N	H
R	S	N	D	W	I	D	W	Q	N	L	R	Q
I	Z	E	T	Q	E	G	J	W	D	N	C	W
E	R	E	S	L	N	S	Z	H	E	B	Q	J
N	W	D	Y	H	D	H	J	T	E	J	D	J
D	Q	C	S	L	L	D	H	Z	D	G	S	Y
E	N	I	Z	U	E	H	R	H	S	H	L	X
Z	Y	S	X	Z	X	O	X	B	T	R	L	S

Direction of words: left to right. Number of words: seven

Y	R	X	N	D	S	L	L	R	Z	R	C	B
H	Q	A	H	J	L	I	T	T	L	E	X	R
X	S	F	Q	X	U	W	M	O	X	S	P	E
N	L	E	A	R	N	I	N	G	M	N	N	H
M	S	C	W	C	E	J	W	Q	L	L	R	J
J	I	S	T	E	J	G	J	W	R	N	C	W
C	Y	D	S	J	I	S	U	H	S	B	A	Z
T	W	Q	Y	Z	T	Q	J	T	R	N	Z	R
D	A	N	G	E	R	O	U	S	C	G	S	Y
E	E	D	S	J	T	J	R	H	S	H	L	X
P	Y	W	X	Q	T	H	I	N	G	L	L	S

```
Z  R  V  N  J  J  Q  L  R  O  R  C  B
Z  X  A  H  J  Z  O  F  B  L  H  X  R
X  S  X  H  P  E  N  N  Y  J  S  P  Z
N  Z  O  T  H  R  J  T  P  M  N  N  H
M  S  C  D  Z  Q  J  S  A  V  E  D  D
E  I  S  T  E  H  G  H  W  R  N  C  Q
C  R  D  S  A  L  S  U  H  S  B  Z  E
T  W  H  Y  H  T  H  W  T  R  N  D  E
C  W  C  S  P  E  N  N  Y  C  G  S  Y
E  N  D  S  W  T  H  R  H  S  H  L  X
X  E  A  R  N  E  D  X  W  Z  L  Q  S
```

In his Sherlock Holmes mysteries, Sir Arthur Conan Doyle often included ciphers for the master detective to unravel as part of the plot.

For the remaining puzzles in this section, you will not be told in which direction the words can be read or how many words there are.

117

J	A	J	N	D	J	L	L	W	E	R	J	Q
H	X	T	J	E	Z	Q	F	I	T	H	X	R
X	S	W	H	X	J	B	M	S	X	S	P	E
J	R	O	L	H	R	R	T	E	M	N	N	N
M	S	R	D	Q	E	D	W	J	L	L	R	O
K	V	D	T	T	R	G	J	W	R	I	C	U
B	R	D	S	O	L	T	U	H	S	S	J	G
T	Q	H	Y	H	T	H	J	T	R	N	D	H
C	J	C	S	L	L	E	H	C	C	G	S	Y
Q	N	D	S	U	T	H	R	H	J	Q	L	X
J	Y	W	X	Q	X	J	X	W	Q	L	L	S

118

K	A	B	S	E	N	C	E	R	E	R	C	B
H	X	T	H	W	Z	P	Y	B	T	H	X	R
X	S	X	H	M	A	K	E	S	X	S	P	E
W	Q	O	T	H	R	R	T	P	Q	N	N	Y
M	S	C	D	W	V	D	T	H	E	L	R	Y
E	R	S	T	U	L	G	N	W	R	N	C	W
C	H	E	A	R	T	D	U	R	S	B	D	E
T	W	Q	Y	H	T	H	K	T	R	N	D	Q
G	R	O	W	O	L	D	H	C	C	G	S	Y
F	N	D	S	U	T	H	R	H	S	H	L	X
W	Y	W	X	J	F	O	N	D	E	R	L	S

Q R X N D R L E R Q R C B
S X A K T Z G F B T H X G
U S L H H U L M Q X S P O
C R L T A V I B P M N N L
K S C P T E T W E N L R D
E Q S T B R T D Q R N C W
C R D S L L E V H N B X Q
T W Q Y H T R B T R N D K
C Q U S L L S H C C N S Y
W N D S B T H R I M O L X
X Y W X V X P X S Q T L S

COGNITION

The Shadow, the 1930s pulp fiction crime-fighting hero, used special symbols to make ciphers, adding considerably to the aura of mystery that enveloped his character.

C	D	O	N	D	D	L	L	R	E	R	C	B
G	X	T	T	N	O	T	F	B	T	H	X	R
D	F	B	H	M	U	V	M	O	Q	S	P	B
Q	R	N	T	H	R	R	T	H	R	O	W	H
O	U	T	G	C	C	W	W	U	L	L	R	O
E	Q	S	T	T	H	E	B	B	A	B	Y	Q
C	R	D	M	L	L	P	U	H	S	B	M	E
T	W	I	T	H	T	H	A	S	R	N	D	P
C	B	C	S	L	L	T	H	E	C	M	L	Y
E	V	D	S	M	T	H	R	H	S	H	L	X
Q	Y	W	X	B	A	T	H	W	A	T	E	R

CRYPTOGRAMS: CAESAR CIPHERS

WHAT IS A CRYPTOGRAM?

Cryptograms are puzzles that hide messages. The original message is called the plaintext; it is transformed by some method, called the code or cipher, into a secret message, called the ciphertext. The code that changes one into the other is called the cryptosystem. In order to convert the ciphertext back into plaintext, you have to figure out the cryptosystem.

HOW TO SOLVE A CAESAR CIPHER PUZZLE

The most common type of cryptogram puzzle is the letter-to-letter substitution, known as a Caesar cipher because it was Julius Caesar who apparently used it as a message-hiding technique in warfare.

Here's how the puzzle works. What simple three-word phrase does the following ciphertext hide?

H M D D C X N T

It hides *I NEED YOU*. It was created by replacing each letter in the plaintext (*I NEED YOU*) with the letter directly preceding it in the alphabet. So *I* was replaced with *H* (the letter just before it), *N* with *M*, *E* with *D*, and so on.

```
H    M D D C    X N T
↑    ↑ ↑ ↑ ↑    ↑ ↑ ↑
I    N E E D    Y O U
```

All ten puzzles below hide common sayings or proverbs. The code used for the first four will be straightforward. From then on, the code will become gradually more complex. Note again that American English spelling will be used.

Here are a few hints. If you see a single-letter word, then the word is either *a* (the article) or *I* (the pronoun). The same kind of reasoning applies to two-letter words. Among the most common are: *so, to, be, is, no, do, of, go, he, me, my, ma, it, in, on, up, we*. Also note that one of the most frequent three-letter words is *the*.

If you see a double-letter at the end, then it will likely be one of these double consonants: *ll* (full, well), *ss* (lass, chess), or *tt* (butt, mutt). Other double consonants are possible, but they occur only in a few words. For example, *dd* occurs mainly in two words, *add* and *odd*. With few exceptions (*boo, too*), the two-letter vowel that is found most commonly at the end is *ee* (*wee, see*).

PUZZLES

121 The following cryptogram hides a three-word saying.

E Z L H K H Z Q H S X   A Q D D C R

_ _ _ _ _ _ _ _ _ _ _   _ _ _ _ _ _

B N M S D L O S

_ _ _ _ _ _ _ _

122 The following cryptogram hides a four-word saying.

Y   B G Y K M L B   G Q   D M P C T C P

_   _ _ _ _ _ _ _   _ _   _ _ _ _ _ _ _

123 The following cryptogram hides a six-word saying.

Q E B   P N R B X H V   T E B B I

_ _ _   _ _ _ _ _ _ _   _ _ _ _ _

D B Q P   Q E B   D O B X P B

_ _ _ _   _ _ _   _ _ _ _ _ _

> The first use of cryptograms for recreational purposes dates back to a ninth century manuscript found at Bamberg, Germany. It contains a cryptogram puzzle that encodes Latin letters into Greek letters.

124 The following cryptogram hides a four-word saying.

E N Q S T M D   E Z U N Q R   S G D

_ _ _ _ _ _ _   _ _ _ _ _ _   _ _ _

A N K C

_ _ _ _

125 The following cryptogram hides a four-word saying.

Z C R R C P   J Y R C   R F Y L

_ _ _ _ _ _   _ _ _ _   _ _ _ _

L C T C P

_ _ _ _ _

Ancient Jewish writers sometimes concealed their messages by substituting one letter of the Hebrew alphabet with another—the last letter in place of the first, the second last for the second, and so on. Their method was called *atbash.*

126 The following cryptogram hides a seven-word saying.

B   Q J D U V S F   J T   X P S U I   B

U I P V T B O E   X P S E T

127 The following cryptogram hides a seven-word saying.

F K U E T G V K Q P   K U   V J G

I T G C V G T   R C T V   Q H   X C N Q T

128 The following cryptogram hides a six-word saying.

W K H   H D U O B   E L U G

F D W F K H V   W K H   Z R U P

The following cryptogram hides a five-word saying.

B D U J P O T   T Q F B L   M P V E F S

_ _ _ _ _ _ _   _ _ _ _ _   _ _ _ _ _ _

U I B O   X P S E T

_ _ _ _   _ _ _ _ _

> Edgar Allan Poe used a cryptogram puzzle in his story "The Gold Bug" (1843). Cryptograms have also appeared in other mysteries, such as Jules Verne's *La Jangada* (1881) and Maurice Leblanc's *The Hollow Needle* (1909).

The following cryptogram hides a six-word saying.

Y T T   R F S D   H T T P X   X U T N Q

_ _ _   _ _ _ _   _ _ _ _ _   _ _ _ _ _

Y M J   G W T Y M

_ _ _   _ _ _ _ _

CRYPTOGRAMS: POLYBIUS CIPHERS

WHAT IS A POLYBIUS CIPHER?

Replacing the letters of a text with numbers is called a Polybius cipher, after the Greek historian Polybius (c. 200–118 BCE), who was among the first to encrypt messages in this way.

HOW TO SOLVE POLYBIUS CIPHERS

One simple Polybius code would be to replace each letter of the plaintext with digits in numerical order. For example, if the plaintext is *I LOVE LOLA,* the code would replace *I* with 1, as *I* is the first letter in the text, *L* with 2, since *L* is the second letter in the text, and so on. The end result is the following ciphertext.

<u>1</u>   <u>2</u> <u>3</u> <u>4</u> <u>5</u>   <u>2</u> <u>3</u> <u>2</u> <u>6</u>

Note that the same number is used for the same letter, no matter where it appears. So, the letter *L* is replaced with 2 in the word *LOVE* once and then is used twice in the word *LOLA:*

I   L O V E   L O L A
↑   ↑ ↑ ↑ ↑   ↑ ↑ ↑ ↑
<u>1</u>   <u>2</u> <u>3</u> <u>4</u> <u>5</u>   <u>2</u> <u>3</u> <u>2</u> <u>6</u>

You will have to figure out the cryptosystem by recognizing partial words as they emerge gradually. Clues will be given for all the puzzles below—more clues for the earlier puzzles, of course. For instance, in the puzzle above, you might be given the following two clues:

L   O
<u>1</u>   <u>2</u> <u>3</u> <u>4</u> <u>5</u>   <u>2</u> <u>3</u> <u>2</u> <u>6</u>

Given that *L* = 2, replace every *L* with the number 2:

L   L O L
<u>1</u>   <u>2</u> <u>3</u> <u>4</u> <u>5</u>   <u>2</u> <u>3</u> <u>2</u> <u>6</u>

Then use the clue that *O* = 3 as shown:

L O   L O L
<u>1</u>   <u>2</u> <u>3</u> <u>4</u> <u>5</u>   <u>2</u> <u>3</u> <u>2</u> <u>6</u>

The rest of the solution involves deducing which letter sequences make legitimate words in English. After a few trial-and-error substitutions, the only solution that is viable linguistically is *I LOVE LOLA*. The hints described above for Caesar ciphers apply here, as well.

Any method of substitution may be used. For example, for the same text, the number assigned to each letter might reflect the position of each letter in the alphabet sequence. So, *A* = 1 because it is the first letter in the alphabet; *B* = 2 because it is the second letter in the alphabet. Note that many numbers in the usual numerical sequence (1, 2, 3, …) will be skipped because of this code: if there is no *B*, the number 2 will not appear; if there is no *C*, the number 3 will not appear; and so on.

I	L	O	V	E		L	O	L	A
↑	↑	↑	↑	↑		↑	↑	↑	↑
9	12	15	22	5		12	15	12	1

Just to make sure you understand:

A = 1 because it is the first letter in the alphabet
E = 5 because it is the fifth letter in the alphabet
I = 9 because it is the ninth letter in the alphabet
L = 12 because it is the twelfth letter in the alphabet
O = 15 because it is the fifteenth letter in the alphabet
V = 22 because it is the twenty-second letter in the alphabet

PUZZLES

131 The following cryptogram hides a three-word saying.

P		C						M								T
1	2	3	4	5	6	4	7		8	3	9	7	10		1	7	2	11	7	4	5

132 The following cryptogram hides a six-word saying.

                    A   E   T

20 23 15   8 5 1 4 19   1 18 5   2 5 20 20 5 18

20 8 1 14   15 14 5

133 The following cryptogram hides a five-word saying. Clue: Note that the numbers are all even.

H   I   E

2 4 6 8 10 12 14   16 10   12 2 8   18 8 10 12

P

20 4 22 16 24 14

> Cryptograms based on substitution patterns involve frequency analysis, or recognizing frequent letter- and word-formation patterns such as double letters (*wood, tool*), single-letter words (*I and a*), and other frequent grammatical and spelling patterns. These are all cognitive processes that are normally subconscious but are brought to awareness by cryptogram puzzles.

134 The following cryptogram hides a seven-word saying. Clue: Note that the numbers are all odd.

G   S   O

1 3 3 5   7 9 11 13 1 15   17 3 19 21   7 3

T

7 9 3 15 21   23 9 3   23 25 11 7

135 The following cryptogram hides a six-word saying.

  N   T   E

3 6 9 6 12 12 15 18 21   15 12   18 24 6

                                             I

27 30 18 24 6 33   30 36   15 3 39 6 3 18 15 30 3

136 The following cryptogram hides an eight-word saying.

  B   E

1 2 3 4 5 6   7 8   7 9   5 10 2   2 6 2

                                           L

11 12   5 10 2   1 2 10 11 13 14 2 15

137 The following cryptogram hides a six-word saying.

  B   S   A

2 9 18 4 19   15 6   1   6 5 1 20 8 5 18

F

6 12 15 3 11   20 15 7 5 20 8 5 18

138 The following cryptogram hides a seven-word saying.

                      T   G

5 10 15   20 15 25 5   5 10 30 35 40 25   30 35

              E   F

45 30 50 15   55 60 15   50 60 15 15

139 The following cryptogram hides a seven-word saying. Clue: The vowels and the consonants are replaced with different patterns.

                I   T   S

6 12 2   18 3 24 30 6   30 6 2 36   3 30

A   H

1 42 48 1 54 30   6 12 2   12 1 24 60 2 30 6

> It was during World War II that the science of cryptography showed its importance. British Intelligence hired thousands of people to crack codes, including the renowned mathematician Alan Turing, a pioneer in computer theory. Because of security restrictions, Turing's role as a cryptographer was not known until long after his death. Although he isn't mentioned explicitly in the film, his contributions to wartime codebreaking were glorified in the movie *Enigma.*

140 The following cryptogram hides a six-word saying.

M   D   N

1 2 3 4 5   6 2 4 7   3 2 8   9 10 2 11

         T

2 3   8 10 4 4 7

CRYPTOGRAMS: TRANSPOSITION CIPHERS

WHAT IS A TRANSPOSITION CIPHER?

The cryptograms you have been deciphering so far are known as substitution ciphers because they involve some form of substitution. Another widely used method of encrypting messages is by transposition, which involves rearranging the letters or words in the plaintext in some way.

HOW TO SOLVE TRANSPOSITION CIPHERS

Let's go through one example. The hidden message *SARA LOVES JIM* might be encrypted by writing the words backward (*SARA LOVES JIM = ARAS SEVOL MIJ*); by separating the vowels from the consonants (*SRAA LVSOE JMI*); by a combination of these two systems (*AARS EOSVL IMJ*); and so on. Transposition cryptograms will get those synapses firing at high rates. As with the previous types of ciphers, all the hidden messages are common sayings or proverbs.

PUZZLES

141 The following cryptogram hides a four-word saying.
SORRY SAFE BETTER THAN

142 The following cryptogram hides a four-word saying.
YTISOIRUC DELLIK EHT TAC

143 The following cryptogram hides a five-word saying.
TI TKSAE TWO TO TNGAO

144 The following cryptogram hides a four-word saying.

LOD ASBHIT IDE AHRD

145 The following cryptogram hides a five-word saying.

NOTHINGHURTSLIKETHETRUTH

146 The following cryptogram hides a six-word saying.

AIEVRTY IS ETH IESPC OF IELF

147 The following cryptogram hides a five-word saying.

UOY PAER TAHW UOY WOS

148 The following cryptogram hides a nine-word saying.

BAD THE WITH GOOD THE TAKE TO HAVE YOU

149 The following cryptogram hides a five-word saying.

NEO OGOD TRUN EDSREVSE NATOHRE

American president Thomas Jefferson built an ingenious device for making Caesar ciphers. It consisted of wooden wheels, each representing the letters of the alphabet printed in different arrangements. He called it the wheel cipher.

150 The following cryptogram hides a nine-word saying.

TUB EHT HSELF SI KAEW EHT TIRIPS SI GNILLIW

4

REASONING

All of our reasoning ends in surrender to feeling.
(BLAISE PASCAL, 1623–1662)

LEWIS CARROLL WAS ONE OF THE GREATEST PUZZLE MAKERS of all time. In his book *The Game of Logic,* he introduced a system of reasoning involving symbols that continue to have implications today for the study of formal logic systems. Basically he showed that abstract reasoning reveals a recognizable structure but is also characterized by the odd twist and turn. Reasoning, along with memory, perception and cognition, is a basic faculty of the mind, allowing us to figure things out in logical, commonsense ways.

PUZZLES AND REASONING

There exists significant research on the neurological benefits that derive from solving reasoning puzzles, such as sudoku. The research shows that such puzzles attenuate or delay the onset of dementia, and Alzheimer's in particular. The latter is a brain disease that causes the progressive loss of memory and other mental abilities. It is the most common cause of severe memory loss in adults over the age of sixty. The disease is named after Alois Alzheimer, a German psychiatrist, who in 1906 first described its deleterious effects on brain cells.

The Alzheimer's Association of the United States endorses puzzles as part of a preventive strategy against the dreaded disease. One of the most relevant of the studies on the subject was published by *The New England Journal of Medicine* in 2003. The study found that 469 participants (aged seventy-five and older) who did puzzles and engaged in other activities for about four days a week were two-thirds less likely to develop Alzheimer's when compared to those who did these activities once a week or less, or not at all. As previously mentioned, any mentally challenging activity gets the brain to establish new synaptic connections or even to grow new cells. This extra brainpower may compensate for any loss of brain cells due to the aging process.

OBJECTIVES OF THIS CHAPTER

The fifty puzzles in this chapter are designed to help you exercise your reasoning skills. They include placement puzzles, lie-detection puzzles, comparison puzzles, cryptarithms (arithmetical problems with numbers missing), and alphametics (arithmetical problems laid out with letter substitutions).

PLACEMENT PUZZLES

WHAT IS A PLACEMENT PUZZLE?

A placement puzzle is any puzzle that involves putting symbols, numbers or letters in cells or in other formats according to some rule or rules. The most popular placement puzzle today is, of course, sudoku. Its origins go back to 1979 when a "number place" puzzle appeared in the May issue of *Dell Pencil Puzzles and Crossword Games*. The inventor of the puzzle was a man named Howard Garns, an editor at the magazine. In 1984, an editor for *Nikoli* magazine in Japan came across one of these puzzles. He loved it so much that he decided to put out an entire magazine devoted to it. He called the puzzle *sudoku*, which is short for the Japanese phrase meaning "only single numbers allowed."

HOW TO SOLVE PLACEMENT PUZZLES

The puzzles below consist of Latin Squares (four puzzles), standard sudoku puzzles (three puzzles) and symbol and figure logic puzzles (three puzzles). A three-by-three Latin Square, for example, is solved by arranging three numbers—in this case 1, 2 and 3—into the nine cells of the square in such a way that each column and row contains each number just once and so that no number is repeated in any row or column. Look at the puzzle below in which three numbers are already inserted. The idea is to complete the rest of the square on the basis of these three clues using reasoning alone:

```
| 1 |   | 3 |
|   |   |   |
|   |   | 2 |
```

Note that the number 2 is missing from the top row. So, to complete it, let's put the number 2 in the empty cell:

```
| 1 | 2 | 3 |
|   |   |   |
|   |   | 2 |
```

The column to the far right has the numbers 3 and 2 in it. Missing from its middle cell is 1. Let's put it there to complete the column:

```
| 1 | 2 | 3 |
|   |   | 1 |
|   |   | 2 |
```

Now, let's complete the left-most column. We could try putting a 3 in the middle cell, but this would mean that 2 must be placed in the bottom cell (to complete the triplet in the column) and, as you can see, there is a 2 already in the bottom row. The rules prohibit us from repeating any number in a row or column in which it already appears.

1	2	3
3		1
2		2

So, the only possibility is shown below:

1	2	3
2		1
3		2

The remaining cells can be completed easily as indicated. Note that the three digits are located in each row and column, but there is no repetition of a number in the row or column in which it has been placed.

1	2	3
2	3	1
3	1	2

Sudoku is a well-known puzzle, having become a veritable craze since 2005. But just in case you are new to it, let's do a simple example. The digits from 1 to 9 have to be placed in each row and column of the grid and in each three-by-three box (outlined in bold). The rules that apply to the Latin Square apply here, as well—no repetition of a digit is allowed in any row, column or box.

1	9	7	4	2	3		6	5
	4			6				9
	5				7		2	1
7	1		5	3	8	2		6
	3	6		1		5	9	8
8			6	4		7	1	
9		2	3		4		5	7
3	7		2			9		4
5	8				1			2

The top row is missing only the digit 8 (all the other digits from 1 to 9 have already been inserted). So, let's put it there:

1	9	7	4	2	3	8	6	5
	4			6				9
	5				7		2	1
7	1		5	3	8	2		6
	3	6		1		5	9	8
8			6	4		7	1	
9		2	3		4		5	7
3	7		2			9		4
5	8				1			2

The right-most column is missing just one number—3. Let's put it in the cell:

1	9	7	4	2	3	8	6	5
	4			6				9
	5				7		2	1
7	1		5	3	8	2		6
	3	6		1		5	9	8
8			6	4		7	1	3
9		2	3		4		5	7
3	7		2			9		4
5	8				1			2

We can now complete the middle right-most box, which, as you can see, is just missing a 4 (since all of the other cells have been populated with numbers between 1 and 9).

1	9	7	4	2	3	8	6	5
	4			6				9
	5				7		2	1
7	1		5	3	8	2	4	6
	3	6		1		5	9	8
8			6	4		7	1	3
9		2	3		4		5	7
3	7		2			9		4
5	8				1			2

Keep reasoning in this fashion until you fill the whole grid, making sure that all rows, columns and boxes contain the nine digits without repeating any digit. The completed sudoku is shown below:

1	9	7	4	2	3	8	6	5
2	4	8	1	6	5	3	7	9
6	5	3	8	9	7	4	2	1
7	1	9	5	3	8	2	4	6
4	3	6	7	1	2	5	9	8
8	2	5	6	4	9	7	1	3
9	6	2	3	8	4	1	5	7
3	7	1	2	5	6	9	8	4
5	8	4	9	7	1	6	3	2

Finally, symbol and figure logic puzzles consist of a grid of symbols or figures. You have to determine logically how to complete the grid. Here is an example:

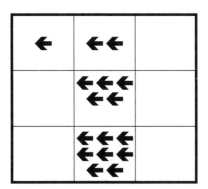

Starting at the top left cell and going from left to right all the way to the bottom right cell, you can see that the placement pattern consists of adding one extra ← to each succeeding cell: one in the first, two in the second, three in the third, and so on.

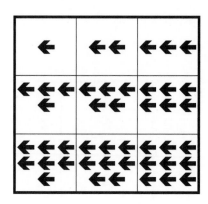

PUZZLES

Puzzles 151–154 are Latin Squares.

151 The puzzle below is a three-by-three square, which means that you have to insert the digits 1, 2 and 3 in each row and column without repetition.

1		
3		
	3	1

152 The puzzle below is a four-by-four square, which means that you have to insert the digits 1, 2, 3 and 4 according to the same rules.

	4	3	
3			4
		1	3
			1

153 The puzzle below is a five-by-five square, which means that you have to insert the digits 1, 2, 3, 4 and 5 according to the same rules.

	4	1		3
			1	
2	5			
	1		5	4
		3	4	5

In 1997, Wayne Gould, a retired judge from New Zealand, picked up a Japanese sudoku puzzle magazine while working in Hong Kong. Gould became intrigued by the puzzle and started making his own. They were published in the *Conway Daily Sun* in New Hampshire starting in 2004. Two months later, they were printed in the *Times of London.* By early 2005, sudoku became a craze in Britain, quickly spreading throughout the world from there.

154 The puzzle below is a six-by-six square, which means that you have to insert the digits 1, 2, 3, 4, 5 and 6 according to the same rules.

6		1	4		2
5	4			6	
	3			2	6
	2			5	4
2		6			
4		3	2		5

Puzzles 155–157 are standard sudoku puzzles.

155

1	2	5	4			7	9	
		9	8			4		
		6	9	2	7	1		3
9	6	8	3	1	4	5		7
2	7				5	3	4	9
4	5				9			1
6	9	4	1		2	8	7	
			7				3	
3				9	6	2	1	4

> The number of sudoku puzzles that can be made with the numbers 1 through 9 is 6,670,903,752,021,072,936,960. It would take a computer more than 211 billion years to solve them all!

156

	6	5		3	1	4	9	
2								5
8	1	3		5			6	7
	3	7		8	6	9	2	
6			7	1			5	4
4	9	1	3		5		7	6
3	2		5					9
		8			2	5	4	3
	5			7	3		8	

		6	9			2		5
			1			4		8
8			3			9	7	1
		5	4		2	3	8	9
				1				
2	3		6	9	8			7
3	4				9	7	5	2
		7			1	8		
5		8	7			1	9	6

Puzzles 158–160 are symbol and figure logic puzzles. Fill in the empty squares with the appropriate number and placement of symbols or figures.

158

À	Á	È
		Í
	Ó	Ù

159

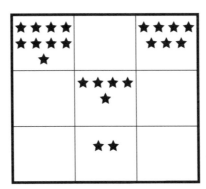

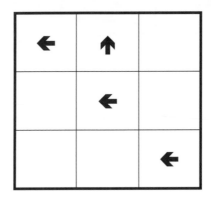

LIE-DETECTION PUZZLES

WHAT IS A LIE-DETECTION PUZZLE?

This type of puzzle involves deducing who the perpetrator of some crime is on the basis of statements made by various people, some of which are true and others false. An example of how to solve one is given below.

HOW TO SOLVE LIE-DETECTION PUZZLES

Five suspicious people were rounded up yesterday by the police. One was suspected of having robbed a bank. Under questioning, here's what each one said.

Annie:	Amelia did not do it.
Arnie:	I agree. Amelia did not do it.
Amy:	Annie did not do it.

Anita:	I did not do it.
Amelia:	I did not do it.

All of them, except the robber who lied, told the truth. Can you identify the bank robber? The answer is Anita. Below is the reasoning.

REASONING:

Annie and Arnie say the same thing, namely that Amelia is innocent. So, the two statements are either both true or both false. Since there is only one liar in the group (the robber), this means that the two statements cannot both be lies. So, they are both true. This also means that Amelia is innocent, as both truthful statements tell us. Not being the robber, Amelia thus told the truth, as well, simply asserting that she did not do it. Amy says that Annie did not do it. This is true because Annie, as we saw, told the truth and we know that only the robber lied. So, the four who told the truth are Amy, Annie, Arnie and Amelia. This leaves Anita as the liar and, thus, the robber. So, despite what she says, which is a lie, Anita is our robber.

PUZZLES

161 Five people were interviewed by the police a few days ago. One of them was suspected of having murdered a person in a fit of rage. Here's what each one said to the police.

Bill:	I didn't kill anyone.
Benny:	Nor did I.
Theresa:	Tamara did it.
Tina:	Yeah, Tamara did do it.
Tamara:	No, Theresa did it.

The three women (Theresa, Tina and Tamara) lied. The two men (Bill and Benny) told the truth. Can you identify the killer?

162 Jake, Diane, Doris, Debby and Jasper were rounded up by the police last week. One of them was suspected of having robbed an automated teller machine. Here's what each one said to the police.

Jake:	I didn't do it.
Diane:	Debby did not do it.
Doris:	I didn't do it.
Debby:	I did not do it.
Jasper:	Jake didn't do it.

Four told the truth. Only the robber lied. Can you identify the robber?

163 Five individuals were brought in by the police yesterday. One of them was suspected of having robbed a bank. Here's what each one said to the police.

Helen:	Vince is innocent.
Vince:	I didn't do it.
Victor:	Van didn't do it.
Van:	I didn't do it.
Harriet:	Van didn't do it.

Three told the truth. Two lied, including the robber. Can you identify the robber?

> **Philosopher Ludwig Wittgenstein (1889–1951) asserted the following about logic: "Logic takes care of itself; all we have to do is to look and see how it does it."**

164 Five insurance company employees were interrogated by the police yesterday. One of them was suspected of embezzlement. Here's what each one said to the police.

Karen:	Katy didn't do it.
Katy:	Karen told the truth. I didn't do it.
Sam:	I know for a fact that Karen didn't do it.

Sal:	Sam didn't do it.
Sid:	Sal didn't do it.

Strangely, everyone told the truth, including the embezzler. Can you identify the embezzler?

165 Five gangsters were rounded up by the police recently. One of them was suspected of having killed a member of a rival gang. Here's what each one said to the police.

Arnie:	Sheila did it.
Andy:	I don't know who did it.
Al:	Sherrie did it.
Sherrie:	Al did it.
Sheila:	Arnie accused me, but it was he who did it.

Everyone lied. Can you identify the killer?

166 The police arrested Eric, Eddy, Ethan, Cara and Cindy yesterday, suspecting one of them of being a cold-case killer. Here's what each one said to the police.

Eric:	Neither woman is the murderer.
Eddy:	Eric is the murderer.
Ethan:	I know who the murderer is.
Cara:	Eric didn't do it.
Cindy:	Eddy didn't do it.

The two women, Cara and Cindy, told the truth. Of the other three suspects, all men, two told the truth and one lied. Can you identify the killer?

> Logical reasoning is often built into popular games. One of these is cribbage. Strangely, the inventor was not a logician or mathematician. It was Sir John Suckling (1609–1642), an English poet of the early seventeenth century.

167 Five people were rounded up and brought in for questioning, since the police suspected one of them of having murdered a rival in romance. Here's what each one said to the police.

Frank:	Flip didn't do it.
Mary:	Frank did it.
Francis:	I didn't do it, believe me.
Flip:	Either Mary or Flavius did it.
Flavius:	I didn't do it.

Everyone told the truth except the only female in the group, Mary, who lied. Can you identify the killer?

168 Five individuals were rounded up a week ago by the police. One of them was suspected of having robbed a bank. Here's what each one said to the police.

Laura:	Lana is innocent.
Ben:	I agree, Lana is innocent.
Lisa:	Laura is innocent.
Liz:	I am innocent.
Lana:	I am innocent.

All of them, except the robber, told the truth. Can you identify the bank robber?

169 Five people—Nora, Nina, Paul, Phil and Pat—were arrested and questioned by the police yesterday. One of them was suspected of having stolen a famous painting. Here's what each one said to the police.

Nora:	Paul is innocent.
Nina:	Yes, it's true. Paul did not do it.
Paul:	I don't know who did it.
Phil:	All I know is that I didn't do it.
Pat:	Paul did not do it.

Three told the truth and two lied. Can you identify the thief?

170 Five individuals were brought in by the police for questioning. One of them was suspected of having killed a fellow gangster. Here's what each one said to the police.

Jack:	Jason did it.
Jason:	No, Jim did it.
Rosa:	I didn't do it for sure.
Jim:	I do not know anything.
Roberta:	Jack didn't do it.

The two women—Rosa and Roberta—both told the truth. All three of the men in the group—Jack, Jason and Jim—lied. Can you identify the killer?

COMPARISON PUZZLES

WHAT IS A COMPARISON PUZZLE?

Everyday life presents us with practical puzzles. Suppose you haven't seen John and Mary since childhood. You are now told that John is taller than you are but that you are taller than Mary. Then who is the shortest? This is, clearly, a puzzle that involves comparison and logical reasoning.

HOW TO SOLVE COMPARISON PUZZLES

Consider the practical puzzle above. John (J) is taller than you are, so he is taller than Mary (M). To put it another way, Mary is shorter than John. We can show this as follows, by putting John before Mary in the line: J—M. Since you (Y) are taller than Mary but shorter than John, you can only be placed between the two in the line: J—Y—M. This shows that you are taller than Mary, but shorter than John. It also shows that Mary is the shortest.

PUZZLES

171 Bill is older than Jane. Sarah is younger than Jane. Who is the oldest?

172 Four people were in a race: Al, Bill, Carrie and Dawn. Al came in behind Bill. Carrie beat Bill, but came in behind Dawn. Who won the race?

173 Four students took the same test. Wayne scored lower than Sheila. Danny scored higher than Shirley. Shirley scored lower than Gina, while Gina scored lower than Danny. Who scored the lowest?

Thomas Edison (1847–1931) remarked that "Genius is one percent inspiration and ninety-nine percent perspiration."

174 There are four siblings in the Charlton family—two brothers, Andy and Ben, and two sisters, Carrie and Darlene. Andy is older than Ben. And Darlene is older than Carrie. Carrie is younger than Ben and Andy is younger than Darlene. Who is the oldest?

175 Four pole-vault jumpers—Sandy, Wes, Mitch and Tara—competed in a tournament recently. Sandy did not win, but she came in before two others. Wes did not win, nor did he come in last. Tara beat Mitch. Who came in first?

176 Five people work in the same bank—Robert, Frieda, Lucy, Carla and Mohan. Each earns a different salary. Robert earns more than Carla but less than Mohan, who earns less than Frieda, who, in turn, earns less than Lucy. Who earns the least?

177 Five brothers are all enrolled at the same university. They were comparing their grades the other day. Bill has a higher overall average than two other brothers. Phil has a lower average than Sam but a higher one than Bill. Jack has a lower average than Mack. Who has the lowest overall average?

178 Six sisters compete every year in the same swimming competition. The outcome this year was the same as it has always been: Bertha was just in front of Martha; Jeannie was just in front of Sonya; Helen was just in front of Norma. To complete the picture, Norma beat Bertha, and Martha beat Jeannie. Who won?

179 Six friends—Andrew, Jake, Earl, Kyle, Sid and Lenny—got together for a friendly foot race. Andrew beat four others, but came in behind Jake. Earl beat Kyle. Sid beat Lenny, but not Kyle. Who came in last?

180 Seven lottery winners got together to compare their winnings. Dick won more than Francesca but less than Karen and Laura. Laura won less than Sally, but Karen won more than Sally. Timothy won more than Francesca but less than Dick. Finally, Nicola won less than Sally but more than Laura. Who won the most?

CRYPTARITHMS

WHAT IS A CRYPTARITHM?

A cryptarithm is an arithmetical layout (of addition, division and so on) with missing numbers that you are supposed to supply by pure reasoning. The inventor was the great American puzzle maker Sam Loyd (1841–1911).

HOW TO SOLVE CRYPTARITHMS

Let's go through a very simple cryptarithm. You are given a layout of an addition problem with missing digits. The objective is to restore the digits logically.

```
    ...  8  ...
+    1   2   3
_____
    ...  1  ...  5
```

It can instantly be established that the empty slot at the extreme left is a carry-over digit equal to 1, because 1 is the only carry-over possible when two digits are added together in the previous column, even if the column has itself a carry-over from the column before it. A little trial and error with different digits will show you this. Let's put 1 into that empty slot:

```
    ...  8  ...
+    1   2   3
_____
 1   1  ...  5
```

Now, look at the right-most column. The empty slot at the top can only be 2, since that is the only digit that, when added to 3 (just below it), produces the 5 below the line. Let's put it in:

```
    ...  8   2
+    1   2   3
_____
 1   1  ...  5
```

This also means that there is no carry-over to the next column over. So, we can safely add 0 in the empty slot below the line since 8 + 2 = 10, and we carry 1 over to the next column:

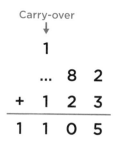

Carry-over
↓
1

```
    ... 8 2
  + 1 2 3
  ─────────
  1 1 0 5
```

Now, we can see that the only number that produces 11 below the line in the second-to-left column is 9 since 1 (carry-over) + 9 + 1 = 11. This completes the solution.

```
    9 8 2
  + 1 2 3
  ─────────
  1 1 0 5
```

PUZZLES

Puzzles 181, 182, 183 and 184 are addition cryptarithms.

181

```
    3 ...
  + ... 1
  ─────────
  ... 1 3
```

182

```
  ... 5 ...
  + 6 ... 2
  ──────────
  ... 0 6 0
```

183

```
    ... 9 0 ...
+   ... ... ... 0
─────────────────
    ... 7 8 1 1
```

184

```
    1 ... ... 4 5
+   ... 0 3 ... 5
─────────────────
    ... 0 2 6 9 0
```

Puzzles 185, 186, 187 and 188 are subtraction cryptarithms.

185

```
      4 3
-   ... ...
─────────
      1 5
```

186

```
    ... 3 ...
-   4 1 2
─────────
    5 ... 9
```

187

```
      7  6  …  …
  –   …  …  1  2
  ─────────────
         1  2  2
```

188

```
   6  5  …  8  …
 – 1  …  9  …  0
 ──────────────
   …  8  0  6  3
```

Puzzles 189 and 190 are multiplication cryptarithms.

189

```
      3  …  6
  ×         …
  ──────────
      7  1  2
```

> The psychologists R. J. Sternberg and J. E. Davidson argued, as far back as 1982, that solving puzzles requires the ability to compare information in a puzzle with information already in memory and then to formulate a solution.

190

```
   …  0  …  9
 ×          3
 ────────────
   6  …  5  …
```

ALPHAMETICS

WHAT IS AN ALPHAMETIC?

An alphametic is a puzzle in which an arithmetical operation is represented with words. The idea is to reconstruct the operation by determining what numbers the letters of the words stand for. The inventor of this puzzle genre is British puzzlist Henry E. Dudeney (1857–1930). Like the cryptarithm above, you will have to hone your reasoning skills. This type of puzzle adds a layer of difficulty because you are not given any numbers at all, just the letters that substitute for them.

HOW TO SOLVE ALPHAMETICS

Let's do a simple addition alphametic. Note that each line of the addition is made up of legitimate words or names. All alphametics work this way. In this case it is *ONE + ONE = KNEE*.

```
    O N E
+   O N E
---------
  K N E E
```

As in the case with the illustrative cryptarithm on page 110, the only possible number that *K* can stand for is 1. The same reasoning applies here. If you have forgotten, just go back and reread the explanation. Let's put it in.

```
    O N E
+   O N E
---------
  1 N E E
```

Now, look at the right-most column. The same two numbers are added together to produce the same number. The only digit that fits that pattern is 0, since 0 + 0 = 0. So, *E* = 0. Let's put this value in wherever *E* occurs:

```
    O N O
+   O N O
─────────
  1 N O O
```

Now, consider the middle column with $N + N = 0$. Clearly, only $N = 5$ fits this pattern. Let's put this value in wherever N occurs:

```
    O 5 O
+   O 5 O
─────────
  1 5 0 0
```

There is a carry-over of 1 in the next column over. Thus, with $O = 7$, we can complete the alphametic since 1 (carry-over) + 7 + 7 = 15.

```
       Carry-over
          ↓
          1
       7 5 0
+      7 5 0
───────────
  1 5 0 0
```

The solution is, therefore:

```
       7 5 0
+      7 5 0
───────────
  1 5 0 0
```

In the ten puzzles below, the occasional Italian word or abbreviation might be used. The solution method, though, is the same.

Puzzles 191–195 are addition alphametics.

191

```
    M E
  + M E
  ─────
  S E E
```

192

```
    T W O
  + T W O
  ───────
  W O O
```

193 One of the words in the puzzle below (*SETRE*) is actually a jumbled word (*TREES*). This does not change the solution method, though.

```
    T E A R
  + S T A R
  ─────────
  S E T R E
```

> Although Dudeney was the inventor of the alphametic, it was likely the puzzlist J. A. H. Hunter who first used the word *alphametic* in his book, *Fun with Figures.*

194 The bottom word of this alphametic is actually two words (*ON*, *TOO*) written together (*ONTOO*).

```
    M   O   O   N
+   M   O   N   O
─────────────────
O   N   T   O   O
```

195 The alphametic below contains the Italian word *MAMMA*, which means mom. The last word is *NANNA* with an extra *A* (*NANNAA*), just like a child would pronounce the endearing word for grandmother.

```
    M   A   M   M   A
+   M   A   M   M   A
─────────────────────
N   A   N   N   A   A
```

Puzzles 196, 197 and 198 are subtraction alphametics.

196 The word *DA* below is the abbreviation for district attorney.

```
    D   A   D
-   O   D   D
─────────────
        D   A
```

197 The puzzle below contains an eclectic mix of words. There is *PAPA*, which is Italian for pope. Then there is the abbreviation *PSAS*, the plural of *PSA*, the enzyme released by the prostate. Finally, there is *PAA*, which is *PA*, colloquial for father, with an extra *A* at the end to show how it might be pronounced by children.

```
    P   A   P   A
-       P   A   A
─────────────────
    P   S   A   S
```

Studies investigating the relationship between puzzle solving and IQ have shown that the two do not always correlate. This is actually good news, since it means that we do not require any particular kind of intelligence to do puzzles. Simply put, puzzles are solved by all kinds of individuals, no matter what their IQs are. Some are better at it than others, but this is true of anything in life.

198

```
    D A R E D
  -   R A R E
  _____
    N E R D
```

Puzzles 199 and 200 are multiplication alphametics.

199 Note that in addition to two words there is the letter *B* as the single-digit multiplier.

```
    B A D
  ×     B
  _____
  A D D
```

200 As random and intractable as the following alphametic seems, it does have a singular solution. Again, note the letter *S* as the single-digit multiplier.

```
    B O S S
  ×       S
  _____
  S I T S
```

5

MODULARITY

I consider that a man's brain originally is like a little empty attic,
and you have to stock it with such furniture as you choose.
(SIR ARTHUR CONAN DOYLE, 1859–1930)

THE TERM *MODULARITY* is used in neuroscience today to describe the presence of units or modules of thought in the brain that, when combined, allow the brain to carry out complex tasks such as problem solving or detecting anomalies or lies. Modularity is evidence that combination, arrangement and blending are intrinsic aspects of the human mind. When we put words together into sentences and sentences into texts we are, in effect, employing modularity to make sense of things.

PUZZLES AND MODULARITY

More technically, the term *modularity* refers to the idea that the mind is composed of independent processing modules that underlie most cognitive states. In a fundamental sense, all the positive research on puzzles has essentially confirmed that the mind is modular. Solving a crossword puzzle, for example, requires the activation of several faculties, including inference and memory. Indeed, if puzzles enhance memory, it is probably because they activate modularity. Our memory system seems to operate as a chain of association modules: concepts, words and ideas are linked so that information can be deciphered meaningfully. Understanding the relationships between different objects and ideas is fundamental to memory.

OBJECTIVES OF THIS CHAPTER

This chapter contains fifty puzzles designed to get various faculties of the brain—inference, association and so on—to work in tandem. Here, you will find puzzles whose solutions seem intractable, but which actually have simple ones. Be careful and good luck!

KNIGHTS AND KNAVES

WHAT IS A KNIGHTS AND KNAVES PUZZLE?

The knights and knaves puzzle, as it is commonly called, is a perfect example of how modular thinking unfolds. Each puzzle in this genre is about a fictional place in which all inhabitants are either knights, who always tell the truth, or knaves, who always lie. From their statements, you are asked to deduce something. Solutions require the use of deductive logic combined with inference. The label *knights and knaves* was given to this genre by master logic puzzlist Raymond Smullyan, mentioned in the previous chapter.

HOW TO SOLVE KNIGHTS AND KNAVES PUZZLES

Here is a paraphrase of the original knights and knaves problem.

The people of a remote island belong to one of two tribes—the Blues or the Maroons (names translated into English). Everyone speaks the same language. Strangely, the members of the Blue tribe always tell the truth, whereas the members of the Maroon tribe always lie. A visitor to the island stopped three islanders. "Are you a Blue?" she asked the first. "Eo don rooma," replied the islander in his native language. "What did he say?" asked the visitor of the second and third individuals, who answered her in English. "He said that he is a Blue," said the second. "No, he said that he is a Maroon," countered the third. To which tribes do the second and third individuals belong?

The solution hinges on figuring out the meaning of the statement *"Eo don rooma."* There are two membership possibilities for the first individual who uttered that statement—he is either a Blue or a Maroon. Now, if he is a Blue and we ask him, "Are you a Blue?" he would say, "Yes, I am a Blue," because he is a truth teller. So, if this is the case, then *"Eo don rooma"* translates as "I am a Blue."

If, instead, he is a Maroon and we ask him the same question—"Are you a Blue?"— he would never say that he is not a Blue and admit to being a Maroon because he is a liar. So, if he is a Maroon, he would lie, and his answer would still be "I am a Blue." Either way, *"Eo don rooma"* translates as "I am a Blue."

Now, the second individual clearly told the truth, while the third individual lied. From this we can deduce that the second one is a Blue and the third a Maroon. Can we tell if the first one is a Blue or a Maroon? There is not enough information to do so.

PUZZLES

201 On an island, the people are divided into two tribes—those who always lie and those who always speak the truth. All individuals speak the same language. Anthropologist Mary Shelley, an ethnographer fascinated by the island culture, ran into three members the other day: two men, Milo and Filo, and one woman, Gila. Dr. Shelley, who does not know the native language of the island, asked Gila, "To which tribe do you belong?" Gila answered her in her native language: *"Duba lo rooba."* "To which tribe does Gila belong?" Dr. Shelley then asked Milo, who answered her in English: "She said that she is a truth teller." To which tribe does Milo belong?

202 Continuing from puzzle 201, Dr. Shelley then asked Filo, "Is Milo a liar?" Filo answered, in English, "Of course he is." To which tribe does Filo belong?

203 Continuing from puzzles 201 and 202, Dr. Shelley went back to Gila and asked her, "To which tribe do the two men belong?" This time Gila answered her in English: "They are both liars." So, to which tribe does Gila belong?

The inventor of this type of puzzle was the British puzzlist Hubert Phillips (1891–1964), who first created them in the 1930s. Phillips was known among his readers as Caliban, the monstrous figure in Shakespeare's play *The Tempest.*

204 Dr. Shelley goes to another part of the island described in puzzles 201, 202 and 203. This time, she runs into four individuals: two men, Dilo and Filo, and two women, Nila and Lila. As she knows, an individual can belong to either the truth tellers or the liars. In this case, she has also found out that the two women are either both liars or both truth tellers, and, similarly, that the two men are either both liars or both truth tellers. She wants to find out, so she asks Dilo, "Are you and Filo truth tellers?" Dilo answers in his native language: "*Duba.*" She then turns to Nila and asks, "Did he say yes?" Nila answers in English, "Yes, he did, but he is a liar." So, who are the liars and who are the truth tellers?

205 Continuing from puzzle 204, Dr. Shelley finds out that the two men and the two women are actually romantic partners. She wants to find out who the couples are, so she asks Filo, "Who is your partner?" He answers, "Lila." On the basis of this answer, Dr. Shelley can now figure out who the couples are. Can you?

206 Dr. Shelley moves on to yet another part of the island, where people are either liars or truth tellers. There she runs into three people: a female, Pila, and two males, Vilo and Zilo. Still fascinated by the situation, she asks Pila, "Are you a truth teller?" "*Hila,*" Pila replies in her native dialect. Dr. Shelley then asks Vilo what Pila said. "She said no," Vilo replies. Shocked, Zilo counters, "She did not say no; she is a truth teller." Can you figure out who the liars and truth tellers are?

207 Continuing from puzzle 206, Dr. Shelley senses that Pila may be a romantic partner of either Vilo or Zilo. To find out, she asks Pila: "Who is your partner?" Pila hesitates and does not answer. So, Dr. Shelley turns to Vilo and asks him, "Are you her partner?" This time, Vilo answers in his native language, "*Orra.*" "What did he say?" Dr. Shelley asks Zilo. "He said yes, but don't believe him." So, who is Pila's partner?

208 Dr. Shelley has fallen in love with one of the men on the island named Rilo. But she does not know to which tribe he belongs—the liars or truth tellers. She wants to join Rilo's tribe so that he, too, can fall in love with her. Rilo has two siblings: a sister, Sila, and a brother, Chilo, who, strangely, belong to different tribes. Rilo belongs to his sister's tribe. Dr. Shelley, however, will not join Rilo's tribe if it is a liar tribe. "Are you a truth teller?" Dr. Shelley asks Sila, who answers in her native language, "*Truba.*" She turns to Chilo and asks him: "What did your sister say?" He answers in English, "She said yes, but do not believe her." Will Dr. Shelley join Rilo's tribe or not?

209 Continuing from puzzle 208, Dr. Shelley has doubts about the situation. She still wants to join Rilo's tribe, because she loves him, so she goes to Sila again and asks her: "Does Rilo belong to the same kind of tribe to which Chilo belongs?" This time, Sila answers in English, "Yes." So, to which tribe does Rilo belong, and will Dr. Shelley join him?

210 Dr. Shelley decides to get into a relationship with Rilo, no matter what tribe he represents. They are planning their marriage when he tells her, "I do not love you, and I do not want to get married." Caught off guard, Dr. Shelley says, "I don't believe you." So, does Rilo love Dr. Shelley?

TRICK PUZZLES

WHAT IS A TRICK PUZZLE?

Trick puzzles play on language and logic, adding an unexpected twist or deceptive information to the puzzle statement. They will keep you on your toes, forcing your brain to sift out the wheat from the chaff, so to speak.

HOW TO SOLVE TRICK PUZZLES

Consider the following paraphrase to a well-known trick puzzle:

A shadow is cast by a very bright red flagpole at the midday sun. What color is the shadow?

Shadows do not possess color. They are always black. Get the idea? Clearly, in this section you will have to really pay attention to all the details presented by a puzzle and analyze them critically.

Some of the puzzles are paraphrases of classic trick puzzles. Others are designed to trick you even more.

PUZZLES

211 Mr. Smith has ten children, but his only female child has just nine brothers. How can this be?

212 If I cook my favorite meal in an old pot, it takes 80 minutes to prepare. But if I cook the same food in the new pot I just bought, it takes an hour and twenty minutes. Why is this so?

213 I have two current U.S. coins in my pocket that add up to thirty cents. One of the two coins is not a nickel. How is this so?

214 Your friends use it, your significant other uses it and even your kids use it. However, even though it belongs to you, you yourself do not generally use it unless it is required of you to do so. What is it?

215 Is it legal in the U.S. for a man to marry his widow's sister?

216 My little boy was given a simple arithmetical problem by his teacher the other day: multiply the first ten digits together and then tell the teacher what he gets. My boy kept on getting zero. Is this possible?

217 Sam's mother's daughter and his brother's sister are one and the same, even though there are three siblings in the family. How is this so?

The late Martin Gardner (1914-2010), whose puzzle column for *Scientific American* was a widely read column in popular science literature, used the expression "Gotcha!" in one of his books to describe the kinds of puzzles in this section—in contrast to the "Aha!" (the name of another of his books) reaction we get from solving puzzles generally.

218 Janet's mother's sister is her brother's aunt. How is this so?

MODULARITY

(219) Doris is looking at a photo of her mother together with a person other than herself. She exclaims, "The person in the photo is my mother's offspring, but that person is not my brother." How is this so?

(220) Mark, an only child, is looking at the photo of a man. At one point he declares, "That man's son is my mother's offspring." Who is he looking at?

PARADOXES

WHAT IS A PARADOX?

Paradoxes are statements or descriptions that seem to defy common sense or go against logic. Perhaps the most famous paradoxes were the ones formulated by the Greek philosopher Zeno of Elea (c. 495–435 BCE). Paradoxes are considered to be types of puzzles because they have either unusual answers or display circular reasoning (no answers). "Which came first, the chicken or the egg?" is an example of circular reasoning, since there is no answer to this question.

HOW TO SOLVE PARADOXES

Here is an example of the kind of paradox you will come across in this section.

I just got an email in my inbox. It had the following statement in it: "This sentence is false."
Is the sentence true or false?

If it is true, then what it says must be true. So, the sentence is false, as the sentence itself says. But this is impossible—a sentence cannot be both true and false. So, let's see if it is false instead. If the sentence is false, then what it says must be false. But the sentence in this case is true—it is false. So, again, it is both true and false. So, we cannot decide its truth value. End of matter.

Unlike this one, some of the puzzles below do have a solution or resolution. So, be careful.

221 Yesterday, I got another email that read: "The previous sentence [the one in the example above] is true." So, is the previous sentence (This sentence is false) true or false on the basis of this new information?

222 Can we decide if the new email (The previous sentence is true) is itself true or false?

223 Yesterday, I got a third email that read: "Both previous sentences were neither true nor false." What do you make of this new email?

> Little is known of Zeno of Elea's life other than he lived in the Greek colony of Elea in southern Italy. His ingenious paradoxes showed that purely logical thinking would force us to conclude that motion is impossible. Despite their mischievous intent, the ideas built into his paradoxes led gradually to the rise of modern philosophy and mathematics.

224 The emails just keep on coming. Here's the next one I got: "This sentence is true, unlike all the previous ones." Is it really true?

225 Guess what? I got yet another email after the one above. It read as follows: "The previous sentence was neither true nor false." What do you make of this email?

Okay, let's get away from this kind of circular reasoning puzzle—and all those emails. Here is a different kind of paradox puzzle.

226 Three boxes contain a total of fifty cents, but we do not know what amount, or how many coins, is in each box—only that each box contains at least one coin. Now, I open one box and find that it contains forty-nine cents. This means that the penny is in one of the other two boxes, while the third one is presumably empty—contrary to what we are told. How can this be explained?

French philosopher René Descartes (1596–1650) refused to accept any belief, even the belief in his own existence, unless he could prove it to be logically true.

227 A gold ring is in one of the following three jewelry cases, each of which has an inscription on it. Can you tell where the ring is if, at most, only one of the inscriptions is true?

A THE RING IS IN HERE.	**B** THE RING IS NOT IN HERE.	**C** THE RING IS NOT IN A.

228 This time we are looking for a precious coin, which is in one of the three boxes below. Strangely, the inscriptions are similar to those in the previous puzzle, but here we are told that there was only one false inscription. So, where is the coin?

A THE COIN IS NOT IN HERE.	**B** THE COIN IS NOT IN C.	**C** THE COIN IS NOT IN HERE.

229 A year ago my friend bought a jewelry box at a flea market. The box bears the following inscription:

THIS BOX WAS MADE BY A TRUTH TELLER.

It is known that the maker of the box belonged to either a truth-telling culture or a liar culture. So, was the box made by a truth teller or a liar?

(230) Last week, I went to the same flea market and bought a similar box. My box bears the following inscription:

> **THIS BOX WAS MADE BY THE MAKER OF THE PREVIOUS BOX.**

What do you make of the inscription?

WEIGHING PUZZLES

WHAT IS A WEIGHING PUZZLE?

The kind of weighing puzzle you will find in this section is the type that asks you how many weighings will be needed to identify a billiard ball that weighs less than others in a set. These puzzles will really test your brain's ability to make inferences.

HOW TO SOLVE WEIGHING PUZZLES

Consider the following puzzle.

> *On a table, there are three billiard balls. One weighs a bit less than the other two; otherwise, they all look exactly the same. With a balance scale, what is the fewest number of weighings you would need to perform in order to be sure that you can identify the one that weighs less?*

Leave one of the balls on the table. Put each of the other two balls on separate pans of the scale—one on the left pan and one on the right one. What will happen? If the culprit ball is the one on the table, then the pans will balance equally. If it is not, then one of the pans will go up—the pan that contains the culprit ball (since it has less weight on it). That's it. With one weighing you have identified the culprit ball—it could be the one on the table or the ball on the pan that went up. There is no other possible outcome.

PUZZLES

231 On a table, there are four billiard balls. One weighs a bit less than the other three; otherwise, they all look exactly the same. With a balance scale, what is the fewest number of weighings you would need to perform in order to be sure that you can safely identify the one that weighs less?

232 Now there are five billiard balls, with one weighing a bit less than the other four. They all look exactly the same. With a balance scale, what is the fewest number of weighings you would need to perform in order to be sure that you can safely identify the one that weighs less?

233 Let's now consider a six-billiard-ball scenario. Again, one weighs a bit less than the other five; otherwise, they all look exactly the same. With a balance scale, what is the fewest number of weighings you would need to perform in order to be sure that you can safely identify the one that weighs less?

> Puzzles are often solved by a process that psychologists call "aha thinking" because a solution might come about spontaneously as the brain makes connections among the various seemingly impossible or disparate elements of a puzzle and, as a modular organ, puts them together into a solution.

234 Now consider thirteen billiard balls, with one weighing a bit less than the other twelve; otherwise, they all look exactly the same. With a balance scale, what is the fewest number of weighings you would need to perform in order to be sure that you can safely identify the one that weighs less?

235 Let's get more complicated with a 100-billiard-ball scenario. Again, one weighs a bit less than the other 99; otherwise, they all look exactly the same. With a balance scale, what is the fewest number of weighings you would need to perform in order to be sure that you can safely identify the one that weighs less?

236 Let's add one ball to the previous puzzle; that is, consider a 101-billiard-ball scenario. One weighs a bit less than the other 100; otherwise, they all look exactly the same. With a balance scale, what is the fewest number of weighings you would need to perform in order to be sure that you can safely identify the one that weighs less?

> Solving the puzzles in this section involves a form of *lateral thinking.* This term was coined by Edward De Bono, a Maltese-born British psychologist. The classic example of lateral thinking is a story about a truck stuck under a low bridge. As a group of people tried to think of some way to force the truck out, a little boy, using lateral thinking, suggested that they simply deflate the tires!

237 Let's see what happens when more than one ball weighs less. On a table there are three billiard balls. Two weigh less than the third one; otherwise, they all look exactly the same. With a balance scale, what is the fewest number of weighings you would need to perform in order to be sure that you can safely identify the lighter pair?

238 Let's do another one of this type. On a table there are four billiard balls. Two weigh the same, say, four pounds each; the other two also weigh the same but less than the first two, say, three pounds each. The four balls all look exactly the same. With a balance scale, what is the fewest number of weighings you would need to perform in order to be sure that you can safely identify the two lighter balls?

239 Let's do one last puzzle of this type. On a table there are five billiard balls. Three weigh three pounds each and two others weigh four pounds each. The five balls all look exactly the same. With a balance scale, what is the fewest number of weighings you would need to perform in order to be sure that you can safely identify the three lighter balls?

240 For the last puzzle in this genre, let's look at a 1,000-billiard-ball scenario. As in most of the puzzles in this section, one weighs a bit less than the other 999; otherwise, they all look exactly the same. With a very large balance scale, what is the fewest number of weighings you would need to perform in order to be sure that you can safely identify the one that weighs less?

DRAW OUT PUZZLES

WHAT IS A DRAW OUT PUZZLE?

This type of puzzle involves a similar kind of hypothesis testing and inferential reasoning as was required by the puzzles in the previous section. You will have to determine how many draws are needed to get a number of balls that match in color from a box of different colored balls. The draws take place with a blindfold on.

HOW TO SOLVE DRAW OUT PUZZLES

Here is a typical example of this kind of puzzle:

In a box there are ten billiard balls, five white and five black. They all weigh the same. With a blindfold on, what is the fewest number you must draw out in order to be sure to get two balls of the same color (two white or two black)?

Three draws are necessary. If we draw out two white or two black in a row, then two draws will do, of course. Lucky! But we cannot assume that luck is on our side. So, let's consider the worst-case scenario. We draw out two balls of different colors—a white one and a black one. It doesn't matter what the order is. The end result will be the same: you will have a white ball and a black ball in hand. Now, the third draw will be either white or black; there is no other choice since there are only white and black balls inside the box (four of each actually). Either way, the ball you draw out will match one of the two balls already out. If it is white, then it matches the white ball outside the box; if it is black, it matches the black ball outside the box. So, three draws will do the trick.

PUZZLES

241 In a box there are fifteen billiard balls, five white, five black and five red. They all weigh the same. With a blindfold on, what is the fewest number you must draw out in order to be sure to get two balls of the same color (two white, two black or two red)?

242 In a box there are thirty-three billiard balls, three white, ten black, eight red and twelve green. They all weigh the same. With a blindfold on, what is the fewest number you must draw out in order to be sure to get two balls of the same color (two white, two black, two red or two green)?

243 In a box there are just seven billiard balls, one white, one black, one red, two green and two blue. They all weigh the same. With a blindfold on, what is the fewest number you must draw out in order to be sure to get two balls of the same color (two green or two blue since these are the only balls that can be paired, of course)?

> **Puzzles have a mystical quality to them. During the Edo period (1603–1867), Japanese puzzles called *sangaku*, meaning "mathematical tablet," were carved on wooden tablets and given as offerings at Shinto shrines or Buddhist temples.**

244 In a box there are twenty-five billiard balls, three white, four black, five red, six green and seven blue. They all weigh the same. With a blindfold on, what is the fewest number you must draw out in order to be sure to get three balls of the same color (three white, three black, three red, three green or three blue)?

245 In another box there are also twenty-five billiard balls, but this time there are exactly five white, five black, five red, five green and five blue. They all weigh the same. Will the outcome be the same under the same conditions? That is, with a blindfold on, what is the fewest number you must draw out in order to be sure to get three balls of the same color (three white, three black, three red, three green or three blue)?

246 Let's alter the conditions a bit. In a box there are ten billiard balls, eight white and two black. They all weigh the same. With a blindfold on, what is the fewest number you must draw out in order to be sure to get the two black balls?

247 What if there were twenty billiard balls, nine white, nine black and two red in the box? They all weigh the same. With a blindfold on, what is the fewest number you must draw out in order to be sure to get the two red balls?

248 Now, let's reverse the situation a bit. Suppose that there are ten billiard balls in a box, nine white and only one black. They all weigh the same. With a blindfold on, what is the fewest number you must draw out in order to be sure to get two white balls?

> The feeling that comes from finding the solution to a puzzle that seems intractable is sometimes called the eureka effect. This term traces its origins to Archimedes who, apparently, found the answer to a difficult physical problem while he took a bath. He was so excited about this that he ran into the streets without putting his clothes back on, shouting, "Eureka!" ("I have found it!")

249 Let's continue along these lines. Suppose, again, that there are ten billiard balls in a box, five white and five black. They all weigh the same. With a blindfold on, what is the fewest number you must draw out in order to be sure to get two white balls?

250 One more. Suppose, again, that there are ten billiard balls in a box, three white, three black, two red and two green. They all weigh the same. With a blindfold on, what is the fewest number you must draw out in order to be sure to get either two red or two green balls?

6

ASSOCIATION

*You know what your problem is, it's that you haven't seen enough movies—
all of life's riddles are answered in the movies.*

(STEVE MARTIN, B. 1945)

RIDDLES ARE AMONG THE OLDEST PUZZLES KNOWN. The riddle form is universal, cutting across time and cultures. The good news is that they are not just part of mischievous word games, but have been found to activate all kinds of brain functions, from purely associative functions to linguistic inferential processes.

RIDDLES AND THE BRAIN

Every lobe of the brain has areas of association cortex that analyze, process and store information. These make possible all our higher mental abilities, such as thinking, speaking and remembering. Riddles appear to be involved directly with association areas of the brain. The research on riddles has borne very positive results, indeed. Because solving a riddle requires knowledge of the extended meanings of words, it activates right-hemisphere functions. The circuits in this hemisphere enable the brain to combine information stored in the memory with information gathered by the senses. In a phrase, riddles are good for the brain.

OBJECTIVES OF THIS CHAPTER

This chapter contains fifty riddles divided into five main thematic areas: riddles based on double entendres and idioms, charade riddles, palindromes (that is, each answer is a palindrome, which means it can be read both forward and backward) and miscellaneous riddles.

DOUBLE ENTENDRE RIDDLES

WHAT IS A DOUBLE ENTENDRE RIDDLE?

Double entendre refers to a word or phrase open to two or more interpretations. In this book, it will be restricted to a word that has more than one meaning. For example, the word *play* can refer to engagement in physical activities for enjoyment, as in "we play tennis every week" or to a dramatic work in theater terminology: "I love the plays of Shakespeare." A double entendre riddle is, simply, a riddle that is based on a double meaning.

HOW TO SOLVE DOUBLE ENTENDRE RIDDLES

Every riddle in this section will be based on two meanings of a word. For example, the double entendre connected to *play* can be translated into the form of a riddle as follows:

> *If observed, it is a theatrical event; if performed, it is a form of recreation. What is it?*

PUZZLES

251 It is something that can be taken for pleasure or for hallucination. What is it?

252 It can be a clue or something taken that we can follow. What could it possibly be?

253 If it's in someone's court, it's that person's move; if we keep it rolling, it preserves momentum. What is it?

According to legend, the ancient Greek poet Homer's death was brought about by the distress he felt at his failure to solve a riddle. It was posed to him by a group of fishermen: "What we caught, we threw away. What we could not catch, we kept." The answer is fleas.

254 To start something they must be wet, but if they are made of clay, they will reveal a basic flaw. What are they?

255 If it's in a storm, it is calm; if it's in the wind, it shows direction. What is it?

256 You take it to see if someone is alive or to determine opinion. What is it?

One of the most famous riddles from the world of the theater can be found in Shakespeare's *Romeo and Juliet*, when Romeo proclaims his love for Juliet in the form of a riddle.

257 Humble persons keep it in their hand; secretive persons put their secrets under it. What is it?

258 You'll appear foolish if it's on your face; if you lay it down, you will fail badly. What is it?

259 If you wear them, they will protect you; if you take them off, you are ready for a fight. What are they?

260 Satisfaction comes by smacking them; curling them, however, shows contempt. What are they?

IDIOM RIDDLES

WHAT IS AN IDIOM RIDDLE?

It was the Greek philosopher Aristotle who coined the term *metaphor*—which comes from the word *metapherein,* meaning "to transfer"—in order to explain how language creates infinite meanings with a limited set of resources. Metaphor is how we create many of our idioms, and in the domain of riddles, idioms are part of the riddle maker's repertoire of wordplay.

Actually, many of the riddles in the section above involve both literal and idiomatic meanings. In this section, only the idiomatic meaning will be used. For example, the word *laugh* is found in idioms such as *laugh in someone's face* (to show contempt for someone) and *laugh out of the other side of one's mouth* (to feel embarrassed after feeling satisfaction wrongly about something).

HOW TO SOLVE IDIOM RIDDLES

To solve such riddles, always think idiomatically, that is, in terms of how a word might be used metaphorically. So, a riddle requiring the answer *laughing* can be based on the two idioms above as follows:

> *You can do it in someone's face or out of the other side of your mouth, but it is neither spitting nor kissing. What is it?*

Note that you will be asked to find the word that makes up the idiom.

PUZZLES

261 If you chase this animal, you are going nowhere. What animal is that?

262 If you chase this instead, you are going after something illusory. What is it?

263 It is not an object, but if you break it, you will cause sadness. What is it?

In the ancient world, riddles were regarded as the means through which the divinities spoke to humans. It was believed that the message could be fully understood only by those equipped with special linguistic knowledge, such as the Greek oracles.

264 If it is broken, it relieves tension between people. What is it?

265 If you see its tip, then the larger part of a problem remains hidden. What could it possibly be?

266 Don't kick it if you want to keep on living. What is it?

Riddles were very popular in the Middle Ages. They dealt with everyday topics such as shops, storms, beer, animals, tools and amorous relations. They provide valuable snapshots into the way people of that era lived and viewed everyday life.

267 A piece of this will make something much easier to do. What is it?

268 If this food item is hot, then you are faced with a controversial situation. What food item is it?

269 The last one of these makes things unbearable. What is it?

Riddle books were among the first books ever printed for popular entertainment after the advent of the printing press in the late 1400s. The 1511 collection of riddles titled *Amusing Questions* was published by a printer called, no pun intended, Wynkyn de Worde.

270 If you do this both ways, the result will be good and bad. What action does this?

CHARADE RIDDLES

WHAT IS A CHARADE RIDDLE?

The charade is a type of riddle. It is solved by deciphering the double meanings suggested by separate syllables, words or lines. In the nineteenth century, it led to the *mime charade,* which has since remained a highly popular game at social gatherings. The mime charade is a riddle in which the syllables of a word, or an entire word or phrase, are acted out by someone. Participants are generally divided into two competing groups, with each group acting out a number of charades that the other group must guess.

HOW TO SOLVE CHARADE RIDDLES

If the answer to the charade is, for example, *baseball*, the riddle might play on the word's syllables *base* and *ball*, as seen in the following example:

This sport is characterized by the use of a "foundation" and a hard version of this "sphere," which can be held and thrown. What sport is it?

A base is a foundation and a ball is a sphere; thus *base + ball = baseball*.

Every riddle in this section will indicate the relevant syllables in quotation marks. You will have to decipher these and then put them together to get the required word.

PUZZLES

271 This transportation system is characterized by a "steel bar" and a "wide way." What system is it?

272 This emotional condition is characterized by an "intense feeling" and a certain "illness." What condition is it?

273 This sport is characterized by a "leg extremity" and an oval "sphere." What sport is it?

A famous appearance of charades is featured in the novel *Vanity Fair* by William Makepeace Thackeray (1811–1863).

274 This vehicle goes through the "atmosphere" in a "level" way. What kind of vehicle could it be?

275 This place may be described as a "water vehicle" with an "enclosure." What place is it?

276 In this place, which is an example of "public grounds," a "sphere" is the main object of interest. What place is it?

277 This tasty seed comes by the name of a "green spherical vegetable" combined with a "hard kernel." What is it?

278 This object is named as a "door opening device" and a "rectangular plane." What is it?

279 This object is also named as a "rectangular plane," but it is "dark." What is it?

280 This is named as both a "printed work" and a "memo." What is it?

PALINDROME RIDDLES

WHAT IS A PALINDROME RIDDLE?

A palindrome is a word, phrase or sentence that reads the same backward and forward with adjustments to the punctuation and spacing if needed. For example, the word *toot* is a word palindrome because it can be read forward or backward. The sentence *A man, a plan, a canal, Panama!* can be read forward or backward if we make adjustments for punctuation and spaces.

There is nothing special to a palindrome riddle other than the answer (a word or name in this case) is a palindrome.

HOW TO SOLVE PALINDROME RIDDLES

Consider the following riddle:

This name was used by Tolstoy for one of his novels and consists of an English article written forward and then backward.

The answer is *Anna*, which is the name used by Tolstoy in his novel *Anna Karenina;* if split into syllables, the name consists of the English indefinite article written forward (*An*) and backward (*na*). *Anna* is a palindrome.

PUZZLES

For riddles 281–285, you will be given the number of letters in the palindrome answer.

281 Three letters: This palindrome refers to an ineffectual person or, in the plural, clothes.

282 Three letters: This palindrome describes a biblical woman or the period before an important event.

283 Five letters: This palindrome describes a duty we should all perform. The last three letters are also the short form of a common male name.

> **Interestingly, the term *palindrome* is used by geneticists to refer to a segment of the DNA in which the nucleotide sequence of one strand reads in reverse order to that of the complementary strand.**

284 Six letters: This palindrome is the name of a famous biblical woman. The last three letters of her name constitute a colloquial way of denying something.

285 Five letters: This palindrome refers to a type of boat. Its last three letters describe a way of talking trivially.

You will not be given the number of letters for the remaining riddles.

286 In one of its many meanings, this palindrome refers to a device for determining flatness. In British English it refers to a type of crossing.

> Benjamin Franklin was a jack-of-all-trades. He composed riddles for his *Poor Richard's Almanac,* an almanac that he published from 1732 to 1758 that became quite popular, in large part because of the riddles.

287 This palindrome refers to something you will have to scoop. Its last two letters can be used as a scholarly abbreviation.

288 This palindrome is a title. Its first three letters refer to a state of mind, and its last two constitute a verb form.

289 This palindrome refers to a machine part. Its first three letters mean "decay."

> For many ancient philosophers, including Plato, riddles were considered to be the language of abstract ideas because they say what cannot be said literally about ultimate truths.

290 This palindrome refers to a principle. Its first three letters refer to a number.

MISCELLANEOUS RIDDLES

WHAT IS A RIDDLE, REALLY?

Riddles are truly fascinating, aren't they? It is hard to pinpoint the reason why they were invented in the first place since they never tell the truth directly, but rather through the play of association of meanings. Solving them requires a large dose of imagination. It would seem that one way to enter the "Thebes" of the human brain is through riddles, which may mirror how thoughts unfold more than any other form of language.

HOW TO SOLVE RIDDLES, AGAIN

The sections above use a theme or method for constructing riddles (double entendres, idioms, charades and palindromes). In this last section, anything goes. You will really have to put your imagination to work here, activating those important cells in the association cortex.

PUZZLES

291 It can go up and it can go down. It can be inside or outside, but it is not an object. What is it?

292 It flies, but it is not an airplane or a bird. And it comes back by itself. What is it?

293 If you keep it, you remain calm; if you lose it, you get angry. What is it?

> The main character of the *Saw* movie series is someone called, rather appropriately, Jigsaw. He poses riddles to his captives, who must solve them in order to save their lives. This is similar to the story of the Sphinx, who spun her famous riddle in ancient times to people entering Thebes. If they could not solve her puzzle, they lost their lives.

294 If you keep it in your hand, it shows your humility; if you take it off, it shows your admiration. What is it?

295 If you take these off, it shows that you are going to be uncompromising.

296 If you lay something on it, you are showing openness; if you put something under it, you are showing the opposite. What is it?

> The ancient Greek priests and priestesses, known as oracles, expressed their more ominous prophecies in the form of riddles. So, too, did many other prophets and seers, such as Nostradamus.

297 Just a piece of this will guarantee success. If someone takes it, that person exceeds all others at something. What is it?

298 You can play it or you can use it to cross over. What is it?

299 If you see it, you will get angry; it also describes the color of a vital body substance. What is it?

300 If you take it away, someone will be astonished; if you waste it, you are having absolutely no effect. What is it?

7

SEMANTIC MEMORY

The words of the world want to make sentences.
(GASTON BACHELARD, 1884–1962)

THE ENGLISH WRITER JOHN DRYDEN (1631–1700) once defined anagrams satirically as the "torturing of one poor word ten thousand ways." Indeed, many words produce multiple anagrams, for some strange reason. The letters of the word *stop*, for example, can be rearranged to produce *pots*, *spot*, *opts* and *tops*. Anagrams involve what psychologists and linguists call semantic memory—the recollection of word and phrase meanings and of concepts generally.

ANAGRAMS AND SEMANTIC MEMORY

The memory of the meanings and uses of words based in part on word association has been found to be critical in "brain maintenance," so to speak. Often, we try to recall a word by going mentally through the alphabet in our brains. This kind of "anagram thinking" is a manifestation of semantic memory for a specific recall purpose. Semantic recall seems to involve processing information over circuits in the association cortex and other parts of the brain. It is also a key factor in the formation of abstract ideas.

It is relevant to note that psychologists use "anagram tests" for assessing intelligence and other cognitive skills. Anagrams thus might activate brainpower because they involve manipulating words and their combinations, and thus activate both sides of the brain.

OBJECTIVES OF THIS CHAPTER

This chapter is all about anagrams. The fifty puzzles are based on the five main types of anagrams: word-to-word, word-to-phrase, phrase-to-word, phrase-to-phrase and names. The goal is to activate the semantic memory in its various forms. You will truly have to sharpen your knowledge of words and word meanings here.

WORD-TO-WORD ANAGRAMS

WHAT IS A WORD-TO-WORD ANAGRAM?

Let's start with the most basic type of anagram puzzle: rearranging the letters of a given word to produce a new word. For example, the letters in the word *evil* can be rearranged to produce *veil*, *vile* or *live*.

HOW TO SOLVE WORD-TO-WORD ANAGRAMS

There really is no one method to solving anagrams. One way is to try letters in combination. So, for example, in *evil* above, ask yourself: Can *e* (as the first letter) be combined with the other letters in different combinations to form a new word? The answer seems to be no. So, move on to the *v*. With this letter as the first letter, we can produce two new words: *veil* and *vile*. Can we do something with *i* as the first letter? Apparently not. Finally, with the last letter *l* we can make the word *live*.

As an aside, in the true spirit of anagram mysticism, note that the three derivative words are mysteriously connected with the original word. In fact, we often pull the *veil* over our eyes not to see *evil*; *evil* is something *vile*; and as you *live* you will come across *evil*. Bizarre, isn't it?

PUZZLES

In each of the puzzles below you are given a single word in which the letters can be rearranged to produce a new word or more than one new word. Every letter in the original or base word must be used—none can be taken away or added to it. Proper names are not allowed. Some of these are well-known among veteran anagram aficionados. Needless to say, you can always find the answers on the internet, but you should of course avoid doing so. As always, the first few are really easy. But they will get much harder as you go along.

301 NIP

302 DEW

303 MEAN

Anagrams go back to ancient times. It was thought that every word, if rearranged to create a new word, would reveal hidden mysteries of the world.

304 TAME

305 STALE

306 SILENT

In the sixth century BCE, the great mathematician Pythagoras is said to have used anagrams to unravel hidden philosophical meanings in words. Plato and his followers also believed that anagrams revealed destiny.

307 FRIEND

308 REPENTS

309 EASTERN

Anagram puzzles became very popular in the medieval ages. One of the best-known creators of these puzzles was the French composer Guillaume de Machault, whose works were a precursor to what we now call classical music.

310 PERTAINS

WORD-TO-PHRASE ANAGRAMS

WHAT IS A WORD-TO-PHRASE ANAGRAM?

The idea in this case is to produce a phrase with the letters of a given word. For example, *dormitory* will yield *dirty room*—how eerily appropriate. This type of anagram puzzle is clearly much more difficult than the previous type. Good luck!

HOW TO SOLVE WORD-TO-PHRASE ANAGRAMS

Again, there is no real method for solving this type of puzzle. Like the anagrams above, the best method may be to try out one letter at a time as a potential first letter in a new combination of letters and as part of a phrase. It would seem that *d* can be easily combined with the letters to produce *dirty*. By taking out the letters *d, i, r, t, y* from *dormitory*, we are left with *o, r, m, o*. Now it is easier to see that these letters can be rearranged to produce *room*. Note that the phrase must make sense and that proper names are not allowed. You might, of course, come up with answers other than the ones given in this book, which are simply the most frequent.

PUZZLES

311 HELPLESS   **312** COURTLY   **313** HOLDING

> Plato apparently believed that the anagrams of people's names revealed their destiny.

314 SEXUAL   **315** CONTROL   **316** EVENING

317 BLUSHED   **318** DESSERT   **319** ENTIRE

320 CREAMY

PHRASE-TO-WORD ANAGRAMS

WHAT IS A PHRASE-TO-WORD ANAGRAM?

This type of anagram is the reverse of the previous one. The idea is to produce a word or words from a phrase. For example, the letters in the phrase *Is pity love?* can be rearranged to form the single word *positively!*—a rather neat answer, no?

HOW TO SOLVE PHRASE-TO-WORD ANAGRAMS

As with the previous types of anagrams, it is not really possible to devise a surefire method for solving such anagrams. Trial and error is basically all you can use here and, again, to consider one letter at a time as a possible first letter in a word. By doing this, you will soon discover in the puzzle above that only by starting with *p* can all the letters be combined to form a word: *positively*. And once again, in the spirit of anagram mysticism, note that even anagrams of this type also seem to provide apt commentaries on the meanings of the original phrases.

Needless to say, you must use all the letters and remember that you can make only single words, not other phrases. Also, proper names do not count. You might, again, come up with answers other than the ones given in this book, which are simply the most frequent.

PUZZLES

321 SLY POP **322** AD FAIR **323** BE LOUD

> The predecessor of Scrabble was a board game called Anagrams. It was invented by a schoolteacher in Salem, Massachusetts, in around 1850. The game gained instant popularity.

324 LED TRIP **325** FLUENT LIP **326** APT LIAR

> A blanagram is the anagram of another word except for one letter. An example is the word *claw*, which has no anagram. But changing the c to k produces *walk*.

327 ROOM BED **328** LEWD SINS **329** LUCID PITY

 ICY PLATES

PHRASE-TO-PHRASE ANAGRAMS

WHAT IS A PHRASE-TO-PHRASE ANAGRAM?

For this type of anagram, the idea is to rearrange the letters of a given phrase to form another phrase or sentence. For example, rearranging the letters of the phrase *the countryside* will yield *No city dust here*!

HOW TO SOLVE PHRASE-TO-PHRASE ANAGRAMS

There is no sure way to solve these anagrams. Trying out individual letters as first letters of different words, as discussed previously, might help. Also, the rearrangement should produce only legitimate phrases, not a set of random words. Once again, you might come up with answers other than the ones given in this book, which are the most frequent.

PUZZLES

 WE MEN

 THE EYES

 SOFT BED

There is only one basic rule in doing anagrams—every letter must be used, with exactly the same number of occurrences as in the original word or phrase. Solutions that fall short of this rule are called "imperfect anagrams."

334 YO, FOUR!   **335** AD BLIGHT   **336** SQUID CAVE

A famous appearance of an anagram in the movies is the one in Roman Polanski's 1968 horror masterpiece *Rosemary's Baby.* Three weeks before her delivery date, Rosemary gets a call informing her that Hutch has tragically died. At the burial ceremony, she is given a book titled *All of Them Witches*, which dealt with the practices of witches and warlocks. One of the warlocks she reads about is named Adrian Marcato. She notices, to her horror, that the name of Adrian Marcato's son Steven is underlined, whereupon she realizes that Steven Marcato is an anagram for Roman Castevet, her neighbor. Rosemary thus starts to realize that the Castevets and their friends are part of a coven and that her unborn baby's blood will be used in one of their rituals.

337 GAG NAUGHT!

In an episode of *The Simpsons* ("Homer's Night Out"), Bart observes a sign at a restaurant with *Cod Platter* on it. He rearranges the letters to spell *Cold Pet Rat.*

338 THIS RUT   **339** GO, IDIOTS!

> The grumpy Dr. Gregory House of the TV program *House, M.D.* states, in one episode, that the letters of his name can be rearranged appropriately to *Huge ego; sorry.*

340 LIES, WOW!

NAME ANAGRAMS

WHAT IS A NAME ANAGRAM?

According to some scholars, anagrams originated in the writings of the Greek poet Lycophron, who lived in Alexandria (285–247 BCE). Lycophron's two most famous anagrams were on the names of Ptolemy and his queen, Arsinoë, in his famous poem on the siege of Troy titled *Cassandra*.

A name anagram is exactly that—an anagram of a name (usually that of a famous person). There are many well-known name anagrams that seem incredibly connected to the individual's life or personality. For example, an anagram of Monica Lewinsky's name is *nice silky woman*. An anagram of Clint Eastwood's name, which describes his early career, is *Old West action*.

HOW TO SOLVE NAME ANAGRAMS

Name anagrams are among the best known in the field of anagram puzzles. Usually, you are given the person's name and then asked to rearrange the letters of the name to get an anagram of it. Here, we will make it a little more challenging by doing the opposite—you will be given the anagram and you must find the name. Keep in mind that the anagram phrase says something about the person, directly, by suggestion or by allusion. As with the previous anagrams, you will have to try the first-letter approach, considering each letter as a potential first letter in a separate word. Trial and error is the only way to do this.

PUZZLES

341 MERRY WARDROBE

342 ME, RADIUM ACE

343 FINE IN TORN JEANS

344 ONLY I CAN THRILL

345 I DEMAND TV LATER

346 A RICH SILENT STAR

347 I LACE WORDS

348 ANGEL OF THE RECLINING

Nature's anagram is the DNA. The nucleotides that make up the DNA are, in fact, not unlike anagrams, since they do indeed predict the individual's destiny, don't they?

349 I LOVE OPERA SINGING!

350 I'LL MAKE A WISE PHRASE

8

VERBAL COGNITION

But if thought corrupts language, language can also corrupt thought.
(GEORGE ORWELL, 1903–1950)

FINDING WORDS HIDDEN IN LETTER ARRAYS is a popular type of puzzle. Called a word search puzzle, it first appeared in the March 1, 1968, issue of the *Selenby Digest* in Norman, Oklahoma. The puzzle caught on quickly, as teachers in the local schools started asking for reprints of the puzzle for their classes. This chapter will have only word search puzzles, responding to many readers of my previous two puzzle books that they enjoyed this type of puzzle enormously and found it very useful for enhancing their brainpower.

PUZZLES AND VERBAL COGNITION

The word search enhances verbal cognition, or the use of language to learn and to store knowledge. International studies from India, Singapore, Canada and the United States have shown that learning new material through word puzzles is very effective. For example, medical and pharmacology students using crossword puzzles as a learning tool to help them remember medical terminology and hard-to-remember concepts tend to retain that information more than the students who do not use them. Although similar studies on word searches do not exist (to the best of my knowledge), it is logical to assume that the same kinds of benefits accrue to the word search solver, as well.

OBJECTIVES OF THIS CHAPTER

The fifty puzzles in this chapter are all based on the word search principle. We will start off with the simplest form of word search puzzle, with the hidden words given to you, then progress to the definitions of the words or the themes that the hidden words encompass.

WORD SEARCHES: GIVEN WORDS

WHAT IS A WORD SEARCH PUZZLE?

A word search puzzle is a puzzle that hides words in an array of letters. These words can be read in any direction—left to right, right to left, top to bottom, bottom to top or diagonally.

HOW TO SOLVE GIVEN WORDS SEARCHES

The most basic kind of word search puzzle is the one that lists the words you will locate in the array. This type clearly sharpens perception of word structure and of identification of words in an amalgam of letters.

For the example below, you are given the seven words—all colors—to find in the array. There is no particular order or arrangement. To simplify matters in this illustrative case, the words can be read only from left to right or top to bottom.

Find the colors blue, orange, green, yellow, brown, red and violet.

B	L	U	E	D	A	L	L	R	E	R	C	B
H	X	T	X	E	Z	O	P	B	T	H	X	R
X	S	X	H	X	R	E	D	O	X	S	P	E
N	Y	O	T	H	R	R	T	P	M	N	N	G
M	E	C	D	C	E	D	W	E	X	L	R	R
E	L	S	X	O	R	A	N	G	E	N	C	E
C	L	D	S	L	L	S	U	H	S	B	X	E
T	O	H	Y	H	T	H	X	T	R	N	D	N
C	W	C	V	I	O	L	E	T	C	G	S	Y
E	P	D	S	U	B	H	R	H	S	H	L	X
X	Y	W	X	A	X	R	B	R	O	W	N	S

The words are highlighted below:

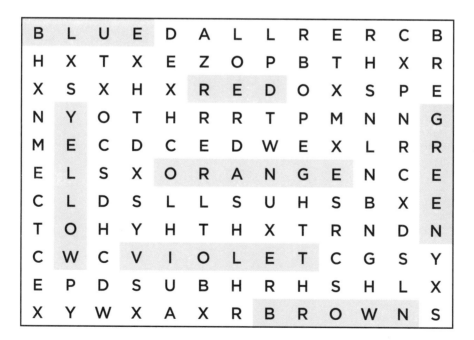

Incidentally, the letters of the hidden words may also crisscross each other. Also there may be extra words in any array. They are there to confuse you.

PUZZLES

For the first five puzzles in this section you will be told how the words can be read (left to right, right to left and so on).

351 Find the following seven flowers in the puzzle below: rose, petunia, orchid, tulip, daisy, geranium, lily. The words are read from left to right.

G	E	R	A	N	I	U	M	R	E	R	C	P
H	Z	T	H	E	Z	D	F	L	I	L	Y	R
Z	S	Z	R	O	S	E	M	O	Z	S	P	E
N	R	O	T	D	R	R	T	P	M	N	N	H
O	R	C	H	I	D	D	W	D	A	I	S	Y
E	I	S	T	O	R	G	D	W	Q	N	C	W
C	R	D	S	L	L	S	U	H	S	B	C	E
T	W	H	E	H	T	T	U	L	I	P	D	I
C	A	C	S	L	L	D	H	C	C	G	S	Y
P	E	T	U	N	I	A	R	H	S	H	A	Z
V	Y	W	Z	A	X	O	Z	W	E	W	L	Q

352 Find the following seven food items in the puzzle below: bread, meat, vegetables, fruit, fish, sweets, pasta. The words are read from left to right and right to left.

V	R	X	N	D	I	L	M	R	E	R	C	B
H	G	V	E	G	E	T	A	B	L	E	S	R
G	S	G	H	G	U	B	M	O	U	S	P	E
N	K	O	T	H	R	R	T	P	M	N	N	H
M	E	A	T	C	E	D	H	S	I	F	R	O
I	I	S	T	E	R	P	O	E	R	N	C	V
C	R	D	S	L	B	R	E	A	D	B	P	E
P	A	S	T	A	Q	L	A	T	R	N	U	I
C	A	F	S	L	L	D	H	C	C	G	S	Y
T	I	U	R	F	T	H	R	H	S	H	L	G
G	Y	W	W	A	S	W	E	E	T	S	L	S

353 Find the following seven clothing items in the puzzle below: scarf, gloves, dress, pants, shirt, jacket, stockings. The words are read from left to right, right to left, and top to bottom, and they might also crisscross.

S	H	I	R	T	A	H	L	O	E	R	C	B
C	B	T	E	M	H	R	F	S	T	N	A	P
A	S	N	H	L	F	B	M	O	T	N	Q	A
R	R	O	G	D	R	R	T	P	M	K	N	H
F	K	C	D	R	E	D	P	E	L	M	R	J
B	I	S	S	E	V	O	L	G	R	N	I	A
R	R	D	S	S	L	K	U	O	S	B	A	C
O	F	H	Y	S	J	L	A	T	R	N	D	K
M	A	C	S	L	L	D	H	C	C	G	S	E
S	T	O	C	K	I	N	G	S	S	H	L	T
E	Y	W	I	A	M	O	C	O	E	L	L	E

Puzzles have always been considered to be tests of intelligence. The great heroes of yore, along with modern-day fictional heroes, have always shown their mettle by solving puzzles, alongside feats of physical prowess.

354 Find the following seven items of footwear in the puzzle below: shoes, boots, sandals, galoshes, slippers, clogs, loafers. The words are read from left to right, right to left, top to bottom and bottom to top, and they might also crisscross.

S	R	T	S	L	I	P	P	E	R	S	Y	T
E	D	T	X	E	B	H	F	B	T	H	X	R
O	S	X	H	X	U	B	M	O	I	S	P	E
H	R	O	G	A	L	O	S	H	E	S	N	D
S	S	C	D	C	E	O	W	E	W	L	R	Z
J	I	M	T	E	R	T	O	H	R	N	C	S
S	L	A	D	N	A	S	U	H	S	B	S	S
T	S	H	Y	H	T	S	A	T	B	N	D	I
C	L	O	G	S	L	D	H	C	C	G	S	L
S	N	D	S	N	T	H	R	H	S	H	L	S
L	O	A	F	E	R	S	Q	B	E	N	L	S

355 Find the following seven items of tableware and table items in the puzzle below: fork, spoon, knife, plate, napkin, bowl, teacup. The words are read from left to right, right to left, top to bottom and bottom to top, and they might also crisscross.

K	R	N	A	P	K	I	N	R	F	R	N	N
N	P	L	H	F	O	B	O	R	T	H	T	O
I	T	C	U	A	P	L	M	O	X	S	P	O
F	R	L	O	W	B	R	T	P	M	N	N	P
E	S	C	D	E	E	D	B	E	P	L	R	S
N	P	A	T	E	R	F	O	R	K	N	C	W
P	U	C	T	L	L	S	W	H	S	B	O	E
K	K	N	Y	E	T	A	L	P	R	N	D	P
R	A	C	S	L	L	D	H	C	C	G	S	O
K	N	D	S	T	E	A	C	U	P	H	L	B
N	A	L	P	N	B	O	N	A	P	L	L	W

For the remaining puzzles in this section you will not be told the direction of the letters.

356 Find the following seven adjectives in the puzzle below: good, clean, happy, great, wonderful, incredible, dreamy.

D	R	E	N	I	N	C	R	R	E	C	L	E
G	R	G	O	O	D	G	R	E	I	N	D	W
W	C	R	N	D	U	E	M	R	X	F	P	O
U	L	E	D	D	R	E	A	M	Y	M	Y	N
C	L	A	N	E	H	A	G	R	E	L	R	D
E	I	T	T	E	R	G	O	W	R	N	C	E
I	N	C	S	Y	P	P	A	H	S	H	A	R
D	R	E	I	N	C	G	R	E	T	A	D	F
C	L	E	A	N	D	R	I	N	C	W	O	U
G	R	G	O	U	W	O	N	I	N	C	L	L
I	N	C	R	E	D	I	B	L	E	L	L	S

A lipogram is a word game that consists of writing paragraphs or entire novels from which a particular letter or group of letters is missing and not allowed to be used. Incredibly, coherent novels have been written in lipogram style.

357 Find the following seven verbs in the puzzle below: discover, enjoy, succeed, perform, sing, play, thrive.

W	R	X	N	D	A	L	L	R	E	R	C	B
H	X	T	D	E	Z	O	G	N	I	S	X	R
X	S	X	I	X	U	B	M	O	X	S	P	E
N	R	O	S	H	R	R	T	P	L	A	Y	H
M	S	C	C	C	E	D	W	E	L	L	R	O
E	N	J	O	Y	R	T	H	R	I	V	E	W
C	R	D	V	L	L	S	U	H	S	B	A	E
T	W	P	E	R	F	O	R	M	R	N	D	I
C	A	C	R	L	L	D	H	C	C	G	S	Y
E	N	D	G	U	T	S	U	C	C	E	E	D
X	Y	W	X	A	X	O	X	W	E	L	L	S

358 Find the following seven print materials in the puzzle below: book, magazine, newspaper, tabloid, poster, sign, flyer.

B	O	K	N	D	M	A	G	A	B	O	O	S
T	B	L	D	O	A	I	D	P	O	S	S	T
F	L	R	E	I	G	N	S	E	L	A	P	A
N	E	W	S	P	A	P	E	R	T	N	A	B
M	A	G	Z	A	Z	N	E	I	S	I	R	L
P	O	S	N	S	I	G	N	B	K	O	O	O
S	G	N	S	L	N	T	V	A	L	I	O	I
T	B	A	Y	R	E	Y	L	F	R	N	D	D
P	S	T	O	K	O	B	N	E	S	W	A	P
Z	I	G	A	M	A	B	L	O	D	I	B	A
B	O	O	K	A	P	O	S	T	E	R	L	S

359 Find the following seven arithmetic terms in the puzzle below: division, addition, subtraction, plus, minus, multiply, factor.

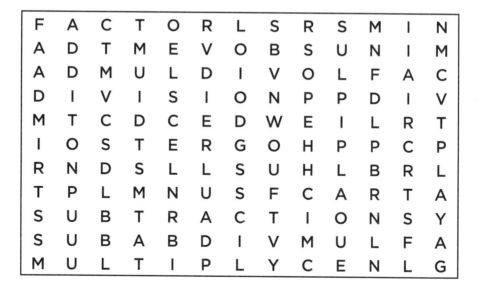

F	A	C	T	O	R	L	S	R	S	M	I	N
A	D	T	M	E	V	O	B	S	U	N	I	M
A	D	M	U	L	D	I	V	O	L	F	A	C
D	I	V	I	S	I	O	N	P	P	D	I	V
M	T	C	D	C	E	D	W	E	I	L	R	T
I	O	S	T	E	R	G	O	H	P	P	C	P
R	N	D	S	L	L	S	U	H	L	B	R	L
T	P	L	M	N	U	S	F	C	A	R	T	A
S	U	B	T	R	A	C	T	I	O	N	S	Y
S	U	B	A	B	D	I	V	M	U	L	F	A
M	U	L	T	I	P	L	Y	C	E	N	L	G

> A heterogram is a sentence or entire text in which no letter of the alphabet occurs more than once. Figuring out how to make heterograms is not as easy as it seems. Try it yourself.

360 Find the following seven tools in the puzzle below: hammer, screwdriver, saw, pliers, wrench, shovel, pick.

```
P  L  P  L  S  H  O  V  E  L  S  W  A
I  W  R  E  C  N  H  S  H  R  L  O  H
C  H  M  A  R  P  L  R  E  I  S  V  I
K  S  C  R  E  D  R  I  S  H  V  E  L
W  R  N  C  W  R  E  N  C  H  C  K  P
S  I  S  T  D  H  M  A  R  A  E  S  W
R  S  C  R  R  D  R  V  E  M  R  I  A
E  H  M  A  I  M  R  E  S  M  H  V  S
I  C  K  P  V  L  H  M  A  E  R  E  M
L  N  D  S  E  S  H  R  O  R  V  E  L
P  L  R  E  R  S  C  R  W  R  I  V  R
```

WORD SEARCHES: THEMES

WHAT IS A THEMATIC WORD SEARCH PUZZLE?

Instead of being given the words to find in an array, a thematic word search puzzle gives you the theme that connects the hidden words. For example, it could be the names of famous writers, colors, types of literature and so on.

HOW TO SOLVE THEMATIC WORD SEARCHES

You are told that there are seven words in the array below that are all connected with the theme of sports. Can you find them? The words can be read only from left to right and top to bottom:

```
T  R  X  B  A  D  M  I  N  T  O  N  B
E  X  T  X  E  Z  X  F  B  T  H  X  S
N  S  X  H  X  U  B  M  X  X  S  P  W
N  R  N  T  G  O  L  F  P  M  O  N  I
I  S  C  D  C  E  D  W  X  L  X  R  M
S  I  S  O  C  C  E  R  W  R  N  C  M
C  R  D  S  L  L  S  U  H  S  B  A  I
T  W  H  Y  B  O  X  I  N  G  N  D  N
C  A  C  S  L  L  D  H  C  C  G  S  G
E  S  K  I  I  N  G  R  H  S  H  L  X
X  Y  W  X  A  X  O  X  W  X  L  L  S
```

The sports, as you can see below, are tennis, golf, boxing, swimming, badminton, skiing and soccer:

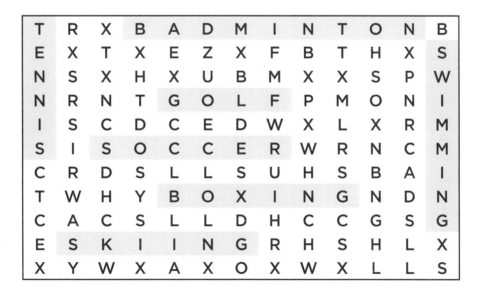

For the first five puzzles in this section you will be told how the words can be read (left to right, right to left and so on).

PUZZLES

361 **Theme: seven words connected to love and lovemaking.** The words are read from left to right. Can you find them?

I	N	F	A	T	U	A	T	I	O	N	C	B
K	V	O	L	H	R	E	A	M	C	H	A	W
H	E	A	R	T	A	C	H	E	D	T	A	E
I	N	F	R	U	R	I	W	N	S	M	I	S
E	M	B	R	A	C	E	G	G	O	L	E	V
E	M	R	A	C	B	E	K	S	S	F	L	I
D	A	T	E	N	F	L	I	R	T	I	N	G
H	R	T	C	H	E	A	F	B	R	A	E	M
K	I	S	S	F	L	R	T	I	N	F	K	R
F	I	D	L	T	Y	I	H	H	E	R	A	T
L	V	E	F	I	D	E	L	I	T	Y	N	S

362 **Theme: seven words connected to the weather.** The words are read from left to right and right to left. Can you find them?

W	O	N	S	D	W	N	S	O	E	R	N	A
H	U	R	C	S	R	E	H	U	N	I	A	R
M	I	L	D	T	C	B	K	L	P	S	P	E
N	J	I	T	H	R	R	T	P	M	N	N	H
M	S	C	O	L	D	D	W	I	D	N	R	O
T	I	S	L	P	R	G	B	W	R	N	C	Y
C	R	D	S	L	L	S	U	H	S	B	A	E
T	W	I	N	D	R	H	A	P	R	N	D	I
H	R	R	U	C	N	E	H	C	H	R	U	Y
S	N	W	O	H	U	R	R	I	C	A	N	E
H	O	T	M	L	D	S	N	W	R	N	S	S

363 **Theme: seven words connected to the automobile.** The words are read from left to right, right to left and top to bottom, and they might crisscross. Can you find them?

M	R	T	O	H	R	D	W	N	D	S	H	I
T	W	H	E	E	L	L	C	S	T	H	R	R
O	I	B	R	A	R	B	R	O	T	O	M	T
R	N	O	T	D	R	R	T	P	M	O	N	N
M	D	C	D	L	E	D	W	E	L	D	R	R
O	S	S	T	I	R	G	R	B	R	N	C	K
R	H	D	S	G	L	S	U	R	S	B	A	B
T	I	H	Y	H	T	H	A	A	R	N	C	R
H	E	C	S	T	R	U	N	K	C	G	S	K
D	L	D	S	U	T	H	R	E	S	H	D	E
O	D	W	H	E	L	E	T	R	U	K	M	S

The expression "connecting the dots" comes from solving a simple and well-known puzzle containing a sequence of numbered dots, which, when connected, reveal the outline of something familiar (for instance, an animal or a face). This is a popular puzzle, especially among children.

364 **Theme: seven words connected to television programming.** The words are read from left to right, right to left, top to bottom and bottom to top, and they might crisscross. Can you find them?

S	T	C	O	M	S	D	O	M	C	U	M	I
H	R	S	E	R	I	E	S	N	W	V	E	N
N	T	I	R	E	U	B	W	R	B	B	L	T
N	A	T	U	R	E	R	E	P	M	R	B	E
M	S	C	D	C	E	D	N	E	L	E	R	R
E	I	O	T	E	R	G	O	W	R	A	S	V
C	R	M	S	L	L	S	U	H	S	L	T	I
T	R	L	E	I	T	Y	A	T	R	I	C	E
I	T	N	Y	V	R	I	E	W	S	T	O	W
D	O	C	U	M	E	N	T	A	R	Y	M	V
D	O	M	C	U	T	R	A	N	E	S	W	S

365 **Theme: seven words connected to time periods (such as night).** The words are read from left to right, right to left, top to bottom and bottom to top, and they might crisscross. Can you find them?

M	R	N	N	I	N	G	N	G	G	H	T	S
T	W	I	L	I	G	H	T	B	N	D	Y	A
E	V	N	I	N	G	E	V	O	I	S	P	O
N	G	H	T	H	G	I	G	T	N	D	A	V
T	W	I	D	L	G	H	T	T	R	M	E	O
E	N	W	A	D	G	E	R	N	O	O	N	C
D	W	A	Y	N	M	R	N	O	M	I	I	N
T	W	I	G	H	T	L	V	E	N	N	G	I
M	R	N	I	N	G	N	O	O	T	G	H	B
E	V	E	N	I	N	G	R	M	S	H	T	X
E	V	M	O	R	N	G	H	T	L	G	H	T

For the remaining puzzles in this section you will not be told the direction of the letters.

366 **Theme: seven American cities.** Can you find them?

C	H	C	G	O	B	R	T	N	D	E	T	H
A	T	L	N	T	A	B	D	L	L	A	S	A
C	H	I	C	A	G	O	M	I	C	H	P	R
N	W	I	S	C	N	S	N	M	M	I	A	T
M	I	C	H	I	C	T	G	O	A	T	L	F
H	O	D	E	T	R	O	I	T	I	P	C	O
C	R	A	S	L	L	N	U	H	I	O	A	R
T	W	L	M	N	N	E	S	T	A	H	R	D
A	T	L	A	N	T	A	H	A	R	T	F	O
B	N	A	S	S	C	A	R	O	B	H	L	K
D	Y	S	X	A	M	I	A	M	I	L	W	S

The expression "to spot a difference" comes from a popular children's puzzle whereby you must find a given number of minute differences between two otherwise similar pictures.

367 **Theme: seven well-known European cities.** Can you find them?

P	R	I	S	R	O	L	E	A	T	H	N	S
L	N	D	P	A	R	I	S	L	N	D	O	N
B	R	L	I	N	U	S	L	S	B	O	N	A
G	N	E	V	E	A	B	D	T	R	O	I	T
R	M	O	D	R	E	O	P	R	I	S	M	A
A	M	S	N	O	D	N	O	L	A	E	A	R
D	A	M	S	M	L	S	U	H	S	B	D	E
L	I	S	B	E	R	L	I	N	R	N	R	I
G	N	E	E	V	A	P	R	I	S	G	I	T
G	N	D	R	I	D	H	L	I	S	H	D	X
M	G	E	N	E	V	A	B	R	E	L	I	N

368 Theme: seven countries. Can you find them?

A	R	G	E	N	T	I	N	A	A	L	C	E
F	R	N	C	E	Z	T	F	R	N	C	H	E
I	T	G	A	L	Y	A	L	G	E	R	I	A
L	R	E	M	N	Y	L	C	H	N	A	N	C
A	R	R	G	E	N	Y	T	I	N	A	A	A
A	L	M	G	E	R	I	A	B	R	T	A	N
M	R	A	N	A	C	O	P	O	R	G	A	L
E	C	N	A	R	F	F	R	N	E	C	D	H
C	A	Y	A	M	R	I	A	C	C	D	N	A
A	R	G	N	T	N	A	I	T	L	I	Y	S
S	W	I	T	Z	E	R	L	A	N	D	L	S

369 Theme: seven American states. Can you find them?

W	I	S	C	T	E	X	M	I	C	H	I	G
H	A	W	A	S	S	I	M	N	T	A	N	A
W	I	W	I	S	C	O	N	S	I	N	O	H
C	A	L	I	F	R	W	N	I	A	E	N	M
T	X	A	T	E	X	A	S	E	L	B	R	O
A	L	A	B	M	A	A	L	A	B	R	M	N
V	C	A	L	I	F	O	R	N	I	A	C	T
O	R	G	O	N	I	L	N	O	I	S	A	A
N	B	R	A	S	K	A	N	E	B	K	S	N
W	S	C	O	N	T	A	M	A	B	A	L	A
W	A	S	N	G	T	O	N	S	T	T	A	S

Mazes are fascinating puzzles, as we have seen in a previous chapter. A particularly interesting genre is a maze in which numbers indicate jumps that form a pathway, rather than a line. This allows the maze to crisscross itself various times.

 370 **Theme: seven school subjects.** Can you find them?

```
M  P  H  S  C  S  S  C  I  S  Y  H  P
A  C  H  H  M  I  S  T  R  Y  G  E  O
T  B  I  L  O  G  Y  M  C  A  T  H  G
H  E  N  G  B  L  I  S  H  M  A  T  E
E  N  G  L  I  S  H  H  E  S  T  R  O
M  I  S  T  O  R  I  O  M  G  E  O  G
A  W  R  I  L  L  S  I  I  N  G  A  R
T  C  H  E  O  M  T  I  S  T  R  Y  A
I  M  T  H  G  L  O  H  T  H  S  S  P
C  N  D  S  Y  T  R  R  R  S  H  L  H
S  T  R  Y  A  B  Y  T  Y  C  L  L  Y
```

WORD SEARCHES: DEFINITIONS

WHAT IS A DEFINITION WORD SEARCH PUZZLE?

In this type of word search puzzle, you are given the definitions of (i.e., the clues for) the hidden words. This type of puzzle thus combines the benefits of acrostics or crosswords with the benefits associated with searching for word forms in a confusing array of letters.

HOW TO SOLVE DEFINITION WORD SEARCHES

You are given one clue for each of the seven hidden words. For this type of puzzle, you may either look for the words and check the clues or, vice versa, answer the clues and then find the words in the array; you can also use a mixture of both strategies. Again, since this puzzle is just for illustrative purposes, the words can be read only from left to right and top to bottom. Note that there are no themes to the puzzles in this section.

1. They allow you to see
2. Typically, you keep this in your pocket or purse
3. It opens a locked door
4. They are used to tighten or fasten shoes
5. The back parts of feet
6. They keep your feet warm
7. You can dance to it

The answers are (1) *eyes*, (2) *wallet*, (3) *key*, (4) *laces*, (5) *heels*, (6) *socks*, (7) *music*. They are found in the array as shown below:

E	Y	E	S	A	L	S	L	W	E	R	C	B
H	X	T	H	P	Z	O	F	A	T	H	X	S
X	S	X	H	X	K	B	M	L	X	S	P	O
J	K	L	P	H	E	R	T	L	M	N	N	C
M	S	C	D	C	Y	D	W	E	L	L	R	K
E	I	S	T	E	E	G	N	T	R	N	C	S
C	R	D	S	L	S	S	N	N	S	B	A	E
H	E	E	L	S	T	H	A	G	R	N	X	I
B	M	K	L	O	F	F	T	S	H	N	S	Y
E	M	U	S	I	C	H	R	H	S	H	L	X
X	Y	W	X	A	X	P	X	L	A	C	E	S

For the first five puzzles in this section, you will be told how the words can be read (left to right, right to left and so on).

PUZZLES

371 The seven words in this puzzle are read from left to right. Can you find them?

CLUES:

1. Room where cooking typically takes place
2. It predicts the future
3. It is taken into the lungs
4. You go there to learn
5. It's above us
6. Device for sweeping floors
7. The day after today

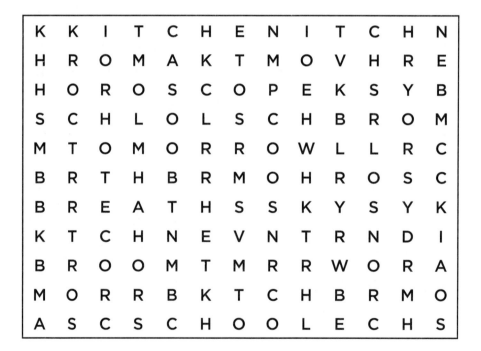

K	K	I	T	C	H	E	N	I	T	C	H	N
H	R	O	M	A	K	T	M	O	V	H	R	E
H	O	R	O	S	C	O	P	E	K	S	Y	B
S	C	H	L	O	L	S	C	H	B	R	O	M
M	T	O	M	O	R	R	O	W	L	L	R	C
B	R	T	H	B	R	M	O	H	R	O	S	C
B	R	E	A	T	H	S	S	K	Y	S	Y	K
K	T	C	H	N	E	V	N	T	R	N	D	I
B	R	O	O	M	T	M	R	R	W	O	R	A
M	O	R	R	B	K	T	C	H	B	R	M	O
A	S	C	S	C	H	O	O	L	E	C	H	S

372 The seven words in this puzzle are read from left to right and right to left. Can you find them?

CLUES:

1. You bring your money there
2. Female parent
3. Male parent
4. Formal union of lovers
5. Regular paid employment
6. You get this when you graduate
7. You put it in your car (complete word)

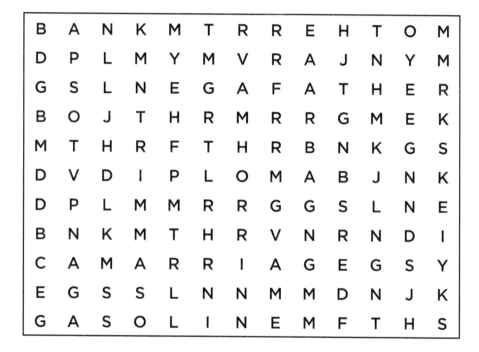

B	A	N	K	M	T	R	R	E	H	T	O	M
D	P	L	M	Y	M	V	R	A	J	N	Y	M
G	S	L	N	E	G	A	F	A	T	H	E	R
B	O	J	T	H	R	M	R	R	G	M	E	K
M	T	H	R	F	T	H	R	B	N	K	G	S
D	V	D	I	P	L	O	M	A	B	J	N	K
D	P	L	M	M	R	R	G	G	S	L	N	E
B	N	K	M	T	H	R	V	N	R	N	D	I
C	A	M	A	R	R	I	A	G	E	G	S	Y
E	G	S	S	L	N	N	M	M	D	N	J	K
G	A	S	O	L	I	N	E	M	F	T	H	S

VERBAL COGNITION

The seven words in this puzzle are read from left to right, right to left and top to bottom, and they might crisscross. Can you find them?

CLUES:

1. It has seven days
2. Male offspring
3. The king's home
4. The art of movies
5. Educator
6. Defender
7. Tooth doctor

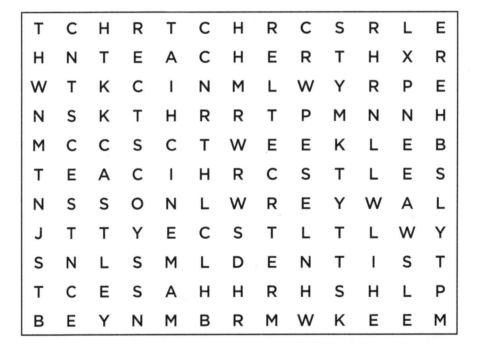

T	C	H	R	T	C	H	R	C	S	R	L	E
H	N	T	E	A	C	H	E	R	T	H	X	R
W	T	K	C	I	N	M	L	W	Y	R	P	E
N	S	K	T	H	R	R	T	P	M	N	N	H
M	C	C	S	C	T	W	E	E	K	L	E	B
T	E	A	C	I	H	R	C	S	T	L	E	S
N	S	S	O	N	L	W	R	E	Y	W	A	L
J	T	T	Y	E	C	S	T	L	T	L	W	Y
S	N	L	S	M	L	D	E	N	T	I	S	T
T	C	E	S	A	H	H	R	H	S	H	L	P
B	E	Y	N	M	B	R	M	W	K	E	E	M

There is evidence to suggest that doing jigsaw puzzles improves hand-to-eye coordination and enhances the ability to reason logically.

374 The seven words in this puzzle are read from left to right, right to left, top to bottom and bottom to top, and they might crisscross. Can you find them?

CLUES:

1. Twelve-month period
2. Female offspring
3. Art place
4. Chiseled art
5. Arbiter
6. M.D.
7. They go to school

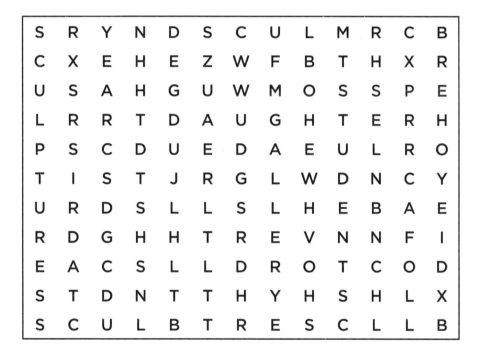

S	R	Y	N	D	S	C	U	L	M	R	C	B
C	X	E	H	E	Z	W	F	B	T	H	X	R
U	S	A	H	G	U	W	M	O	S	S	P	E
L	R	R	T	D	A	U	G	H	T	E	R	H
P	S	C	D	U	E	D	A	E	U	L	R	O
T	I	S	T	J	R	G	L	W	D	N	C	Y
U	R	D	S	L	L	S	L	H	E	B	A	E
R	D	G	H	H	T	R	E	V	N	N	F	I
E	A	C	S	L	L	D	R	O	T	C	O	D
S	T	D	N	T	T	H	Y	H	S	H	L	X
S	C	U	L	B	T	R	E	S	C	L	L	B

375 The seven words in this puzzle are read from left to right, right to left, top to bottom and bottom to top, and they might crisscross. Can you find them?

CLUES:

1. There are twelve of these in a year
2. Your mother's brother
3. Artifacts are displayed in this place
4. Person who is good at sports
5. Twelve people obliged to give a verdict
6. Person who looks after patients
7. Your father's legal relation to his wife

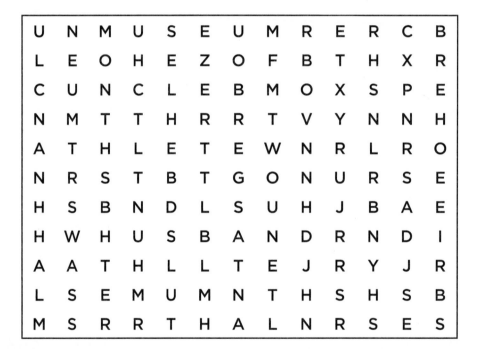

U	N	M	U	S	E	U	M	R	E	R	C	B
L	E	O	H	E	Z	O	F	B	T	H	X	R
C	U	N	C	L	E	B	M	O	X	S	P	E
N	M	T	T	H	R	R	T	V	Y	N	N	H
A	T	H	L	E	T	E	W	N	R	L	R	O
N	R	S	T	B	T	G	O	N	U	R	S	E
H	S	B	N	D	L	S	U	H	J	B	A	E
H	W	H	U	S	B	A	N	D	R	N	D	I
A	A	T	H	L	L	T	E	J	R	Y	J	R
L	S	E	M	U	M	N	T	H	S	H	S	B
M	S	R	R	T	H	A	L	N	R	S	E	S

For the remaining puzzles in this section you will not be told the direction of the letters.

376 There are seven words hidden in the puzzle below. Can you find them?

CLUES:

1. There are twenty-four of these in a day
2. An upper body limb
3. It helps you walk if you have a limp
4. The flesh of an animal
5. A design plan or technical drawing
6. A place with many stores
7. A portable cloth shelter

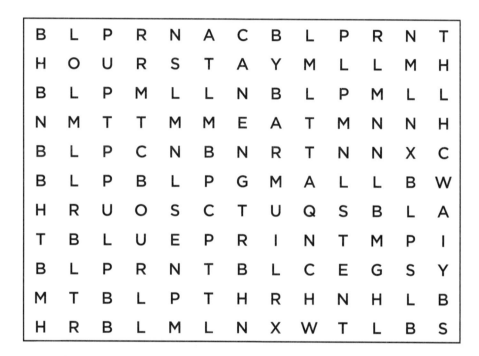

B	L	P	R	N	A	C	B	L	P	R	N	T
H	O	U	R	S	T	A	Y	M	L	L	M	H
B	L	P	M	L	L	N	B	L	P	M	L	L
N	M	T	T	M	M	E	A	T	M	N	N	H
B	L	P	C	N	B	N	R	T	N	N	X	C
B	L	P	B	L	P	G	M	A	L	L	B	W
H	R	U	O	S	C	T	U	Q	S	B	L	A
T	B	L	U	E	P	R	I	N	T	M	P	I
B	L	P	R	N	T	B	L	C	E	G	S	Y
M	T	B	L	P	T	H	R	H	N	H	L	B
H	R	B	L	M	L	N	X	W	T	L	B	S

VERBAL COGNITION

377 There are seven words hidden in the puzzle below. Can you find them?

CLUES:

1. There are sixty of these in an hour
2. The grasping limb
3. You sleep in it
4. They are often eaten with meat
5. White fluid secreted by female mammals
6. Place where some sports are played
7. A very tall building

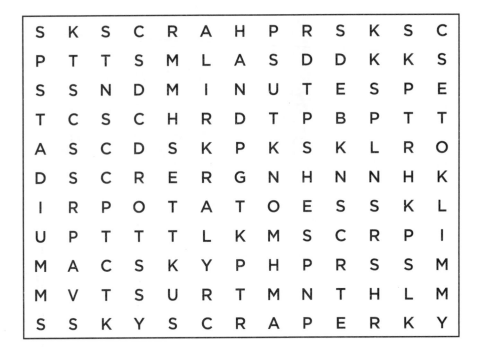

S	K	S	C	R	A	H	P	R	S	K	S	C
P	T	T	S	M	L	A	S	D	D	K	K	S
S	S	N	D	M	I	N	U	T	E	S	P	E
T	C	S	C	H	R	D	T	P	B	P	T	T
A	S	C	D	S	K	P	K	S	K	L	R	O
D	S	C	R	E	R	G	N	H	N	N	H	K
I	R	P	O	T	A	T	O	E	S	S	K	L
U	P	T	T	T	L	K	M	S	C	R	P	I
M	A	C	S	K	Y	P	H	P	R	S	S	M
M	V	T	S	U	R	T	M	N	T	H	L	M
S	S	K	Y	S	C	R	A	P	E	R	K	Y

378 There are seven words hidden in the puzzle below. Can you find them?

CLUES:

1. There are sixty of these in a minute
2. A lower limb of the body
3. You listen to it typically in the car
4. What coffee or cocoa seeds are called
5. Hot drink, consumed typically at breakfast or after meals
6. Place where a legal case is argued
7. Large road vehicle

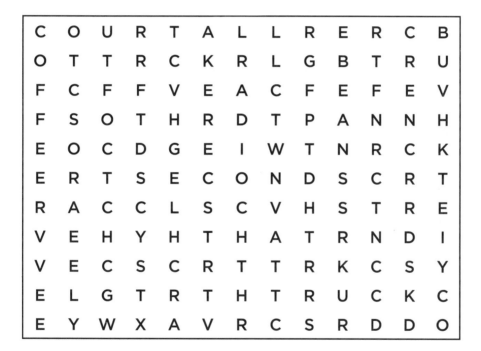

C	O	U	R	T	A	L	L	R	E	R	C	B
O	T	T	R	C	K	R	L	G	B	T	R	U
F	C	F	F	V	E	A	C	F	E	F	E	V
F	S	O	T	H	R	D	T	P	A	N	N	H
E	O	C	D	G	E	I	W	T	N	R	C	K
E	R	T	S	E	C	O	N	D	S	C	R	T
R	A	C	C	L	S	C	V	H	S	T	R	E
V	E	H	Y	T	H	A	T	R	N	D	I
V	E	C	S	C	R	T	T	R	K	C	S	Y
E	L	G	T	R	T	H	T	R	U	C	K	C
E	Y	W	X	A	V	R	C	S	R	D	D	O

379 There are seven words hidden in the puzzle below. Can you find them?

CLUES:

1. It covers a building
2. A common type of seat
3. Classical dance form
4. A cold dish of various mixtures, usually served with a dressing
5. Colorless, tasteless liquid necessary to sustain life
6. Large room used typically for meetings, dances and other events
7. A sandy or pebbly shore

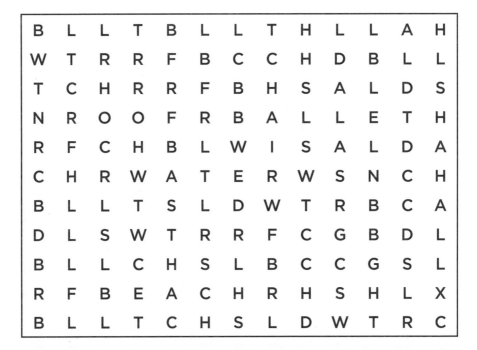

B	L	L	T	B	L	L	T	H	L	L	A	H
W	T	R	R	F	B	C	C	H	D	B	L	L
T	C	H	R	R	F	B	H	S	A	L	D	S
N	R	O	O	F	R	B	A	L	L	E	T	H
R	F	C	H	B	L	W	I	S	A	L	D	A
C	H	R	W	A	T	E	R	W	S	N	C	H
B	L	L	T	S	L	D	W	T	R	B	C	A
D	L	S	W	T	R	R	F	C	G	B	D	L
B	L	L	C	H	S	L	B	C	C	G	S	L
R	F	B	E	A	C	H	R	H	S	H	L	X
B	L	L	T	C	H	S	L	D	W	T	R	C

One of the first video games, called *Noughts and Crosses,* goes back to 1952. It allowed players to test their tic-tac-toe skills against a computer (in an early era of computers). Nowadays, online venues and video game devices of all kinds are highly popular. Do they enhance brainpower? The answer would seem to be yes.

380 There are seven words hidden in the puzzle below. Can you find them?

CLUES:

1. A glass frame in a building that allows you to look outside
2. Panel that operates a computer and other digital devices
3. Classical type of composition for full orchestra
4. It tastes good with fries on the side
5. It is intended to make people laugh
6. Place where classes take place
7. They are the hearing organs

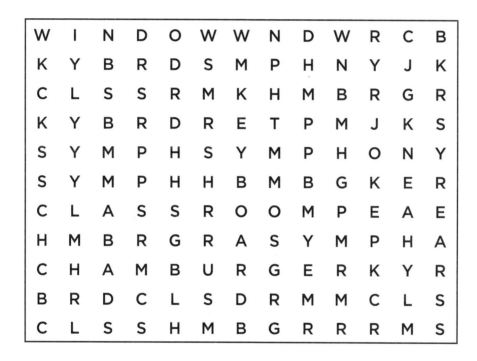

W	I	N	D	O	W	W	N	D	W	R	C	B
K	Y	B	R	D	S	M	P	H	N	Y	J	K
C	L	S	S	R	M	K	H	M	B	R	G	R
K	Y	B	R	D	R	E	T	P	M	J	K	S
S	Y	M	P	H	S	Y	M	P	H	O	N	Y
S	Y	M	P	H	H	B	M	B	G	K	E	R
C	L	A	S	S	R	O	O	M	P	E	A	E
H	M	B	R	G	R	A	S	Y	M	P	H	A
C	H	A	M	B	U	R	G	E	R	K	Y	R
B	R	D	C	L	S	D	R	M	M	C	L	S
C	L	S	S	H	M	B	G	R	R	R	M	S

WORD SEARCHES: SYNONYMS

WHAT IS A SYNONYM WORD SEARCH PUZZLE?

In this variant of the word search puzzle, you are given synonyms for the hidden words. Again, this type of mental activity is bound to sharpen your verbal skills since it, too, combines the cognitive skills used to solve acrostics or crosswords with the benefits connected to searching for word forms in an array of letters.

HOW TO SOLVE SYNONYM WORD SEARCHES

You are given synonyms for the seven hidden words. In the puzzle below the words can be read from left to right and top to bottom:

1. smooth
2. round
3. delicious
4. angry
5. happy
6. sad
7. lively

The answers are (1) *flat*, (2) *circular*, (3) *tasty*, (4) *mad*, (5) *glad*, (6) *gloomy*, (7) *energetic*. They are found in the array as shown below:

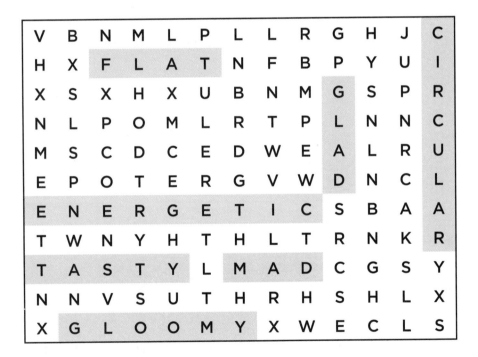

For the first five puzzles in this section you are given the direction in which the letters can be read. Also, keep in mind that there really is no one synonym for a word and, thus, that you will have to guess which ones were chosen for the purpose of the puzzles below. You will have to sharpen your thesaurus skills here.

PUZZLES

381 The seven words in this puzzle are read from left to right. Can you find them?

SYNONYMS:

1. big
2. glad
3. loyal
4. hard
5. rich
6. weak
7. cunning

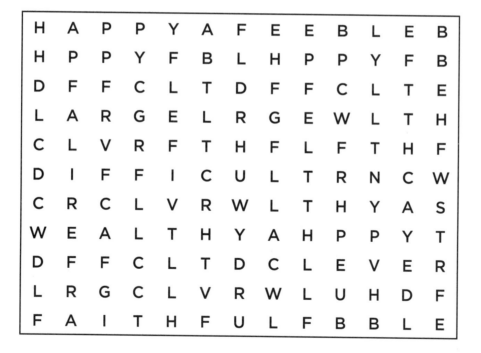

H	A	P	P	Y	A	F	E	E	B	L	E	B
H	P	P	Y	F	B	L	H	P	P	Y	F	B
D	F	F	C	L	T	D	F	F	C	L	T	E
L	A	R	G	E	L	R	G	E	W	L	T	H
C	L	V	R	F	T	H	F	L	F	T	H	F
D	I	F	F	I	C	U	L	T	R	N	C	W
C	R	C	L	V	R	W	L	T	H	Y	A	S
W	E	A	L	T	H	Y	A	H	P	P	Y	T
D	F	F	C	L	T	D	C	L	E	V	E	R
L	R	G	C	L	V	R	W	L	U	H	D	F
F	A	I	T	H	F	U	L	F	B	B	L	E

382 The seven words in this puzzle are read from left to right and right to left. Can you find them?

SYNONYMS:

1. usual
2. polite
3. small
4. rare
5. well-known
6. safe
7. vacant

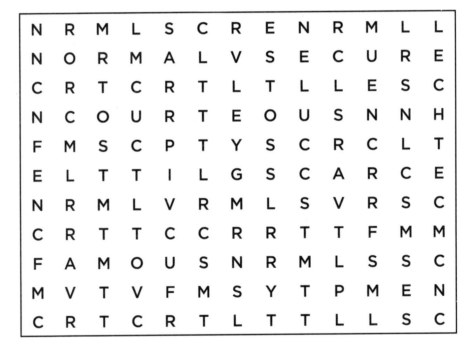

N	R	M	L	S	C	R	E	N	R	M	L	L
N	O	R	M	A	L	V	S	E	C	U	R	E
C	R	T	C	R	T	L	T	L	L	E	S	C
N	C	O	U	R	T	E	O	U	S	N	N	H
F	M	S	C	P	T	Y	S	C	R	C	L	T
E	L	T	T	I	L	G	S	C	A	R	C	E
N	R	M	L	V	R	M	L	S	V	R	S	C
C	R	T	T	C	C	R	R	T	T	F	M	M
F	A	M	O	U	S	N	R	M	L	S	S	C
M	V	T	V	F	M	S	Y	T	P	M	E	N
C	R	T	C	R	T	L	T	T	L	L	S	C

383 The seven words in this puzzle are read from left to right, right to left and top to bottom, and they might crisscross. Can you find them?

SYNONYMS:

1. beautiful
2. comical
3. intelligent
4. fortunate
5. legitimate
6. almost
7. anyway

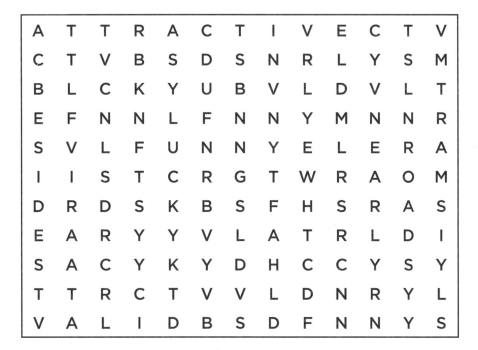

A	T	T	R	A	C	T	I	V	E	C	T	V
C	T	V	B	S	D	S	N	R	L	Y	S	M
B	L	C	K	Y	U	B	V	L	D	V	L	T
E	F	N	N	L	F	N	N	Y	M	N	N	R
S	V	L	F	U	N	N	Y	E	L	E	R	A
I	I	S	T	C	R	G	T	W	R	A	O	M
D	R	D	S	K	B	S	F	H	S	R	A	S
E	A	R	Y	Y	V	L	A	T	R	L	D	I
S	A	C	Y	K	Y	D	H	C	C	Y	S	Y
T	T	R	C	T	V	V	L	D	N	R	Y	L
V	A	L	I	D	B	S	D	F	N	N	Y	S

A pangram is a sentence using every letter of the alphabet at least once. The best-known English example is *The quick brown fox jumps over the lazy dog*, which uses all twenty-six letters.

VERBAL COGNITION

384 The seven words in this puzzle are read from left to right, right to left, top to bottom and bottom to top, and they might crisscross. Can you find them?

SYNONYMS:

1. courageous
2. opposite
3. fate
4. keen
5. silly
6. tip
7. good-looking

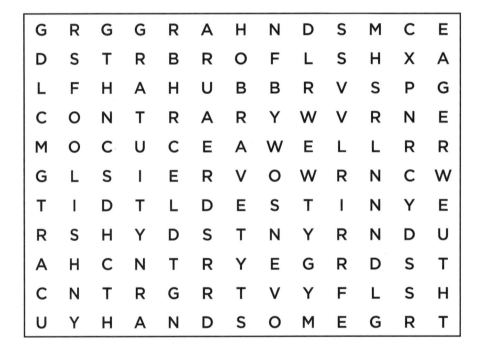

G	R	G	G	R	A	H	N	D	S	M	C	E
D	S	T	R	B	R	O	F	L	S	H	X	A
L	F	H	A	H	U	B	B	R	V	S	P	G
C	O	N	T	R	A	R	Y	W	V	R	N	E
M	O	C	U	C	E	A	W	E	L	L	R	R
G	L	S	I	E	R	V	O	W	R	N	C	W
T	I	D	T	L	D	E	S	T	I	N	Y	E
R	S	H	Y	D	S	T	N	Y	R	N	D	U
A	H	C	N	T	R	Y	E	G	R	D	S	T
C	N	T	R	G	R	T	V	Y	F	L	S	H
U	Y	H	A	N	D	S	O	M	E	G	R	T

The seven words in this puzzle are read from left to right, right to left, top to bottom and bottom to top, and they might crisscross. Can you find them?

SYNONYMS:

1. maybe
2. film
3. noon
4. out-of-date
5. remark
6. select
7. zenith

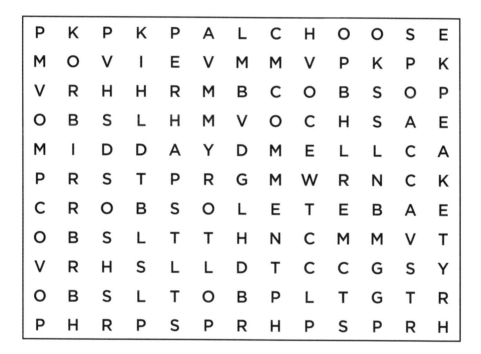

P	K	P	K	P	A	L	C	H	O	O	S	E
M	O	V	I	E	V	M	M	V	P	K	P	K
V	R	H	H	R	M	B	C	O	B	S	O	P
O	B	S	L	H	M	V	O	C	H	S	A	E
M	I	D	D	A	Y	D	M	E	L	L	C	A
P	R	S	T	P	R	G	M	W	R	N	C	K
C	R	O	B	S	O	L	E	T	E	B	A	E
O	B	S	L	T	T	H	N	C	M	M	V	T
V	R	H	S	L	L	D	T	C	C	G	S	Y
O	B	S	L	T	O	B	P	L	T	G	T	R
P	H	R	P	S	P	R	H	P	S	P	R	H

For the remaining puzzles in this section you will not be told the direction of the letters.

386 There are seven words hidden in the puzzle below. Can you find them?

SYNONYMS:

1. above
2. stop
3. exit
4. gift
5. bunny
6. garbage
7. rug

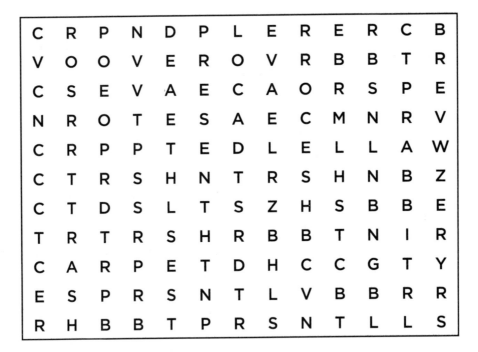

C	R	P	N	D	P	L	E	R	E	R	C	B
V	O	O	V	E	R	O	V	R	B	B	T	R
C	S	E	V	A	E	C	A	O	R	S	P	E
N	R	O	T	E	S	A	E	C	M	N	R	V
C	R	P	P	T	E	D	L	E	L	L	A	W
C	T	R	S	H	N	T	R	S	H	N	B	Z
C	T	D	S	L	T	S	Z	H	S	B	B	E
T	R	T	R	S	H	R	B	B	T	N	I	R
C	A	R	P	E	T	D	H	C	C	G	T	Y
E	S	P	R	S	N	T	L	V	B	B	R	R
R	H	B	B	T	P	R	S	N	T	L	L	S

Puzzles and games have been around for as long as humans have lived in groups. It is estimated that the origin of games goes back at least ten thousand years.

387 There are seven words hidden in the puzzle below. Can you find them?

SYNONYMS:

1. close
2. chef
3. reply
4. need
5. reach
6. buy
7. understand

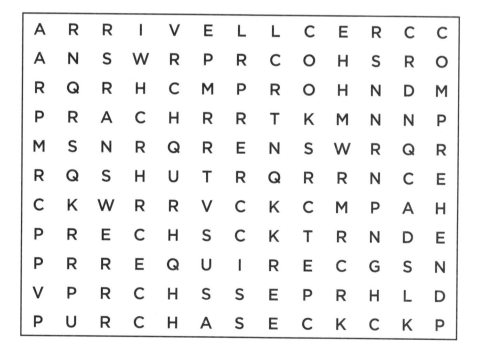

A	R	R	I	V	E	L	L	C	E	R	C	C
A	N	S	W	R	P	R	C	O	H	S	R	O
R	Q	R	H	C	M	P	R	O	H	N	D	M
P	R	A	C	H	R	R	T	K	M	N	N	P
M	S	N	R	Q	R	E	N	S	W	R	Q	R
R	Q	S	H	U	T	R	Q	R	R	N	C	E
C	K	W	R	R	V	C	K	C	M	P	A	H
P	R	E	C	H	S	C	K	T	R	N	D	E
P	R	R	E	Q	U	I	R	E	C	G	S	N
V	P	R	C	H	S	S	E	P	R	H	L	D
P	U	R	C	H	A	S	E	C	K	C	K	P

There are seven words hidden in the puzzle below. Can you find them?

SYNONYMS:

1. superb
2. weird
3. conceited
4. spoiled
5. advance
6. suggest
7. concede

P	R	A	D	M	I	T	C	D	E	R	R	P
R	R	G	N	T	R	N	D	S	Q	R	U	Q
E	S	X	C	L	L	N	T	P	E	R	I	E
P	P	O	T	H	A	R	R	O	G	A	N	T
R	R	P	S	E	E	X	C	E	N	L	E	O
E	O	R	R	G	N	T	R	W	A	N	D	X
D	C	R	R	V	N	L	L	E	R	N	T	V
T	E	X	C	E	L	L	E	N	T	N	D	V
R	E	P	R	P	S	D	H	C	S	G	S	P
E	D	X	C	L	L	N	T	S	T	R	N	G
S	D	R	P	R	O	P	O	S	E	N	G	E

389 There are seven words hidden in the puzzle below. Can you find them?

SYNONYMS:

1. deny
2. deceive
3. betrayal
4. affection
5. narcissism
6. achievement
7. well-liked

D	I	S	L	O	Y	A	L	T	Y	R	C	C
F	N	D	N	S	S	P	P	L	R	P	V	R
M	S	L	D	R	F	T	D	S	L	S	A	V
V	N	T	R	E	F	U	T	E	N	N	N	Y
M	S	C	A	C	E	D	G	E	L	L	I	O
M	I	S	L	E	A	D	O	W	R	N	T	G
S	C	D	U	S	C	C	S	S	S	L	Y	E
P	P	L	P	R	C	V	A	S	R	N	D	G
D	S	F	O	N	D	N	E	S	S	G	S	Y
E	S	D	P	U	C	H	R	H	S	H	L	X
V	S	L	Y	S	U	C	C	E	S	S	L	S

Sam Loyd (1841–1911) was one of the greatest puzzle makers of all time. He started out as a chess player and then transferred what he learned from playing chess to the creation of puzzles. Loyd's puzzles remain among the most ingenious ever created.

There are seven words hidden in the puzzle below. Can you find them?

SYNONYMS:

1. build
2. destroy
3. comment
4. abscond
5. collect
6. throw away
7. proof

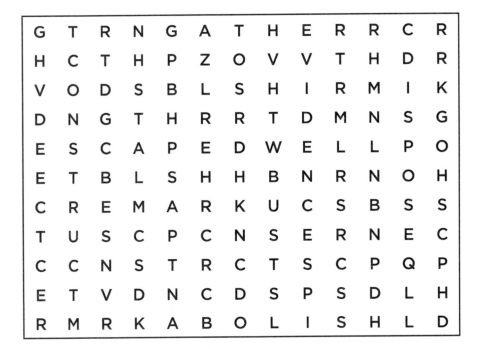

```
G  T  R  N  G  A  T  H  E  R  R  C  R
H  C  T  H  P  Z  O  V  V  T  H  D  R
V  O  D  S  B  L  S  H  I  R  M  I  K
D  N  G  T  H  R  R  T  D  M  N  S  G
E  S  C  A  P  E  D  W  E  L  L  P  O
E  T  B  L  S  H  H  B  N  R  N  O  H
C  R  E  M  A  R  K  U  C  S  B  S  S
T  U  S  C  P  C  N  S  E  R  N  E  C
C  C  N  S  T  R  C  T  S  C  P  Q  P
E  T  V  D  N  C  D  S  P  S  D  L  H
R  M  R  K  A  B  O  L  I  S  H  L  D
```

WORD SEARCHES: ANTONYMS

WHAT IS AN ANTONYM WORD SEARCH PUZZLE?

In this version of the word search puzzle, you are given antonyms (opposite meanings) for the hidden words. Here, you will need to sharpen your thesaurus skills and try to infer which antonym was chosen for a particular word and then look for it in the array of letters below.

HOW TO SOLVE ANTONYM WORD SEARCHES

You are given seven antonyms for the seven hidden words. The words in the puzzle below can be read from left to right and top to bottom:

1. tall
2. young
3. generous
4. night
5. open
6. fast
7. kind

The answers are (1) *short*, (2) *old*, (3) *greedy*, (4) *day*, (5) *closed*, (6) *slow*, (7) *mean*. They are found in the array as shown below:

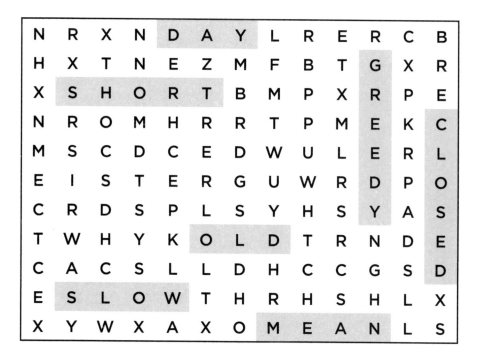

For the first five puzzles in this section you will be told how the words can be read (left to right, right to left and so on).

PUZZLES

391 The seven words in this puzzle are read from left to right. Can you find them?

ANTONYMS:

1. bad
2. dangerous
3. unique
4. easy
5. finish
6. take
7. go

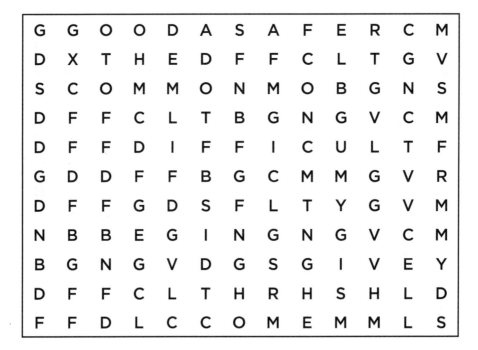

G	G	O	O	D	A	S	A	F	E	R	C	M
D	X	T	H	E	D	F	F	C	L	T	G	V
S	C	O	M	M	O	N	M	O	B	G	N	S
D	F	F	C	L	T	B	G	N	G	V	C	M
D	F	F	D	I	F	F	I	C	U	L	T	F
G	D	D	F	F	B	G	C	M	M	G	V	R
D	F	F	G	D	S	F	L	T	Y	G	V	M
N	B	B	E	G	I	N	G	N	G	V	C	M
B	G	N	G	V	D	G	S	G	I	V	E	Y
D	F	F	C	L	T	H	R	H	S	H	L	D
F	F	D	L	C	C	O	M	E	M	M	L	S

The seven words in this puzzle are read from left to right and right to left. Can you find them?

ANTONYMS:

1. neat
2. early
3. special
4. dreary
5. increase
6. allow
7. sever

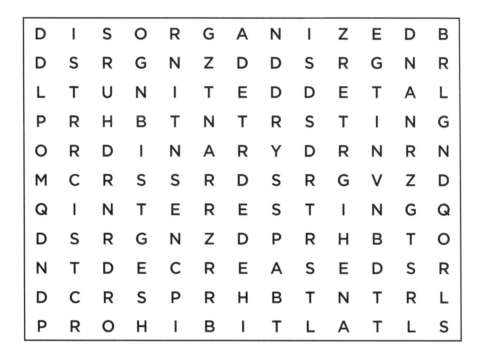

D	I	S	O	R	G	A	N	I	Z	E	D	B
D	S	R	G	N	Z	D	D	S	R	G	N	R
L	T	U	N	I	T	E	D	D	E	T	A	L
P	R	H	B	T	N	T	R	S	T	I	N	G
O	R	D	I	N	A	R	Y	D	R	N	R	N
M	C	R	S	S	R	D	S	R	G	V	Z	D
Q	I	N	T	E	R	E	S	T	I	N	G	Q
D	S	R	G	N	Z	D	P	R	H	B	T	O
N	T	D	E	C	R	E	A	S	E	D	S	R
D	C	R	S	P	R	H	B	T	N	T	R	L
P	R	O	H	I	B	I	T	L	A	T	L	S

The seven words in this puzzle are read from left to right, right to left, top to bottom, and they might crisscross. Can you find them?

ANTONYMS:

1. dirty
2. long
3. city
4. weak

5. over
6. wrong
7. always

C	L	N	N	D	R	R	G	H	T	N	V	R
C	N	C	L	E	A	N	G	R	Y	S	T	R
N	G	O	F	T	L	B	M	U	N	D	E	R
N	R	U	T	S	R	R	T	P	E	N	O	I
V	S	N	D	H	E	D	V	E	V	L	R	G
T	S	T	R	O	N	G	V	W	E	N	C	H
S	H	R	S	R	L	S	B	N	R	B	R	T
C	W	Y	Y	T	G	H	A	T	R	N	D	V
Q	W	R	T	P	S	F	B	N	M	M	N	B
T	R	R	T	P	Y	Y	P	M	N	N	M	V
S	W	V	B	A	L	O	L	P	E	Y	L	S

The number of puzzle genres (riddles, anagrams, word squares, sudoku, crosswords, acrostics, and so on and so forth) exceeds the number of genres in many other areas of human creativity, such as music and literature.

The seven words in this puzzle are read from left to right, right to left, top to bottom and bottom to top, and they might crisscross. Can you find them?

ANTONYMS:

1. hard
2. above
3. smile
4. abundant
5. enemy
6. natural
7. blame

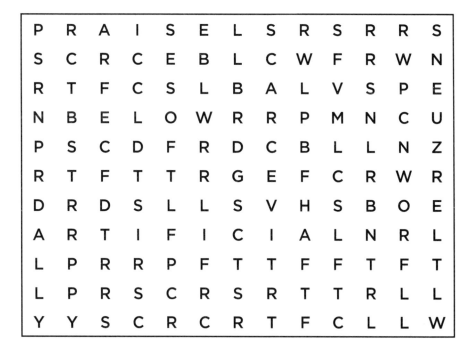

P	R	A	I	S	E	L	S	R	S	R	R	S
S	C	R	C	E	B	L	C	W	F	R	W	N
R	T	F	C	S	L	B	A	L	V	S	P	E
N	B	E	L	O	W	R	R	P	M	N	C	U
P	S	C	D	F	R	D	C	B	L	L	N	Z
R	T	F	T	T	R	G	E	F	C	R	W	R
D	R	D	S	L	L	S	V	H	S	B	O	E
A	R	T	I	F	I	C	I	A	L	N	R	L
L	P	R	R	P	F	T	T	F	F	T	F	T
L	P	R	S	C	R	S	R	T	T	R	L	L
Y	Y	S	C	R	C	R	T	F	C	L	L	W

395 The seven words in this puzzle are read from left to right, right to left, top to bottom and bottom to top, and they might crisscross. Can you find them?

ANTONYMS:

1. cowardly
2. timid
3. broad
4. lend
5. cheap
6. deep
7. expand

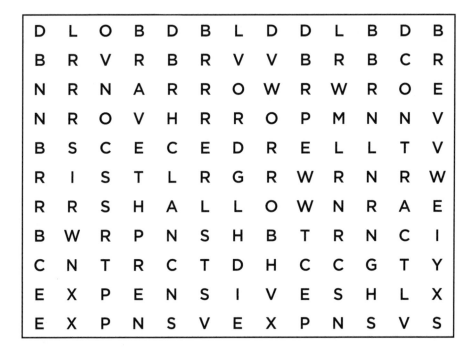

D	L	O	B	D	B	L	D	D	L	B	D	B
B	R	V	R	B	R	V	V	B	R	B	C	R
N	R	N	A	R	R	O	W	R	W	R	O	E
N	R	O	V	H	R	R	O	P	M	N	N	V
B	S	C	E	C	E	D	R	E	L	L	T	V
R	I	S	T	L	R	G	R	W	R	N	R	W
R	R	S	H	A	L	L	O	W	N	R	A	E
B	W	R	P	N	S	H	B	T	R	N	C	I
C	N	T	R	C	T	D	H	C	C	G	T	Y
E	X	P	E	N	S	I	V	E	S	H	L	X
E	X	P	N	S	V	E	X	P	N	S	V	S

For the remaining puzzles in this section, you will not be told the direction of the letters.

396 There are seven words hidden in the puzzle below. Can you find them?

ANTONYMS:

1. false
2. exit
3. frequent
4. forget

5. wise
6. lost
7. stingy

R	M	B	T	F	L	S	H	R	E	R	C	V
R	T	T	R	E	M	E	M	B	E	R	X	R
G	N	E	U	R	M	B	M	B	R	S	P	V
N	R	G	E	N	E	R	O	U	S	N	N	H
G	N	R	S	C	N	D	W	E	E	L	R	O
R	M	B	M	B	T	R	M	E	L	B	R	V
G	N	R	S	L	E	H	G	N	D	R	S	E
R	M	M	B	R	R	H	A	F	O	U	N	D
S	L	D	M	G	N	R	V	S	M	V	N	S
G	N	R	S	E	N	T	R	R	M	B	B	R
F	O	O	L	I	S	H	F	N	D	S	L	D

In their classic 1940 book, *Mathematics and the Imagination,* Kasner and Newman wrote about how classic puzzles have led to discovery: "the theory of equations, of probability, the infinitesimal calculus, the theory of point sets, of topology, all have grown out of problems first expressed in puzzle form."

397 There are seven words hidden in the puzzle below. Can you find them?

ANTONYMS:

1. knowledge
2. lenient
3. maximum
4. major
5. melt
6. noisy
7. sober

M	N	I	N	F	R	Z	L	D	F	R	Z	B
H	G	G	Q	U	T	T	F	R	E	E	Z	E
M	I	N	O	R	U	B	M	U	D	R	N	K
I	D	O	D	R	N	K	T	N	S	T	R	C
N	R	R	Q	U	E	T	W	K	L	L	R	O
I	N	A	T	E	Q	S	T	R	S	T	R	Q
M	K	N	S	L	U	F	R	Z	I	G	N	O
U	S	C	Y	H	I	M	I	M	M	I	M	N
M	T	E	S	L	E	D	H	L	C	M	S	N
I	G	N	S	S	T	R	I	C	T	I	G	N
M	N	M	M	N	R	M	N	M	M	M	N	R

398 There are seven words hidden in the puzzle below. Can you find them?

ANTONYMS:

1. sour
2. cloudy
3. occupied
4. compulsory
5. yin
6. volatile
7. energetic

S	S	S	U	N	N	Y	P	R	E	R	C	B
W	N	W	P	V	L	A	L	V	T	H	X	R
T	N	E	L	N	T	N	C	O	Y	N	A	G
S	Y	E	C	T	H	G	D	L	M	N	N	H
W	S	T	D	R	R	D	P	U	S	W	S	T
T	N	V	T	Y	G	G	L	N	Y	N	P	G
S	N	C	V	A	C	A	N	T	V	C	L	T
W	Y	N	Y	H	T	H	A	A	Y	N	A	G
T	S	T	L	E	T	H	A	R	G	I	C	Y
S	N	N	S	T	T	H	R	Y	S	H	I	X
W	Y	G	D	S	C	O	D	S	W	W	D	S

399 There are seven words hidden in the puzzle below. Can you find them?

ANTONYMS:

1. future
2. enthusiasm
3. glib
4. unpleasant
5. reward
6. throw
7. withdraw

R	R	E	C	E	I	V	E	R	E	R	P	S
C	P	N	S	H	M	N	T	P	N	S	R	R
V	P	R	V	D	P	R	V	D	R	S	O	E
P	R	O	A	P	A	T	H	Y	M	N	V	H
T	S	C	D	A	P	N	S	H	M	N	I	T
P	P	R	O	F	O	U	N	D	R	N	D	T
H	R	D	S	T	L	S	I	H	S	B	E	E
Y	W	H	Y	H	T	H	C	T	R	N	D	K
P	U	N	I	S	H	M	E	N	T	G	S	Y
R	N	D	P	R	V	D	P	N	S	M	N	T
V	Y	W	P	M	S	N	V	P	A	S	T	S

400 There are seven words hidden in the puzzle below. Can you find them?

ANTONYMS:

1. fake
2. persist
3. let go
4. sincere
5. drawback
6. receive
7. humility

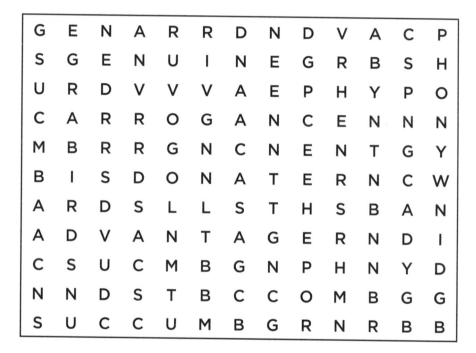

G	E	N	A	R	R	D	N	D	V	A	C	P
S	G	E	N	U	I	N	E	G	R	B	S	H
U	R	D	V	V	V	A	E	P	H	Y	P	O
C	A	R	R	O	G	A	N	C	E	N	N	N
M	B	R	R	G	N	C	N	E	N	T	G	Y
B	I	S	D	O	N	A	T	E	R	N	C	W
A	R	D	S	L	L	S	T	H	S	B	A	N
A	D	V	A	N	T	A	G	E	R	N	D	I
C	S	U	C	M	B	G	N	P	H	N	Y	D
N	N	D	S	T	B	C	C	O	M	B	G	G
S	U	C	C	U	M	B	G	R	N	R	B	B

9

BIMODALITY

One forgets words as one forgets names.
One's vocabulary needs constant fertilizing or it will die.
(EVELYN WAUGH, 1903–1966)

AS YOU KNOW, THERE ARE TWO BRAIN HEMISPHERES—the left and the right. Over more than two centuries, it has been found that they process information and carry out thinking differently. The left hemisphere is involved in logical and purely linguistic cognition, while the right hemisphere is involved in more imaginative, visual and inferential thinking. These are called *modes* of thought. Many puzzles involve the use of both modes, as we have seen throughout this book. In other words, they activate *bimodal* thinking—logical and imaginative, linguistic and visual, and so on, in tandem.

PUZZLES AND BIMODALITY

In a 2012 study published in *Developmental Psychology*, it was found that children entering kindergarten displayed a range of differences in their spatial skills. The study examined the relationship between children's early puzzle play and these skills. Children who were observed playing with puzzles performed better on regular spatial tasks than those who did not. Moreover, among those children who engaged in puzzles, the frequency of puzzle play predicted performance on complex spatial tasks. These are right hemispheric activities, while the puzzles involve several bimodal functions. In other words, puzzles can, from childhood onward, activate bimodality and this is crucial for the brain at any age.

OBJECTIVES OF THIS CHAPTER

This chapter contains fifty puzzles involving word logic of various kinds, such as synonyms, completions and the like. The words are arranged within the given geometrical figures, and solving the puzzles involves spotting patterns among the words themselves or in the way the words are laid out within the figures. The combination of word logic with spatial perception is what makes these puzzles bimodal.

WORD CIRCLES

WHAT IS A WORD CIRCLE PUZZLE?

This is a puzzle with four words inserted into the four segments of the circle in some way. One of the words is missing. You will have to figure out what that word is on the basis of the other three. Anything goes. For example, the words could be antonym pairs (*night-day, good-bad*), or they could be legitimate words that have a letter less than the previous word (*mates, mate, mat, ma*). You might find the puzzles in this section a bit easier than many of the ones you have solved in previous chapters. But they are not as easy as they may seem. You will still have to put your bimodal brain to work.

HOW TO SOLVE WORD CIRCLE PUZZLES

Let's do a very simple circle puzzle. What is the missing word based on the other three?

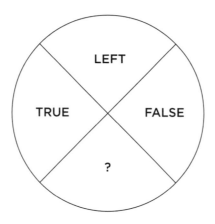

TRUE-FALSE are antonyms and opposite each other. So, by deduction, the word opposite *LEFT* is *RIGHT.*

PUZZLES

401 Provide the missing word based on the other words.

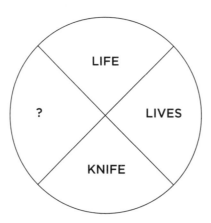

402 Provide the missing word based on the other words.

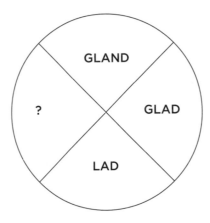

403 Provide the missing word based on the other words.

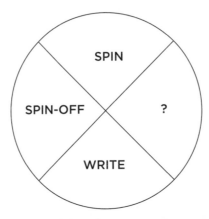

To use a metaphor, the brain is the master control center of the body and the organ of thought. It is at its best when both hemispheres are engaged. Puzzles seem to enable the brain to do this consistently.

404 Provide the missing word based on the other words.

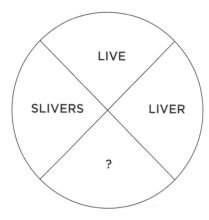

405 Provide the missing word based on the other words.

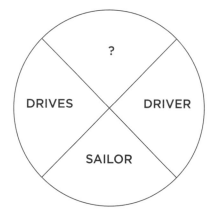

406 Provide the missing word based on the other words.

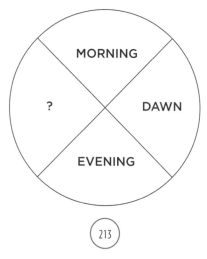

The right and left hemispheres of the brain are connected by bundles of nerve fibers, the largest of which is called the corpus callosum. Each hemisphere, in turn, is divided into four lobes (regions). Each one has the same name as the bone of the skull that lies above it. Neuroscientists believe that bimodality emerges through the corpus callosum; when the hemispheres are disconnected, as in the treatment of epilepsy, the affected individuals cannot process information bimodally.

407 Provide the missing word based on the other words.

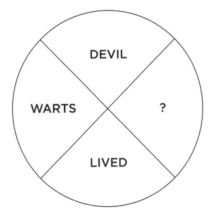

408 Provide the missing word based on the other words.

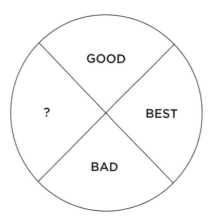

The brain has billions of neurons that are connected to one another in complex networks. All physical and mental functions depend on the establishment and maintenance of these networks. As research has started to show, puzzles seem to contribute to the maintenance of these networks.

410 Provide the missing word based on the other words.

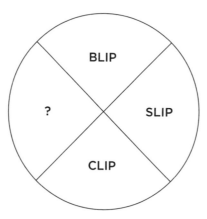

BIMODALITY

WORD RECTANGLES

WHAT IS A WORD RECTANGLE PUZZLE?

This is a puzzle with four words inserted into boxes (smaller rectangles) within a rectangle according to some principle. One of the words is missing. You will have to figure out what that word is on the basis of some pattern present in the other boxes. Basically, this is a different geometrical version of the circle puzzle. But the challenge is different. For example, the words in the boxes could be anagrams of each other, they could describe some sequence, they could refer to sets that come in four (*north, south, east, west*), and so on. For instance, the words *spot, tops, pots* and *opts* are anagrams of each other; the four words *two, four, eight, sixteen* describe a sequence of 2 (two), 2^2 (four), 2^3 (eight), 2^4 (sixteen) and so on. You might also be given bits and pieces of words that, when combined, form an authentic word.

HOW TO SOLVE WORD RECTANGLE PUZZLES

In this type of puzzle, you should always start with the box in the top left corner:

NE	?
FUL	NESS

These are parts of the word *needfulness: NE+ED+FUL+NESS.* Missing from the word is *ED*.

PUZZLES

411 Complete the following rectangle logically.

LIVE	VEIL
VILE	?

412 Complete the following rectangle logically.

DES	PER
?	TION

413 Complete the following rectangle logically.

G	O
N	?

Our habits and skills, such as nail-biting or playing the piano, become part of neuron networks. When we stop performing an activity, the networks for that activity fall into disuse and eventually may disappear. There is an obvious lesson for puzzle solvers in this—keep on solving puzzles to keep the brain functioning efficiently.

414 Complete the following rectangle logically.

TRIANGLE	SQUARE
PENTAGON	?

415 Complete the following rectangle logically.

CLUBS	?
DIAMONDS	SPADES

416 Complete the following rectangle logically.

UNHAPPINESS	?
HAPPY	NESS

In the late 1800s, scientists found that damage to particular parts of the brain caused the same pattern of language disabilities in patients. Damage to the left frontal lobe in Broca's area, named for the French surgeon Pierre Paul Broca, destroyed the ability to articulate words. Damage to the left temporal lobe in Wernicke's area, named for the German neurologist Carl Wernicke, caused difficulties in understanding language. Today, new imaging technologies enable neuroscientists to observe the brain directly while people speak, listen, read and think. This technology shows that language processing is extremely complex and that the language-related areas of the brain are spread out widely, with different types of language tasks activating these areas in many sequences and patterns.

417 Complete the following rectangle logically.

ARMS	LEGS
EARS	?

418 Complete the following rectangle logically.

BELGIUM	GERMANY
NETHERLANDS	?

419 Complete the following rectangle logically.

?	AIR
WIND	FIRE

The brain's functions depend on the action of neurotransmitters, which are distributors of a chemical substance that is released at the end of a nerve fiber when a nerve impulse arrives from the synapses. An excess or deficiency of a specific transmitter may lead to a serious disorder in thought, mood or behavior.

420 Complete the following rectangle logically.

SIN	?
RE	LY

WORD TRIANGLES

WHAT IS A WORD TRIANGLE PUZZLE?

A word triangle consists of words in a triangle inserted to the left and to the right of the perpendicular according to some principle or rule. However, one word per side belongs to the other side. You have to find the two culprit words.

HOW TO SOLVE WORD TRIANGLE PUZZLES

Here's a simple puzzle. The three words on each side of the perpendicular should belong to the same category, but in the triangle below, one word per side is misplaced. What are the two misplaced words?

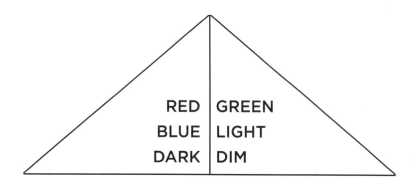

On the left side, the words *RED* and *BLUE* are actual colors, whereas *DARK* describes a shade. On the right side, *LIGHT* and *DIM* refer to shades, and there is one color, *GREEN*. So, it would seem that colors belong on the left and shades on the right. *DARK* and *GREEN* are the misplaced words.

PUZZLES

421 The three words on each side of the perpendicular should belong to the same category, but in the triangle below, one word per side is misplaced. What are the two misplaced words?

422 The three words on each side of the perpendicular should belong to the same category, but in the triangle below, one word per side is misplaced. What are the two misplaced words?

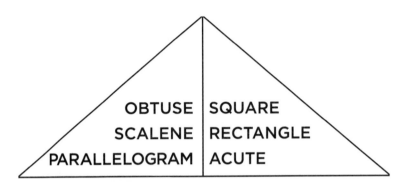

OBTUSE | SQUARE
SCALENE | RECTANGLE
PARALLELOGRAM | ACUTE

423 The three words on each side of the perpendicular should belong to the same category, but in the triangle below, one word per side is misplaced. What are the two misplaced words?

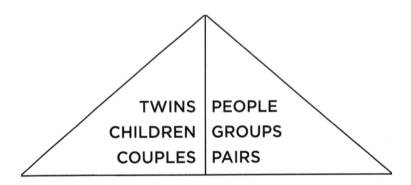

TWINS | PEOPLE
CHILDREN | GROUPS
COUPLES | PAIRS

Experts believe that during our lifetime, our long-term memory will store hundreds of times the amount of information in a comprehensive multivolume encyclopedia. If the estimate is correct, then doing word puzzles keeps access to that information going for a long time.

424 The three words on each side of the perpendicular should belong to the same category, but in the triangle below, one word per side is misplaced. What are the two misplaced words?

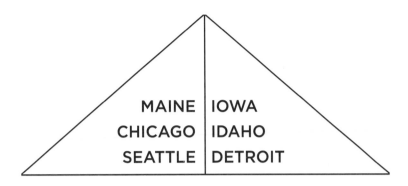

MAINE | IOWA
CHICAGO | IDAHO
SEATTLE | DETROIT

425 The three words on each side of the perpendicular should belong to the same category, but in the triangle below, one word per side is misplaced. What are the two misplaced words?

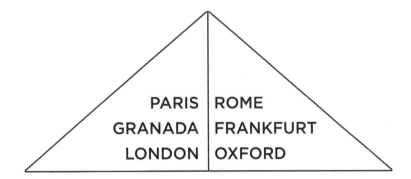

PARIS | ROME
GRANADA | FRANKFURT
LONDON | OXFORD

426 The three words on each side of the perpendicular should belong to the same category, but in the triangle below, one word per side is misplaced. What are the two misplaced words?

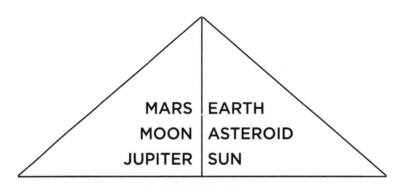

MARS | EARTH
MOON | ASTEROID
JUPITER | SUN

In general, we forget more and more with the passing of time. An hour after a party ends, we can probably remember most of the guests who were there. A few days later, however, we might recall only a few of the guests. As time goes by, we will remember even fewer. Neuroscientists have devoted much effort to understanding why the passage of time makes us unable to remember things. It seems that doing puzzles of all kinds is a good antidote to the memory-damaging effects of time.

427 The three words on each side of the perpendicular should belong to the same category, but in the triangle below, one word per side is misplaced. What are the two misplaced words?

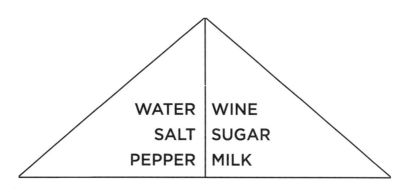

WATER | WINE
SALT | SUGAR
PEPPER | MILK

428 The three words on each side of the perpendicular should belong to the same category, but in the triangle below, one word per side is misplaced. What are the two misplaced words? Be careful! This is a really tricky one. Hint: Look at the words themselves, not their meanings.

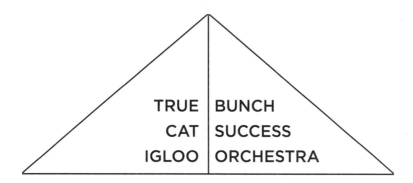

TRUE | BUNCH
CAT | SUCCESS
IGLOO | ORCHESTRA

429 The three words on each side of the perpendicular should belong to the same category, but in the triangle below, one word per side is misplaced. What are the two misplaced words? As with puzzle 428, be careful!

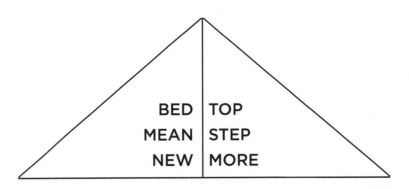

BED | TOP
MEAN | STEP
NEW | MORE

Memory experts now believe that people can, with practice, increase their ability to remember by doing crosswords or word games such as those in this chapter.

430 The three words on each side of the perpendicular should belong to the same category, but in the triangle below, one word per side is misplaced. What are the two misplaced words? After the last two puzzles, you are going to find this one very easy.

MATISSE | DALÍ
SALINGER | CARAVAGGIO
CHEKHOV | PIRANDELLO

WORD CELLS

WHAT IS A WORD CELL PUZZLE?

A word cell puzzle is a square with nine cells in which words are located. The idea is to find the row, column or diagonal in which the words are related in some way (three synonyms, three colors and so on). This is really a verbal version of tic-tac-toe.

HOW TO SOLVE WORD CELL PUZZLES

Let's do a simple puzzle. Indicate the row, column or diagonal that contains words that are related according to some rule or principle:

RUN	BOX	FOOD
JUMP	EASILY	FUN
WALK	YOU	GREEN

The left column contains three verbs of motion. The other rows, columns or diagonals have nothing in common. So the answer is the left column: *RUN—JUMP—WALK*.

PUZZLES

431 Indicate the row, column or diagonal that contains words connected by some rule or principle.

JACKET	SHORTS	PAJAMAS
BEDROOM	NICE	DAY
CARRY	OVER	DUTY

432 Indicate the row, column or diagonal that contains words connected by some rule or principle.

POPCORN	KEY	LARGE
BREAD	GLADLY	MALE
ARTICHOKE	WE	ARE

433 Indicate the row, column or diagonal that contains words connected by some rule or principle.

GREAT	DAYLIGHT	DRIVE
TENNIS	GOLF	SOCCER
PURPLE	NEVER	LET

The puzzles in this chapter essentially involve association. For example, we are more likely to connect two things that are almost the same or are different. This principle is found in the solution to the puzzles of this chapter.

434 Indicate the row, column or diagonal that contains words connected by some rule or principle.

VERY	FIND	TIME
HOME	MOVE	THEM
ONLY	SEND	RATHER

435 Indicate the row, column or diagonal that contains words connected by some rule or principle.

SOLD	OFTEN	NEW
SHE	ANYONE	SPEND
TOO	FREE	TATTOO

436 Indicate the row, column or diagonal that contains words connected by some rule or principle.

ARE	CRUX	BILL
DREAMS	EASY	OFF
INCREDIBLE	GYPSY	PURR

By doing puzzles, our "puzzle instinct" seems to kick in and allows us to enjoy and do all genres. This argues anecdotally in favor of the idea that puzzles and bimodality are intertwined.

437 Indicate the row, column or diagonal that contains words connected by some rule or principle.

NEVER	COVER	GOOD
TAKE	NOBODY	GIVE
LIKELY	WHO	NOTHING

438 Indicate the row, column or diagonal that contains words connected by some rule or principle.

FRIEND	STAY	SILLY
FREQUENT	ALLY	MORE
JELLY	WHATEVER	LAZY

439 Indicate the row, column or diagonal that contains words connected by some rule or principle.

CRIME	SCENE	INVESTIGATION
BEND	UNIQUENESS	STILL
CONFESS	WHICHEVER	TRULY

440 Indicate the row, column or diagonal that contains words connected by some rule or principle.

ROCK	NAME	CLEARLY
AND	SURELY	TYPE
ROLL	THOSE	OPEN

WORD PYRAMIDS

WHAT IS A WORD PYRAMID PUZZLE?

A word pyramid is a puzzle consisting of four words stacked on top of each other according to some principle or rule. The overarching rule is that each word in the pyramid belongs there for a couple of reasons, not just one. You are also given two words to choose from at the very bottom that will complete the puzzle. It looks simpler than it really is, although statistically you have a fifty-fifty chance of guessing the right answer. Of course, the point is not to guess but to figure out logically which of the two alternatives makes up the base of the pyramid.

HOW TO SOLVE WORD PYRAMID PUZZLES

Let's do a simple word pyramid:

VIOLET
WHITE
BLUE
RED or GREEN?

Which of the two words *RED* or *GREEN* completes the pyramid? Clearly, all the words in the pyramid refer to colors. In addition, note that the word at the top (*VIOLET*) has six letters; the one below it (*WHITE*) has five letters; the one below that (*BLUE*) has four letters. So, logically, the bottom word should be a color and have three letters. That word is *RED*.

This "double whammy" characterizes all the puzzles in this section: (1) you will have to figure out what category of things the pyramid represents and (2) what structural feature the words share.

PUZZLES

441 Which of the two words *CUP* or *GLASS* completes the pyramid?

NAPKIN
SPOON
FORK
CUP or GLASS?

442 Which of the two words *MAIL* or *SPECIAL* completes the pyramid?

MENIAL
TRIVIAL
CORDIAL
MAIL or SPECIAL?

BIMODALITY

443 Which of the two words *FIVE* or *SIX* completes the pyramid?

ONE
NINE
THREE
FIVE or SIX?

444 Which of the two words *DECATHLON* or *FOOTBALL* completes the pyramid?

ARCHERY
BASEBALL
CURLING
DECATHLON or FOOTBALL?

445 Which of the two words *SURGE* or *SLUSH* completes the pyramid?

SNOW
SLEET
SQUALL
SURGE or SLUSH?

446 Which of the two words *DRIVER* or *DRIVEN* completes the pyramid?

DRIVE
DRIVING
DRIVES
DRIVER or DRIVEN?

Which of the two words *NECKLACE* or *BROOCH* completes the pyramid?

PIN
RING
WATCH
NECKLACE or BROOCH?

Which of the two words *EURO* or *POUND* completes the pyramid?

DOLLAR
YEN
MARK
EURO or POUND?

Which of the two words *TEN* or *FORTY* completes the pyramid?

THREE
SEVEN
EIGHT
TEN or FORTY?

Which of the two words *ITALIAN* or *PORTUGUESE* completes the pyramid?

ENGLISH
GERMAN
GREEK
ITALIAN or PORTUGUESE?

10

WHOLE BRAIN HEALTH

Methinks the human method of expression by sound of tongue is very elementary, and ought to be substituted for some ingenious invention which should be able to give vent to at least six coherent sentences at once.

(VIRGINIA WOOLF, 1882–1941)

THE OVERALL OBJECTIVE OF THIS BOOK has been to provide puzzles for promoting brain health, with the underlying motto being "puzzle power for brainpower." I have used the ongoing research in neuroscience to organize the puzzles into chapters designed to activate (in theory) specific brain areas or functions—memory, perception, cognition, association and so on. The assumption is that there is a correlation between attempting the puzzles and the functions of the brain. Of course, doing puzzles for the pleasure of it may be all you have been looking for, and I hope you have been able to derive some satisfaction from the puzzles here.

PUZZLES AND WHOLE BRAIN HEALTH

I should mention that the literature on the correlation between puzzles and brain fitness really has not been established, as I mentioned on my own *Psychology Today* blog. In *From Square One: A Meditation, with Digressions, on Crosswords* (2009), Dean Olsher indicates that even studies that have found a correlation between crossword puzzles and mental acuity admit that the two are only marginally related. The reason is that doing a certain genre of puzzle, such as crosswords, over and over, as most people are inclined to do, does not provide enough diversity to activate all the different areas of the brain.

Individual brains differ dramatically, depending not only on the individual's genetic inheritance, but also on his or her life experiences and individual talents. The fingers activate the same general area of the cortex in everyone's brain, but this area is larger in people who use their fingers often, such as those who play musical instruments. So, by extension, I would argue that the areas of the brain activated by puzzles of particular kinds might be larger than normal, but I do not know this for sure; however, after reading the relevant studies, I would think this to be a logical assumption.

OBJECTIVES OF THIS CHAPTER

This chapter contains fifty puzzles of the kinds that readers of my previous books have told me they really enjoyed, such as doublets and rebuses. Therefore, this chapter contains twenty doublets, twenty rebuses and ten deduction puzzles. They are designed to promote "whole brain" health.

DOUBLETS

WHAT IS A DOUBLET?

This is one of the most well-liked types of puzzles, providing both challenge and recreation. The doublet is an invention of Lewis Carroll. The challenge is to transform one word into another by changing only one letter at a time, and forming a genuine new word (not a proper name) with each letter change. Turning the word *HEAD* into *TAIL* is a famous example; it is worth repeating here for illustrative purposes.

HOW TO SOLVE DOUBLETS

Doublets are also known as word ladders, and each new word is called a step. In case you have never done one, let's go through the solution to the aforementioned example, which involves four steps:

HEAD ← initial word

heal ← change the *D* of *HEAD* above to *L* in order to get *heal* (a cure)

teal ← change the *H* of *heal* to *T* in order to get *teal* (a color)

tell ← change the *A* of *teal* to *L* in order to get *tell* (a synonym of say)

tall ← change the *E* of *tell* to *A* in order to get *tall* (opposite of short)

TAIL ← finally, change the first *L* of *tall* to *I* and you'll get *TAIL*

That's all there is to it. Simply change one letter at a time going down the ladder in steps. Note that the words in the doublet are not included in the number of steps: the four steps above are the words in between: *heal—teal—tell—tall*.

These puzzles will really get the whole brain working. They involve association (connecting one word to another), inference (anticipating what changes need to be made down the ladder), deduction (using logic to figure out which letter is needed on some steps) and other faculties in tandem. The number of steps is given to you. But there may be other ways to solve the doublets. So, if you come up with different answers than the ones provided at the back, it probably means that your brainpower is better than mine!

PUZZLES

As usual, we will start off with very easy puzzles, progressing gradually to more complicated ones. NOTE: No abbreviations or proper names are allowed.

451 Change GOOD to GOAL in one step.

452 Change WINTER to DINNER in one step.

453 Change BALL to PARK in two steps.

454 Change LOVE to HATE in two steps.

455 Change SCARY to STORY in three steps.

456 Change MALE to PUNK in four steps.

457 Change FLIP to TRAY in five steps.

458 Change LIVER to POWER in four steps.

459 Change SPILL to SCOPE in five steps.

460 Change BRAVE to PLUNK in five steps.

COMPLEX DOUBLETS

WHAT IS A COMPLEX DOUBLET?

Starting in 1879, Lewis Carroll published his doublet puzzles in *Vanity Fair*, which offered prizes for solutions. He later amended the rules to make the puzzles more difficult. One of these changes was the use of anagrams in one or more of the steps. His first puzzle of this kind was: Change IRON into LEAD by either introducing a new letter to create a new word on a step or by rearranging the letters of the word at any step. You may not do both in the same step. This type of doublet can be called a complex doublet.

HOW TO SOLVE COMPLEX DOUBLETS

Let's go through the solution to Carroll's puzzle. Note that you may or may not be told which step or steps require an anagram rather than a letter change. In the solution, there is just one anagram step, as you can see:

IRON ← initial word
icon ← change the *R* of *IRON* to C in order to get *icon*
coin ← rearrange the letters of *icon* in order to get *coin*
     (= anagram step)
corn ← change the *I* of *coin* to R in order to get *corn*
cord ← change the *N* of *corn* to D in order to get *cord*
lord ← change the *C* of *cord* to L in order to get *lord*
load ← change the *R* of *lord* to A in order to get *load*
LEAD ← finally, change the *O* of *load* to E in order to get *LEAD*

Note that the number of steps required in this case is six. The anagram steps will be pointed out in the answers section at the back of the book.

PUZZLES

461 Change SMALL to PULLS in two steps.

462 Change PLATES to TABLES in two steps.

463 Change VEIL to MINE in three steps.

464 Change PLAN to POTS in six steps.

> The doublet became an instant craze in London. In 1879, the publisher Macmillan assembled the *Vanity Fair* puzzles into a booklet titled *Doublets: A Word Puzzle,* which sold out quickly. It was followed by two other editions, each containing more puzzles than the one prior.

465 Change LOVE to TRAP in five steps.

466 Change TRAPS to WORDS in four steps.

467 Change FRIEND to TESTED in five steps.

> Carroll's two collections, *Pillow Problems* and *A Tangled Tale,* contain puzzles that have become classics, being used over and over in various disguises, variations and elaborations in collections ever since.

468 Change SMART to STRAW in six steps.

469 Change DEVIL to KILLS in five steps.

> In his book *Language on Vacation* (1965), Dmitri A. Borgmann claimed that the ideal form of the doublet puzzle was the one that involved the transformation of *n* letters in *n* moves. He was the one who renamed the puzzle a word ladder. An example would be to change COLD to WARM. There are four letters in the two words and, thus, an "ideal" solution is one that consists of four changes, which means inserting three steps between the words, with the fourth change producing WARM. It works in this case: COLD-cord-card-ward-WARM.

470 Change PARTY to CLAPS in six steps.

WORD REBUSES

WHAT IS A WORD REBUS?

A word rebus is a puzzle in which pictures, letters, layout or juxtaposition are used in combination to hide some message. The encrypted message might consist of a play on the sound of letters, on their location with respect to others, and so on. The trick is to "read" the message in verbal language to see what it yields.

HOW TO SOLVE WORD REBUSES

A word rebus is one in which numbers, other words or parts of words are combined with another word in some way (before, within or after) to hide a message or a phrase. Here's an example:

W1111HILE

We see several ones in the word *while*. So, with a little phonetic adjustment we get "once in a while." Get it? These puzzles really will put your whole brain on alert.

PUZZLES

471 What message or phrase is suggested by the following rebus?

4GETit

472 What message or phrase is suggested by the following rebus?

OholeNE

473 What message or phrase is suggested by the following rebus?

LIFE—LIFE

> Alcuin (734-804) was a scholar and an adviser to Charlemagne. He transformed Charlemagne's court into a cultural center. He also put together one of the first popular mathematical puzzle collections in history, which he wrote to sharpen the minds of young people.

474 What message or phrase is suggested by the following rebus?

ONCE—ONCE

475 What message or phrase is suggested by the following rebus?

HAbirdND is worth BU2SH

476 What message or phrase is suggested by the following rebus?

CAMfootPS—CAMfootPS

> Research has shown that brain shrinkage is especially symptomatic of Alzheimer's disease. New studies now show that physical exercise combined with puzzles constitutes a powerful strategy for preventing shrinkage.

(477) What message or phrase is suggested by the following rebus?
THINK—THINK

(478) What message or phrase is suggested by the following rebus?
TIME—TIME

(479) What message or phrase is suggested by the following rebus?
ICE^3

> Research has shown that visual puzzles, such as rebuses, stimulate centers in the right hemisphere of the brain. This means, potentially, that holistic thinking is utilized as you solve these puzzles.

(480) What message or phrase is suggested by the following rebus?
FUNNY FUNNY 4 WORDS

LAYOUT REBUSES

WHAT IS A LAYOUT REBUS?

A layout rebus is based on deciphering what message or phrase the layout or juxtaposition of words suggests. The difference between this type and the previous one is minimal—in effect, a rebus is a rebus. The difference is that positioning is more prominent in the construction of the hidden message or phrase. Actually, a few of the puzzles above were based on the layout principle, preparing you for the puzzles in this section. Again, you will have to make some adjustments linguistically to produce the suggested message.

HOW TO SOLVE LAYOUT REBUSES

What phrase does the following rebus suggest?

WATER
BREATHE

The answer is "Breathe under water." This is because the word BREATHE is under the word WATER. Get it? Some of the puzzles below are well-known among rebus enthusiasts.

PUZZLES

481 What message or phrase is suggested by the following rebus?

HEAD
HEELS

482 What message or phrase is suggested by the following rebus?

ONCE
TIME

483 What message or phrase is suggested by the following rebus?

YRAROPMET

The French writer and philosopher Voltaire (1694–1778) composed many rebuses. He would often send invitations to people in rebus form to see if they could figure out what his message was.

484 What message or phrase is suggested by the following rebus?

GOOD GOOD BE BE TRUE

485 What message or phrase is suggested by the following rebus?

MANY MANY TIMES

486 What message or phrase is suggested by the following rebus?

HAI | RS

Coins with rebuses, representing famous people or cities, inscribed on them were common in ancient Greece and Rome.

487 What message or phrase is suggested by the following rebus?

PLAY
PLAY PLAY
PLAY

488 What message or phrase is suggested by the following rebus?

APPEAR JUDGE

489 What message or phrase is suggested by the following rebus?

_____GO_____

In Renaissance Italy, Pope Paul III (1468-1549) suggested the use of rebuses to teach literacy to the masses.

490 What message or phrase is suggested by the following rebus?

B B / NOT B B

DEDUCTION PUZZLES

WHAT IS A DEDUCTION PUZZLE?

Deduction puzzles involve logical thinking and inference. Basically, you have to solve the puzzle based on the information you are given. For example, you might have to match professions to certain people, dress colors to certain women and so on.

HOW TO SOLVE DEDUCTION PUZZLES

Let's do a simple deduction puzzle:

> *Three women, whose names are Ms. Violet, Ms. Brown and Ms. White, came to a dance party dressed in violet, brown and white. No woman wore the color of dress that corresponded to her name. Ms. Violet sat next to the woman dressed in white. What color dress did each woman wear?*

We know that Ms. Violet did not wear violet, nor did she wear white because she sat next to someone else who wore that color. So, by the process of elimination, she wore brown. Let's jot this down in chart form.

Woman	Dress
Ms. Violet	brown
Ms. Brown	?
Ms. White	?

Now the brown dress is eliminated as a possibility for the remaining two women. Also, we know that Ms. White did not wear white, so the only color left for her is violet:

Woman	Dress
Ms. Violet	brown
Ms. Brown	?
Ms. White	violet

As you can see, the only color left for Ms. Brown is white:

Woman	Dress
Ms. Violet	brown
Ms. Brown	white
Ms. White	violet

The first puzzles will be relatively easy, allowing you to get the hang of what to do. The last three or four will really get your logical brain working.

PUZZLES

491 **Two men, Sam and Frank, and two women, Gina and Veronica, get together every Tuesday night to play cards.** They play in pairs, one man and one woman per pair. Gina is unhappy tonight because she rarely wins when Frank plays with the other woman. How are the pairs made up tonight?

492 **Three men—Mark, Bill and Jack—work in a factory.** One is the machinist, another is the foreman and the third is the accountant. Mark cannot stand the accountant, but he gets along very well with Bill. Bill and the machinist earn the same. What job does each man perform?

493 **In the Walker family, there are two brothers, two sisters and, of course, a mother and a father.** The male names are Frank, Phil and Will; the female names are Penny, Chantelle and Danielle. Chantelle and Danielle are the youngest members of the family. Will is older than Phil, but neither one is the oldest. What are the father's and mother's names?

494 **In the Sorrentino family, the father, the mother and the daughter call each other by their nicknames—Sunny, Dreamy and Funny—but not necessarily in that order.** Sunny is not the mother, and Funny is not the daughter. Sunny is the oldest member of the family. What is each person's nickname?

495 **The drummer, bassist and pianist of a jazz trio are called Marcel, Robert and Wes, but not necessarily in that order.** Here's what we know about them. The pianist, an only child, goes out often with the drummer. Wes is not the pianist. Robert has a sister. Wes would like to play the bass, but finds it too difficult. Which instrument does each man play?

496 **Seven women—Anna, Bertha, Cathy, Debbie, Ella, Franca and Gillian—always get together to play cards.** A few of them are only children, including Ella. Tonight, they decided to play in pairs, leaving one of them out to be the referee. Anna played with her best friend. Bertha's pair beat Franca's pair. Cathy and Debbie were losers. The referee was not an only child. Who was the odd female out (the referee)?

497 **Last week, three couples went on a disco date.** One woman was dressed in red, one in green and one in blue. The men also wore outfits in the same three colors. Strangely, their surnames matched the colors they wore: Mr. and Ms. Red wore red; Mr. and Ms. Green wore green; Mr. and Ms. Blue wore blue. While the three couples were dancing, Mr. Red said to Ms. Green and to her partner, "Not one of us is dancing with a partner dressed in the same color." What were the dance pairings?

498 **Three men—Nick, Joe and Gill—and three women—Mary, Shirley and Dina—work in the same office in the roles of comptroller, technician, programmer, manager, publicist and marketer.** Nick, Mary and Dina are only children. The comptroller has two sisters. Joe has one sibling, a brother. Gill is the technician. One of the only children is the programmer. Joe is neither the marketer nor the publicist. Of the three only children, the male is neither the programmer nor the marketer. The marketer works next to Dina. What is each person's job?

499 **Three married couples get together to play canasta every Saturday night.** The men are Paul, Rob and Lou; the women are Barb, Hillary and Lola. Last Saturday night, the pairs were made up of men and women who were not married to each other. Here's what happened. Barb lost, while her husband, she states, was in the winning couple. Lou and Paul lost. Hillary won. She is not married to Paul. Who are the married couples?

You have almost reached the end of this brain workout. One more puzzle to go. Even if you have been successful at solving most of these puzzles, it is good exercise to go back and redo them all, learning from the insights you gained the first time around.

(500) **Three sisters—Nora, Dora and Cora—and three brothers—Nick, Dick and Cam— get along with each other extremely well.** The oldest one of the six is a female, as is the youngest one. Nick is older than Cora. Nora is younger than Dick, who is younger than Cora. Cam is the second oldest. Can you put the siblings in order from oldest to youngest?

ANSWERS

1 Hidden word: **Christmas**

```
S O L S T I C E
  M O N T H S
    S P R I N G
    W I N T E R
    S N O W
  A U T U M N
  S U M M E R
    L E A P
W E E K S
```

2 Hidden word: **Matrimony**

```
  H O N E Y M O O N
        M A R R I A G E
  I N F A T U A T I O N
          R I N G
        K I S S
  G R O O M
    D I V O R C E
V A L E N T I N E
  M A R R Y
```

3 Hidden word: **Olympics**

```
      B O X I N G
F O O T B A L L
  H O C K E Y
    S W I M M I N G
        P O L O
  T E N N I S
    S O C C E R
    B A S E B A L L
```

4 Hidden word: **Cyberspace**

```
        C O M P U T E R S
M E M O R Y
    G L O B A L
      W E B
  I N T E R N E T
        S C R E E N
  C E L L P H O N E
        S A T E L L I T E
      F A C E B O O K
T W I T T E R
```

5 Hidden word: **Maserati**

```
  A U T O M O B I L E
          A I R P L A N E
          S H I P
B I C Y C L E
          T R A I N
  S U B W A Y
      M O T O R C Y C L E
    H E L I C O P T E R
```

6 Hidden word: **Euphoria**

```
    G L E E
P L E A S U R E
      R A P T U R E
D E L I G H T
      J O Y
  C H E E R F U L N E S S
      B L I S S
  G L A D N E S S
```

7 Hidden word: **Shakespeare**

```
      S O N N E T
G O T H I C
    D R A M A
H A I K U
C O M E D Y
    S A T I R E
    P O E T R Y
  M E M O I R
  N A R R A T I V E
B I O G R A P H Y
N O V E L
```

8 Hidden word: **Mediterranean**

```
  S W A M P
    O C E A N
P O N D
      I N L E T
      T A R N
  C R E E K
      R I V E R
  S T R E A M
      L A K E
  C H A N N E L
      S E A
      B A Y
L A G O O N
```

9 Hidden word: **Pomiculture**

```
    A P P L E
      O R A N G E
    L E M O N
  A P R I C O T
      C R A N B E R R Y
G R A P E F R U I T
        P L U M
    T O M A T O
  C O C O N U T
      S T R A W B E R R Y
    P E A R
```

10 Hidden word: **Horticulture**

```
      H E D G E S
  F L O W E R S
    G R A S S
    T R E E S
    I N S E C T S
  R O C K S
    B U S H E S
    P L A N T S
V E G E T A B L E S
  S H R U B S
  H E R B S
    W E E D S
```

11 Words from top to bottom row: **era, rat, ate**

E	R	A
R	A	T
A	T	E

12 Words from top to bottom row: **top, oil, ply**

T	O	P
O	I	L
P	L	Y

13 Words from top to bottom row: **fall, area, lean, lane**

F	A	L	L
A	R	E	A
L	E	A	N
L	A	N	E

14 Words from top to bottom row: **more, open, read, ends**

M	O	R	E
O	P	E	N
R	E	A	D
E	N	D	S

15 Words from top to bottom row: **parts, aloha, rotor, those, saree** (spelling alternative of **sari**)

P	A	R	T	S
A	L	O	H	A
R	O	T	O	R
T	H	O	S	E
S	A	R	E	E

16 Words from top to bottom row: **nor, one, red**

N	O	R
O	N	E
R	E	D

17 Words from top to bottom row: **wet, era, tap**

W	E	T
E	R	A
T	A	P

18 Words from top to bottom row: **wall, area, lead, lads**

W	A	L	L
A	R	E	A
L	E	A	D
L	A	D	S

19 Words from top to bottom row: **main, also, isle, noel**

M	A	I	N
A	L	S	O
I	S	L	E
N	O	E	L

20 Words from top to bottom row: **picks, inane, canoe, knock, seeks**

P	I	C	K	S
I	N	A	N	E
C	A	N	O	E
K	N	O	C	K
S	E	E	K	S

21 The odd one out is **FLOUR**; it is the only word that is not a flower.

22 The odd one out is **LADY**; it is the only singular noun (all the other nouns are plural).

23 The odd one out is **WATER**; it is the only liquid substance, all the others are solids.

24 The odd one out is **TABLE**; it is the only word with more than three letters.

25 The odd one out is **TOOL**; it is the only word that does not refer to a geometrical figure.

26 The odd one out is **MASSES**; it is the only word that does not end in *is*.

27 The odd one out is **THING**; it is the only word that is not an adjective (it is a noun).

28 The odd one out is **FORK**; it is the only word that does not have a double vowel in it (*EE, OO, AA*).

29 The odd one out is **BOLD**; it is the only word that does not have a double consonant in it (*LL, TT, NN*).

30 The odd one out is **JACKET**; it is the only word that does not refer to a part of the human body.

31 Theme: **sports**

S	K	I	I	N	G		
P	I	N	G	-	P	O	N	G
R	O	W	I	N	G		
R	U	G	B	Y			
T	E	N	N	I	S		
S	O	C	C	E	R		

32 Theme: **cinema**

A	C	T	O	R			
D	I	R	E	C	T	O	R
A	N	I	M	A	T	I	O	N
M	O	V	I	E	S		
F	I	L	M				
O	S	C	A	R	S		

33 Theme: **colors**

S	C	A	R	L	E	T	
I	N	D	I	G	O		
V	I	O	L	E	T		
C	R	I	M	S	O	N	
A	Z	U	R	E			
C	E	L	E	S	T	E	

34 Theme: animals

```
C H E E T A H
L I O N
T I G E R
M O O S E
O R A N G U T A N
E L E P H A N T
S N A K E
```

35 Theme: anatomy

```
H E A R T
I N T E S T I N E
M A N D I B L E
T H Y R O I D
N O S T R I L S
M U S C L E S
L A R Y N X
```

36 Theme: money

```
I N C O M E
D O L L A R
C U R R E N C Y
E U R O
Y E N
```

37 Theme: sweets

```
C A N D I E S
W A F F L E S
C A R A M E L
C A K E
T O F F E E
B O N B O N S
```

38 Theme: science

```
A T O M S
E L E C T R O N
G R A V I T Y
E N E R G Y
Q U A N T A
M O L E C U L E
R E L A T I V I T Y
```

39 Theme painting

```
P O R T R A I T U R E
D A D A I S M
C U B I S M
L A N D S C A P E
A B S T R A C T
C H I A R O S C U R O
M O D E R N I S M
G O T H I C
```

40 Theme: literature

```
N O V E L L A
F I C T I O N
P O E T R Y
R O M A N C E
D R A M A
F A B L E
N A R R A T I V E
A U T H O R
P R O S E
M Y S T E R Y
```

41

```
B E A T
A L S O
    I N
    A S
```

42

```
H O T E L
E A R N S
N T   D D
  H O E
  S A D
```

43

```
E N V Y   T V
L I A R   A A
I L L     B L
    I G L O O
    D O N O R
```

44

W	E	A	T	H	E	R
A	N	C	H	O	R	S
I	D	■	I	O	U	
T	O	W	N	■	P	I
S	W	I	G	■	T	O

45

T	R	Y	■	A	S	
E	A	R	■	W	O	
N	D	■	O	V	A	L
D	I	N	N	E	R	■
E	U	C	L	I	D	
R	S	■	Y	N		

46

B	A	L	L	A	D
A	B	O	U	N	D
M	O	U	N	D	■	N	O
■	V	I	A	■	F	O	R
■	E	E	R	■	A	T	E

47

S	U	C	C	E	S	S
A	L	O	O	F	N	E	S	S
I	C	E	D	■	E	X	C	E	L
L	E	D	■	M	E	■	A	N	D
■	R	S	■	M	R	■	R	D

48

T	R	U	T	H	■	L	O	V	E
B	A	T	H	E	■	O	R	A	L
A	K	A	I	■	S	O	A	P
■	E	H	S	■	A	T	T	I	C
						E	D	I

49

A	B	I	D	E	S	■	S	P	E	C	I	A	L
C	A	N	O	N	S	■	S	T	R	A	N	G	E
A	D	U	L	T	■	■	B	E	D
C	D	I	■	R	O	P	E	■	C	E	O
I	E	T	■	A	R	E	A	■	A	R	R	A	Y
A	R	■	P	E	A	R	■	T	A	N	G	O

50

A	M	I	C	A	B	L	E	■	I	F	■	U	R
N	A	S	H	V	I	L	L	E	■	F	L	I	P	S
T	N	■	A	O	■	O	N	E	■	Y	O
■	I	N	■	O	P	E	R	A	■	T
R	E	A	R	■	P	E	R	■	S	O	A	P
A	R	E	■	T	O	E	■	G	U	S	H	■	E	P
P	E	R	■	A	N	N	■	Y	P	■	X	E

51 Number of Circles: **3**

52 Number of Circles: **4**

53 Number of Circles: **5**

54 Number of Circles: **5**

55 Number of Circles: **5**

56 Number of Circles: **6**

57 Number of Circles: **6**

58 Number of Circles: **7**

59 Number of Circles: **7**

60 Number of Circles: **8**

61 Number of Four-Sided Figures: **12**

1	2	
3	4	5

SOLUTION:

1. 1
2. 1+2
3. 1+2+3+4+5
4. 1+3
5. 2
6. 2+4+5
7. 3
8. 3+4
9. 3+4+5
10. 4
11. 4+5
12. 5

62 Number of Four-Sided Figures: 15

SOLUTION:

1. 1
2. 1+2
3. 1+2+3
4. 1+2+3+4+5+6
5. 1+2+3+5+6
6. 1+2+5
7. 2
8. 2+5
9. 3
10. 3+4+6
11. 3+6
12. 4
13. 5
14. 5+6
15. 6

63 Number of Four-Sided Figures: 29

SOLUTION:

1. 1
2. 1+2
3. 1+2+3+4
4. 1+2+3+4+5
5. 1+2+3+4+5+6+7+8+9
6. 1+2+3+4+6+7+8
7. 1+2+6
8. 2
9. 2+4
10. 2+4+6+7
11. 2+6
12. 3+4
13. 3+4+5
14. 3+4+5+7+8+9
15. 3+4+7+8
16. 4
17. 4+7
18. 5
19. 5+9
20. 6
21. 6+7
22. 6+7+8
23. 6+7+8+9
24. 7
25. 7+8
26. 7+8+9
27. 8
28. 8+9
29. 9

64 Number of Four-Sided Figures: 28

SOLUTION:

1. 1+2
2. 1+2+3
3. 1+2+3+4
4. 1+2+3+4+5+6+7+8+9
5. 1+2+3+5+6+8
6. 1+2+5
7. 2
8. 3
9. 3+4
10. 3+4+6+7
11. 3+4+6+7+8+9
12. 3+6
13. 3+6+8
14. 4
15. 4+7
16. 4+7+9
17. 5
18. 5+6+8
19. 5+6+7+8+9
20. 6
21. 6+7
22. 6+7+8+9
23. 6+8
24. 7
25. 7+9
26. 8
27. 8+9
28. 9

65 Number of Four-Sided Figures: 33

SOLUTION:

1. 1
2. 1+2
3. 1+2+3+4+5+6
4. 1+2+3+4+5+6+7+8+9+10
5. 1+2+4+5+6
6. 1+2+4+5+6+7+8
7. 1+4
8. 1+4+7
9. 2
10. 2+3+5+6
11. 2+3+5+6+8+9+10
12. 2+5+6
13. 2+5+6+8
14. 3
15. 3+9
16. 3+9+10
17. 4
18. 4+5
19. 4+5+6
20. 4+5+6+7+8
21. 4+7
22. 5
23. 5+6
24. 5+6+8
25. 6
26. 7
27. 7+8
28. 7+8+9+10
29. 8
30. 8+9+10
31. 9
32. 9+10
33. 10

66 Number of Four-Sided Figures: **20**

SOLUTION:

1. 1+4
2. 1+2+3+4
3. 1+2+3+4+5+6+7+8+9
4. 1+4+5+6+7+8
5. 2
6. 2+3
7. 2+3+9
8. 3
9. 3+9
10. 4
11. 4+5+6
12. 5
13. 5+6
14. 5+6+7+8
15. 5+6+7+8+9
16. 5+7
17. 6
18. 6+8
19. 7
20. 9

67 Number of Four-Sided Figures: **41**

SOLUTION:

1. 1
2. 1+2
3. 1+2+3
4. 1+2+3+4+5+6
5. 1+2+3+4+5+6+7+8+9+10+11+12
6. 1+2+3+7+8+9+10
7. 1+2+7
8. 1+2+7+8
9. 2
10. 2+7
11. 2+7+8
12. 3
13. 3+4+5+6
14. 3+4+5+6+9+10+11+12
15. 3+9+10
16. 4
17. 4+5
18. 4+5+6
19. 4+5+6+11
20. 4+5+6+11+12
21. 5
22. 5+6
23. 5+6+11
24. 5+6+11+12
25. 6
26. 6+11
27. 6+11+12
28. 7
29. 7+8
30. 7+8+9
31. 7+8+9+10
32. 7+8+9+10+11+12
33. 8
34. 9
35. 9+10
36. 9+10+11+12
37. 10
38. 10+11+12
39. 11
40. 11+12
41. 12

68 Number of Four-Sided Figures: **45**

SOLUTION:

1. 1
2. 1+2
3. 1+2+3+4+5+6
4. 1+2+3+4+5+6+7+8+9+10+11+12
5. 1+2+4+5
6. 1+2+4+5+7+8
7. 1+4
8. 1+4+7
9. 2
10. 2+3+5+6
11. 2+3+5+6+8+9+10+11+12
12. 2+5
13. 2+5+8
14. 3+6
15. 3+6+9+10
16. 3+6+9+10+11+12
17. 4
18. 4+5
19. 4+5+6
20. 4+5+6+7+8+9+11
21. 4+5+7+8
22. 4+7
23. 5
24. 5+6
25. 5+6+8+9+11
26. 5+8
27. 6
28. 6+9
29. 6+9+11
30. 7
31. 7+8
32. 7+8+9+11
33. 7+8+9+10+11+12
34. 8
35. 8+9+10+11+12
36. 8+9+11
37. 9
38. 9+10
39. 9+10+11+12
40. 9+11
41. 10
42. 10+12
43. 11
44. 11+12
45. 12

69 Number of Four-Sided Figures: **31**

SOLUTION:

1. 1+4+5
2. 1+2+4+5
3. 1+2+3+4+5
4. 1+2+3+4+5+6+7+8+9+10+11
5. 1+2+4+5+6+7+8+9
6. 1+4+5+6+7+8
7. 2
8. 2+3
9. 2+3+9+10+11
10. 2+9
11. 3
12. 3+10
13. 3+10+11
14. 4
15. 4+5

16. 4+6
17. 5
18. 6
19. 6+7+8
20. 6+7+8+9
21. 6+7+8+9+10+11
22. 7
23. 7+8

24. 7+8+9
25. 7+8+9+10+11
26. 8
27. 9
28. 9+10+11
29. 10
30. 10+11
31. 11

70 Number of Four-Sided Figures: **61**

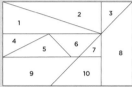

SOLUTION:

1. 1
2. 1+5
3. 1+2+5+8
4. 1+2+3+5+6+8
5. 1+2+3+4+5+6+7+8
6. 1+2+3+4+5+6+7+8+9+10+11+12+13+14+15+16
7. 1+2+3+5+6+8+9+10+11+12+13+15
8. 1+2+5+8+9+10+11+12
9. 1+5+9
10. 1+5+9+10
11. 2+8
12. 2+3+6+8
13. 2+3+4+6+7+8
14. 2+3+4+6+7+8+11+12+13+14+15+16
15. 2+3+6+8+11+12+13+15
16. 2+8+11+12
17. 3
18. 3+4
19. 3+4+6+7
20. 3+4+6+7+13+14
21. 3+4+6+7+13+14+15+16
22. 3+6
23. 3+6+13
24. 3+6+13+15
25. 4
26. 4+7
27. 4+7+14
28. 4+7+14+16
29. 5

30. 5+9
31. 5+9+10
32. 6
33. 6+7
34. 6+7+13+14
35. 6+7+13+14+15+16
36. 6+13
37. 6+13+15
38. 7
39. 7+14
40. 7+14+16
41. 8
42. 8+12
43. 9
44. 9+10
45. 9+10+11+12
46. 9+10+11+12+13+14+15+16
47. 9+10+11+12+13+15
48. 10
49. 11+12
50. 11+12+13+14+15+16
51. 11+12+13+15
52. 12
53. 13
54. 13+14
55. 13+14+15+16
56. 13+15
57. 14
58. 14+16
59. 15
60. 15+16
61. 16

71 Number of Triangles: **9**

SOLUTION: Note that not all numbered segments figure into the solution.

1. 2
2. 3
3. 4+8
4. 5
5. 5+9

6. 6+10
7. 7
8. 8
9. 10

72 Number of Triangles: **9**

SOLUTION: Note again that not all numbered segments figure into the solution.

1. 1
2. 2
3. 2+3
4. 3
5. 4

6. 5
7. 7
8. 7+8+10
9. 7+10

73 Number of Triangles: **17**

SOLUTION: Note again that not all numbered segments figure into the solution.

1. 1+7
2. 2
3. 3+10
4. 4
5. 4+8+9
6. 4+9
7. 6
8. 6+11
9. 7

10. 8
11. 9
12. 9+10
13. 9+10+11
14. 10
15. 10+11
16. 11
17. 12

74 Number of Triangles: **16**

SOLUTION:

1. 1
2. 2
3. 2+3
4. 3
5. 4
6. 4+5
7. 5
8. 6
9. 7
10. 8
11. 8+9
12. 9
13. 10
14. 10+11
15. 11
16. 12

75 Number of Triangles: **41**

SOLUTION:

1. 1
2. 2
3. 2+3+6
4. 2+12+13
5. 3
6. 3+4
7. 3+6
8. 4
9. 4+5
10. 4+5+7+8
11. 5
12. 5+6
13. 5+6+16
14. 5+6+7+10
15. 5+6+13+14+
    15+16+17
16. 6
17. 7
18. 7+8
19. 7+10
20. 7+10+18
21. 8
22. 8+9
23. 9
24. 9+10
25. 10
26. 11
27. 11+12
28. 11+14
29. 12
30. 12+13
31. 13
32. 13+14
33. 13+14+15+17
34. 14
35. 15
36. 15+17
37. 16
38. 16+18
39. 17
40. 18
41. 19

76 Number of Triangles: **26**

SOLUTION:

1. 1+4
2. 2
3. 2+3
4. 4
5. 5+18
6. 6
7. 6+7+12
8. 6+12
9. 6+12+13
10. 7
11. 7+8+14
12. 8
13. 8+9
14. 8+9+13+14+15
15. 8+13+14
16. 8+14
17. 9
18. 9+15
19. 10+16
20. 11
21. 11+17
22. 12
23. 13
24. 14
25. 16
26. 18

77 Number of Triangles: **33**

SOLUTION: Note again that not all numbered segments figure into the solution.

1. 1
2. 1+2
3. 1+4
4. 1+4+10+11+13
5. 2
6. 2+3
7. 3
8. 3+4
9. 3+4+5
10. 3+4+11+12+14
11. 4
12. 5
13. 6
14. 7
15. 7+8
16. 8
17. 9
18. 10
19. 10+11+13
20. 10+13
21. 10+13+15
22. 11
23. 11+12+14
24. 12
25. 12+14
26. 12+14+15
27. 13
28. 14
29. 15
30. 17
31. 17+19
32. 18+19+20
33. 20

78 Number of Triangles: **25**

SOLUTION: Note again that not all numbered segments figure into the solution.

1. 1
2. 1+2
3. 1+3
4. 2
5. 2+4
6. 3
7. 3+4
8. 3+4+5
9. 4
10. 5
11. 6
12. 7
13. 7+8

14. 8
15. 9
16. 11
17. 11+13
18. 12
19. 14+17
20. 15
21. 15+18+19+20
22. 16+21
23. 17
24. 19
25. 21

80 Number of Triangles: **30**

SOLUTION: Note again that not all numbered segments figure into the solution.

1. 1+3
2. 1+3+10+11+17+18
3. 1+10+17
4. 2
5. 2+4
6. 3
7. 3+11+18
8. 6
9. 6+7
10. 7
11. 9
12. 9+24+26
13. 10+11+17+18
14. 10+17
15. 11+18

16. 12
17. 12+13
18. 12+13+19+20+21
19. 12+19
20. 13+20+21
21. 15
22. 15+25
23. 17
24. 17+18
25. 18
26. 20
27. 22
28. 23
29. 24+26
30. 26

79 Number of Triangles: **25**

SOLUTION:

1. 1+5
2. 2
3. 2+3+6
4. 3+6
5. 4
6. 4+7
7. 5
8. 6
9. 6+7
10. 7
11. 8+13+18
12. 9
13. 9+14

14. 9+14+19
15. 10+15+20
16. 11
17. 11+16
18. 11+16+21
19. 12+17+22
20. 13+18
21. 15+20
22. 17+22
23. 18
24. 20
25. 22

81 1 – 1 equals 0

82 11 – 1 equals 10

83 The square root of 1 (√1) is, of course, equal to 1

84 111 – 1 equals 110

85 11 × 1 equals 11

86 11 + 11 equals 22

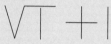

87 √1 + 1 equals 2

88 111 − 111 equals 0

89 1 × 1 + 11 equals 12 **OR** 11 × 1 + 1 equals 12

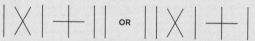

90 1 × 1 × 1 × 1 equals 1

91

0	9	8	2
0	5	1	1
4	4	1	0
1	0	3	6

92

6	1	1	3	4
7	2	0	1	0
1	0	3	9	8
1	1	3	5	1
6	0	3	2	3

93

1	1	2	3	4
4	2	0	1	6
7	1	0	3	2
1	0	3	6	2
8	9	7	5	1

94

6	1	3	4	5
7	0	1	0	6
0	8	2	2	2
1	3	6	1	1
8	0	0	3	5

95

9	1	1	0	4	5
7	0	0	2	0	1
0	2	3	9	8	2
3	0	4	0	5	3
1	0	3	0	1	5
8	0	7	2	3	0

96

6	1	1	3	1	1
7	2	0	1	0	0
4	5	7	0	9	3
1	0	3	0	1	5
5	6	1	1	1	1
8	9	0	1	9	5

97

1	6	1	0	1	5
4	5	0	8	2	9
4	5	0	8	1	1
1	0	1	0	1	5
5	6	7	0	9	1
0	0	1	1	3	5

98

5	1	1	3	4	0	5
7	2	0	1	0	3	6
7	8	3	3	8	1	2
3	4	4	0	5	1	6
7	8	9	1	2	0	7
0	9	8	2	9	2	9
8	9	7	6	3	1	5

99

6	1	1	3	4	0	7	5
7	2	0	1	0	3	7	6
7	8	3	9	9	1	0	2
3	4	1	0	5	0	1	6
7	8	9	1	2	1	8	7
1	0	3	6	1	1	6	5
5	6	7	5	1	2	0	9
8	9	7	6	3	3	1	5

100

7	1	1	3	0	1	7	8	4	5
7	2	0	1	0	1	2	4	0	6
7	8	3	9	1	0	0	5	8	2
3	4	4	0	1	1	2	0	5	6
7	8	9	1	0	8	3	0	2	7
0	9	8	2	0	1	2	0	2	2
4	5	7	8	1	0	0	1	2	9
4	5	7	8	0	1	1	1	1	9
1	0	3	6	4	1	0	1	1	5
8	9	7	6	0	9	2	3	3	5

101 $2 - 2 = 0$ **OR** $2 + 0 = 2$

102 $(20 \div 5)/4 = 1$ **OR** $(5 \times 4)/20 = 1$

103 $(\sqrt{9}) \div 3 = 1$

104 $\sqrt{16} = 2 \times 2$

105 $3^2 = 7 + 2$ **OR** $2^2 + 3 = 7$

106 $36 \div 6 = 5 + 1$ **OR** $(5 + 1) \times 6 = 36$

107 $49 \div 7 = 9 - 2$ **OR** $(9 - 2) \times 7 = 49$

108 $5 \times 5 = 23 + 2$ **OR** $(5 \times 5) - 2 = 23$

109 $7 \times 7 \times 1 = 42 + 7$

110 $(3 - 2) \div 1 = 5 - 4$ **OR** $3 - 2 = (5 - 4) \div 1$ **OR** $(5 + 2) - 4 = 3 \div 1$

111 Let your hair down.

W	R	X	N	D	A	L	K	R	E	R	C	B
H	X	T	Z	E	Z	N	F	B	T	H	X	R
X	S	X	H	X	Z	B	M	Q	X	S	P	E
N	R	L	E	T	R	R	T	P	M	N	N	H
M	S	C	D	Z	E	J	W	Q	L	L	R	Q
E	Z	S	T	E	R	G	Z	W	R	N	C	W
Y	O	U	R	Z	L	S	Z	H	S	B	Z	Z
T	J	H	Y	H	A	I	R	T	J	N	D	J
C	X	C	S	L	L	V	H	C	C	G	S	Y
E	Q	D	S	U	T	H	R	H	S	H	L	X
H	Y	W	D	O	W	N	X	W	Q	L	L	S

112 Go the whole nine yards.

R	R	X	N	D	J	L	L	R	E	R	C	B
H	G	O	Q	E	Z	T	H	E	T	H	X	R
X	S	X	H	X	U	B	M	Q	S	S	P	E
N	R	O	T	Z	R	R	T	P	M	N	N	H
M	S	C	D	C	E	D	W	H	O	L	E	O
E	Q	S	T	E	R	G	Z	W	R	N	C	Q
C	R	D	S	L	L	S	U	H	S	B	Z	E
T	W	H	Z	H	T	H	J	T	R	N	D	J
C	J	C	S	L	B	D	H	C	C	G	S	Y
E	N	I	N	E	N	H	R	Y	A	R	D	S
X	Y	W	X	J	X	O	X	Q	E	Z	L	S

113 Blood is thicker than water.

T	R	X	N	D	X	T	L	R	E	R	C	M
H	X	B	H	B	Z	H	F	B	T	H	X	R
X	S	L	H	I	U	I	M	J	X	S	P	E
N	K	O	T	S	R	C	T	P	M	N	N	H
M	S	O	K	B	K	K	Z	K	L	L	W	Z
L	B	D	T	E	R	E	O	W	R	N	A	W
C	R	K	S	L	L	R	B	T	S	B	T	E
T	T	H	Y	H	T	H	Z	H	R	N	E	Z
C	Z	C	S	L	T	D	H	A	Q	G	R	Y
T	N	T	S	U	T	H	R	N	S	H	L	X
T	Q	W	T	A	Q	K	T	W	Z	T	L	S

116 A penny saved is a penny earned.

Z	R	V	N	J	J	J	Q	L	R	O	R	C	B
Z	X	A	H	J	Z	O	F	B	L	H	X	R	
X	S	X	H	P	E	N	N	Y	J	S	P	Z	
N	Z	O	T	H	R	J	T	P	M	N	N	H	
M	S	C	D	Z	Q	J	S	A	V	E	D	D	
E	I	S	T	E	H	G	H	W	R	N	C	Q	
C	R	D	S	A	L	S	U	H	S	B	Z	E	
T	W	H	Y	H	T	H	W	T	R	N	D	E	
C	W	C	S	P	E	N	N	Y	C	G	S	Y	
E	N	D	S	W	T	H	R	H	S	H	L	X	
X	E	A	R	N	E	D	X	W	Z	L	Q	S	

114 A friend in need is a friend indeed.

C	R	I	J	D	A	K	L	R	J	R	C	B
A	X	N	H	J	Z	O	F	B	T	H	X	R
X	S	X	H	X	F	B	M	L	X	S	P	E
F	R	O	J	H	R	R	T	P	I	Q	N	H
R	S	N	D	W	I	D	W	Q	N	L	R	Q
I	Z	E	T	Q	E	G	J	W	D	N	C	W
E	R	E	S	L	N	S	Z	H	E	B	Q	J
N	W	D	Y	H	D	H	J	T	E	J	D	J
D	Q	C	S	L	L	D	H	Z	D	G	S	Y
E	N	I	Z	U	E	H	R	H	S	H	L	X
Z	Y	S	X	Z	X	O	X	B	T	R	L	S

117 A word to the wise is enough.

J	A	J	N	D	J	L	L	W	E	R	J	Q
H	X	T	J	E	Z	Q	F	I	T	H	X	R
X	S	W	H	X	J	B	M	S	X	S	P	E
J	R	O	L	H	R	R	T	E	M	N	N	N
M	S	R	D	Q	E	D	W	J	L	L	R	O
K	V	D	T	T	R	G	J	W	R	I	C	U
B	R	D	S	O	L	T	U	H	S	S	J	G
T	Q	H	Y	H	T	H	J	T	R	N	D	H
C	J	C	S	L	L	E	H	C	C	G	S	Y
Q	N	D	S	U	T	H	R	H	J	Q	L	X
J	Y	W	X	Q	X	J	X	W	Q	L	L	S

115 A little learning is a dangerous thing.

Y	R	X	N	D	S	L	L	R	Z	R	C	B
H	Q	A	H	J	L	I	T	T	L	E	X	R
X	S	F	Q	X	U	W	M	O	X	S	P	E
N	L	E	A	R	N	I	N	G	M	N	N	H
M	S	C	W	C	E	J	W	Q	L	L	R	J
J	I	S	T	E	J	G	J	W	R	N	C	W
C	Y	D	S	J	I	S	U	H	S	B	A	Z
T	W	Q	Y	Z	T	Q	J	T	R	N	Z	R
D	A	N	G	E	R	O	U	S	C	G	S	Y
E	E	D	S	J	T	J	R	H	S	H	L	X
P	Y	W	X	Q	T	H	I	N	G	L	L	S

118 Absence makes the heart grow fonder.

K	A	B	S	E	N	C	E	R	E	R	C	B
H	X	T	H	W	Z	P	Y	B	T	H	X	R
X	S	X	H	M	A	K	E	S	X	S	P	E
W	Q	O	T	H	R	R	T	P	Q	N	N	Y
M	S	C	D	W	V	D	T	H	E	L	R	Y
E	R	S	T	U	L	G	N	W	R	N	C	W
C	H	E	A	R	T	D	U	R	S	B	D	E
T	W	Q	Y	H	T	H	K	T	R	N	D	Q
G	R	O	W	O	L	D	H	C	C	G	S	Y
F	N	D	S	U	T	H	R	H	S	H	L	X
W	Y	W	X	J	F	O	N	D	E	R	L	S

265

All that glitters is not gold.

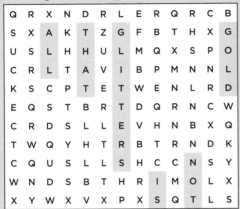

Q	R	X	N	D	R	L	E	R	Q	R	C	B
S	X	A	K	T	Z	G	F	B	T	H	X	G
U	S	L	H	H	U	L	M	Q	X	S	P	O
C	R	L	T	A	V	I	B	P	M	N	N	L
K	S	C	P	T	E	T	W	E	N	L	R	D
E	Q	S	T	B	R	T	D	Q	R	N	C	W
C	R	D	S	L	L	E	V	H	N	B	X	Q
T	W	Q	Y	H	T	R	B	T	R	N	D	K
C	Q	U	S	L	L	S	H	C	C	N	S	Y
W	N	D	S	B	T	H	R	I	M	O	L	X
X	Y	W	X	V	X	P	X	S	Q	T	L	S

120 Do not throw out the baby with the bathwater.

C	D	O	N	D	D	L	L	R	E	R	C	B
G	X	T	T	N	O	T	F	B	T	H	X	R
D	F	B	H	M	U	V	M	O	Q	S	P	B
Q	R	N	T	H	R	R	T	H	R	O	W	H
O	U	T	G	C	C	W	W	U	L	L	R	O
E	Q	S	T	T	H	E	B	B	A	B	Y	Q
C	R	D	M	L	L	P	U	H	S	B	M	E
T	W	I	T	H	T	H	A	S	R	N	D	P
C	B	C	S	L	L	T	H	E	C	M	L	Y
E	V	D	S	M	T	H	R	H	S	H	L	X
Q	Y	W	X	B	A	T	H	W	A	T	E	R

121 Familiarity breeds contempt.

Code: Each letter is replaced with the one before it in the alphabet (just like the illustrative puzzle). For example, F is replaced with E because it occurs just before it. Note that the letter before A is Z— the last letter of the alphabet, and thus the one just before starting over with A.

E Z L H K H Z Q H S X   A Q D D C R
↓ ↓ ↓ ↓ ↓ ↓ ↓ ↓ ↓ ↓ ↓   ↓ ↓ ↓ ↓ ↓ ↓
F A M I L I A R I T Y   B R E E D S

B N M S D L O S
↓ ↓ ↓ ↓ ↓ ↓ ↓ ↓
C O N T E M P T

122 A diamond is forever.

Code: Each letter is replaced with the letter that is located two before it in the alphabet. For example, D is replaced with B because it occurs two letters just before it (B, C, D). Also, note that A is replaced with Y (Y, Z, A [starting over]).

Y   B G Y K M L B   G Q   D M P C T C P
↓   ↓ ↓ ↓ ↓ ↓ ↓ ↓   ↓ ↓   ↓ ↓ ↓ ↓ ↓ ↓ ↓
A   D I A M O N D   I S   F O R E V E R

123 The squeaky wheel gets the grease.

Code: Each letter is replaced with the letter that is located three before it in the alphabet. For example, T is replaced with Q (Q, R, S, T). Note again that A is replaced with X (X, Y, Z, A [starting over]).

Q E B   P N R B X H V   T E B B I
↓ ↓ ↓   ↓ ↓ ↓ ↓ ↓ ↓ ↓   ↓ ↓ ↓ ↓ ↓
T H E   S Q U E A K Y   W H E E L

D B Q P   Q E B   D O B X P B
↓ ↓ ↓ ↓   ↓ ↓ ↓   ↓ ↓ ↓ ↓ ↓ ↓
G E T S   T H E   G R E A S E

124 Fortune favors the bold.

Code: Fooled you? This one goes back simply to the puzzle with which we started off this section—namely, each letter is replaced with the one before it in the alphabet. So, *F* is replaced by *E*, and so on. Did you miss it?

E N Q S T M D   E Z U N Q R   S G D
↓ ↓ ↓ ↓ ↓ ↓ ↓   ↓ ↓ ↓ ↓ ↓ ↓   ↓ ↓ ↓
F O R T U N E   F A V O R S   T H E

A N K C
↓ ↓ ↓ ↓
B O L D

125 Better late than never.

Code: Once again, a code used previously applies here—just to keep you on your toes. This goes back to the code used in puzzle 122. Each letter is replaced with the letter that is located two before it in the alphabet. For example, *E* is replaced with *C* because it occurs two letters just before it, and so on. Note that *Z* is two letters before *B* (*Z, A, B*).

Z C R R C P   J Y R C   R F Y L
↓ ↓ ↓ ↓ ↓ ↓   ↓ ↓ ↓ ↓   ↓ ↓ ↓ ↓
B E T T E R   L A T E   T H A N

L C T C P
↓ ↓ ↓ ↓ ↓
N E V E R

126 A picture is worth a thousand words.

Code: Each letter is replaced with the one after it in the alphabet. For example, the letter *A* is replaced by *B*, which is the letter after it.

B   Q J D U V S F   J T   X P S U I   B
↓   ↓ ↓ ↓ ↓ ↓ ↓ ↓   ↓ ↓   ↓ ↓ ↓ ↓ ↓   ↓
A   P I C T U R E   I S   W O R T H   A

U I P V T B O E   X P S E T
↓ ↓ ↓ ↓ ↓ ↓ ↓ ↓   ↓ ↓ ↓ ↓ ↓
T H O U S A N D   W O R D S

127 Discretion is the greater part of valor.

Code: Each letter is replaced with the second one after it in the alphabet. For example, *D* is replaced by *F*, the second letter after *D* in the alphabet.

F K U E T G V K Q P   K U   V J G
↓ ↓ ↓ ↓ ↓ ↓ ↓ ↓ ↓ ↓   ↓ ↓   ↓ ↓ ↓
D I S C R E T I O N   I S   T H E

I T G C V G T   R C T V   Q H   X C N Q T
↓ ↓ ↓ ↓ ↓ ↓ ↓   ↓ ↓ ↓ ↓   ↓ ↓   ↓ ↓ ↓ ↓ ↓
G R E A T E R   P A R T   O F   V A L O R

128 The early bird catches the worm.

Code: Each letter is replaced with the third one after it in the alphabet. For example, *T* is replaced with the third letter after it in the alphabet, which is *W* (*T, U, V, W*). Note that the third letter after *Y* is *B*, because of starting over in the alphabet (*Y, Z, A, B*).

```
W K H      H D U O B      E L U G
↓ ↓ ↓      ↓ ↓ ↓ ↓ ↓      ↓ ↓ ↓ ↓
T H E      E A R L Y      B I R D

F D W F K H V      W K H      Z R U P
↓ ↓ ↓ ↓ ↓ ↓ ↓      ↓ ↓ ↓      ↓ ↓ ↓ ↓
C A T C H E S      T H E      W O R M
```

129 Actions speak louder than words.

Code: We wanted again to keep you on your toes with this one by using an already-used code—each letter is replaced with the one after it. So, *A* is replaced by *B*, and so on. Part of the fascination and challenge of puzzle solving is being aware of little traps like this one—that is, going back unexpectedly to a previously used code.

```
B D U J P O T      T Q F B L      M P V E F S
↓ ↓ ↓ ↓ ↓ ↓ ↓      ↓ ↓ ↓ ↓ ↓      ↓ ↓ ↓ ↓ ↓ ↓
A C T I O N S      S P E A K      L O U D E R

U I B O      X P S E T
↓ ↓ ↓ ↓      ↓ ↓ ↓ ↓ ↓
T H A N      W O R D S
```

130 Too many cooks spoil the broth.

Code: Each letter is replaced with the fifth one after it. For example, *O* is replaced by *T* (*O, P, Q, R, S, T*). Note that the fifth letter after *Y*, after restarting the alphabet, is *D* (*Y, Z, A, B, C, D*).

```
Y T T      R F S D      H T T P X      X U T N Q
↓ ↓ ↓      ↓ ↓ ↓ ↓      ↓ ↓ ↓ ↓ ↓      ↓ ↓ ↓ ↓ ↓
T O O      M A N Y      C O O K S      S P O I L

Y M J      G W T Y M
↓ ↓ ↓      ↓ ↓ ↓ ↓ ↓
T H E      B R O T H
```

131 Practice makes perfect.

Code: As in the illustrative puzzle, the letter occurring first is assigned 1, the letter occurring second is assigned 2, and so on. So, *P* = 1, *R* = 2, and so on.

```
P R A C T I C E      M A K E S      P E R F E C T
↑ ↑ ↑ ↑ ↑ ↑ ↑ ↑      ↑ ↑ ↑ ↑ ↑      ↑ ↑ ↑ ↑ ↑ ↑ ↑
1 2 3 4 5 6 4 7      8 3 9 7 10      1 7 2 11 7 4 5
```

132 Two heads are better than one.

Code: The number assigned to each letter reflects the position of each letter in the alphabet sequence. So, *A* = 1 because it is the first letter in the alphabet; *B* = 2 because it is the second letter in the alphabet; and so on. Note that numbers in the normal numerical sequence will be skipped because of this code; if there is no *C* then the number 3 will not appear.

```
T  W  O      H  E  A  D  S      A  R  E      B  E  T  T  E  R
↑  ↑  ↑      ↑  ↑  ↑  ↑  ↑      ↑  ↑  ↑      ↑  ↑  ↑  ↑  ↑  ↑
20 23 15     8  5  1  4  19     1  18 5      2  5  20 20 5  18

T  H  A  N      O  N  E
↑  ↑  ↑  ↑      ↑  ↑  ↑
20 8  1  14     15 14 5
```

133 Honesty is the best policy.

Code: Each letter as it occurs is replaced with the even numbers in order. *H* appears first and the first even number is 2, so *H* = 2; *O* appears second and the second even number is 4, so *O* = 4, and so on.

H	O	N	E	S	T	Y		I	S		T	H	E		B	E	S	T
↑	↑	↑	↑	↑	↑	↑		↑	↑		↑	↑	↑		↑	↑	↑	↑
2	4	6	8	10	12	14		16	10		12	2	8		18	8	10	12

P	O	L	I	C	Y
↑	↑	↑	↑	↑	↑
20	4	22	16	24	14

134 Good things come to those who wait.

Code: Each letter as it occurs is replaced with the odd numbers in order. *G* appears first and the first odd number is 1, so *G* = 1; *O* appears second and the second odd number is 3, so *O* = 3, and so on.

G	O	O	D		T	H	I	N	G	S		C	O	M	E		T	O
↑	↑	↑	↑		↑	↑	↑	↑	↑	↑		↑	↑	↑	↑		↑	↑
1	3	3	5		7	9	11	13	1	15		17	3	19	21		7	3

T	H	O	S	E		W	H	O		W	A	I	T
↑	↑	↑	↑	↑		↑	↑	↑		↑	↑	↑	↑
7	9	3	15	21		23	9	3		23	25	11	7

135 Necessity is the mother of invention.

Code: Each letter is replaced by a factor of three in order. *N* appears first and the first factor is 3, so *N* = 3; *E* appears second and the second factor is 6, so *E* = 6, and so on.

N	E	C	E	S	S	I	T	Y		I	S		T	H	E
↑	↑	↑	↑	↑	↑	↑	↑	↑		↑	↑		↑	↑	↑
3	6	9	6	12	12	15	18	21		15	12		18	24	6

M	O	T	H	E	R		O	F		I	N	V	E	N	T	I	O	N
↑	↑	↑	↑	↑	↑		↑	↑		↑	↑	↑	↑	↑	↑	↑	↑	↑
27	30	18	24	6	33		30	36		15	3	39	6	3	18	15	30	3

136 Beauty is in the eye of the beholder.

Code: Just to make sure you are on your toes, the code used here is exactly the same as the one used for puzzle 131. The letter occurring first is assigned 1, the letter occurring second is assigned 2, and so on. So, *B* = 1, *E* = 2 and so on.

B	E	A	U	T	Y		I	S		I	N		T	H	E		E	Y	E
↑	↑	↑	↑	↑	↑		↑	↑		↑	↑		↑	↑	↑		↑	↑	↑
1	2	3	4	5	6		7	8		7	9		5	10	2		2	6	2

O	F		T	H	E		B	E	H	O	L	D	E	R
↑	↑		↑	↑	↑		↑	↑	↑	↑	↑	↑	↑	↑
11	12		5	10	2		1	2	10	11	13	14	2	15

137 Birds of a feather flock together.

Code: Once again, we are just checking to see if you are on your toes. The code used here is exactly the same as the one used for puzzle 132. The number assigned to each letter reflects the position of each letter in the alphabet sequence. So, *A* = 1 because it is the first letter in the alphabet; *B* = 2 because it is the second letter in the alphabet; and so on. Note that numbers in the normal numerical sequence will be skipped because of this code; for instance, if there is no *D* then the number 4 will not appear.

B	I	R	D	S		O	F		A		F	E	A	T	H	E	R
↑	↑	↑	↑	↑		↑	↑		↑		↑	↑	↑	↑	↑	↑	↑
2	9	18	4	19		15	6		1		6	5	1	20	8	5	18

F	L	O	C	K		T	O	G	E	T	H	E	R
↑	↑	↑	↑	↑		↑	↑	↑	↑	↑	↑	↑	↑
6	12	15	3	11		20	15	7	5	20	8	5	18

138 The best things in life are free.

Code: Each letter is replaced by a factor of five in order. *T* appears first and the first factor is 5, so *T* = 5; *H* appears second and the second factor is 10, so *H* = 10, and so on.

T	H	E		B	E	S	T		T	H	I	N	G	S		I	N
↑	↑	↑		↑	↑	↑	↑		↑	↑	↑	↑	↑	↑		↑	↑
5	10	15		20	15	25	5		5	10	30	35	40	25		30	35

L	I	F	E		A	R	E		F	R	E	E
↑	↑	↑	↑		↑	↑	↑		↑	↑	↑	↑
45	30	50	15		55	60	15		50	60	15	15

139 The first step is always the hardest.

Code: The vowels are replaced by 1, 2, 3, 4, 5 in order: *A* = 1, *E* = 2, *I* = 3, *O* = 4 (not present in the text), *U* = 5 (not present in the text). The consonants are replaced by factors of 6 in order. *T* appears first and the first factor is 6, so *T* = 6; *H* appears second and the second factor is 12, so *H* = 12, and so on.

T	H	E		F	I	R	S	T		S	T	E	P		I	S
↑	↑	↑		↑	↑	↑	↑	↑		↑	↑	↑	↑		↑	↑
6	12	2		18	3	24	30	6		30	6	2	36		3	30

A	L	W	A	Y	S		T	H	E		H	A	R	D	E	S	T
↑	↑	↑	↑	↑	↑		↑	↑	↑		↑	↑	↑	↑	↑	↑	↑
1	42	48	1	54	30		6	12	2		12	1	24	60	2	30	6

140 Money does not grow on trees.

Code: Just to make sure you are on your toes one last time, the code used here is exactly the same as the one used for puzzle 131 and others. The letter occurring first is assigned 1, the letter occurring second is assigned 2, and so on. So, *M* = 1, *O* = 2, and so on.

M	O	N	E	Y		D	O	E	S		N	O	T		G	R	O	W
↑	↑	↑	↑	↑		↑	↑	↑	↑		↑	↑	↑		↑	↑	↑	↑
1	2	3	4	5		6	2	4	7		3	2	8		9	10	2	11

O	N		T	R	E	E	S
↑	↑		↑	↑	↑	↑	↑
2	3		8	10	4	4	7

141 Better safe than sorry.
Code: The order of the words is scrambled.

142 Curiosity killed the cat.
Code: Each word is written backward.

143 It takes two to tango.
Code: The vowels in each word are separated from the consonants and placed at the end of each word.

144 Old habits die hard.
Code: The letters of each word are scrambled.

145 Nothing hurts like the truth.
Code: The words are written without spaces to separate them.

146 Variety is the spice of life.
Code: The vowels in each word are separated from the consonants and placed at the beginning of each word.

147 You reap what you sow.
Code: Each word is written backward.

148 You have to take the good with the bad.
Code: The sentence is written backward.

149 One good turn deserves another.
Code: The vowels in each word are scrambled randomly in the word.

150 The spirit is willing but the flesh is weak.
Code: First, the first four words are put at the end: *BUT THE FLESH IS WEAK THE SPIRIT IS WILLING.* Second, the words are written backward.

151

1	2	3
3	1	2
2	3	1

152

1	4	3	2
3	1	2	4
4	2	1	3
2	3	4	1

153

5	4	1	2	3
4	3	5	1	2
2	5	4	3	1
3	1	2	5	4
1	2	3	4	5

154

6	5	1	4	3	2
5	4	2	3	6	1
1	3	4	5	2	6
3	2	6	1	5	4
2	1	5	6	4	3
4	6	3	2	1	5

155

1	2	5	4	6	3	7	9	8
7	3	9	8	5	1	4	6	2
8	4	6	9	2	7	1	5	3
9	6	8	3	1	4	5	2	7
2	7	1	6	8	5	3	4	9
4	5	3	2	7	9	6	8	1
6	9	4	1	3	2	8	7	5
5	1	2	7	4	8	9	3	6
3	8	7	5	9	6	2	1	4

156

7	6	5	2	3	1	4	9	8
2	4	9	8	6	7	1	3	5
8	1	3	9	5	4	2	6	7
5	3	7	4	8	6	9	2	1
6	8	2	7	1	9	3	5	4
4	9	1	3	2	5	8	7	6
3	2	6	5	4	8	7	1	9
1	7	8	6	9	2	5	4	3
9	5	4	1	7	3	6	8	2

157

4	1	6	9	8	7	2	3	5
9	7	3	1	2	5	4	6	8
8	5	2	3	4	6	9	7	1
1	6	5	4	7	2	3	8	9
7	8	9	5	1	3	6	2	4
2	3	4	6	9	8	5	1	7
3	4	1	8	6	9	7	5	2
6	9	7	2	5	1	8	4	3
5	2	8	7	3	4	1	9	6

158 The accent mark is alternating from left to right on the same letter (À, Á) starting from the top left corner to the bottom right corner.

À	Á	È
É	Ì	Í
Ò	Ó	Ù

159 The number of ★ symbols starts at 9 in the top left corner and diminishes by one in each subsequent cell (9, 8, 7, 6, ...), ending with one of the symbols in the bottom right corner.

★★★★ ★★★★ ★	★★★★ ★★★★	★★★★ ★★★
★★★★ ★★	★★★★ ★	★★★★
★★★	★★	★

160 The arrow is rotating in a clockwise direction from the top left corner to the bottom right corner.

←	↑	→
↓	←	↑
→	↓	←

161 Tina
The men told the truth. Since Bill and Benny are the two men, therefore they told the truth. From their statements we can thus eliminate both as the killer since they say that they were innocent (which we know is true). Theresa and Tina blame Tamara. But we know that the women lied. So, contrary to what they say, we can eliminate Tamara, as well. Tamara accuses Theresa. This is, of course, a lie. So, contrary to what Tamara says, Theresa is not our killer. We have now eliminated Bill, Benny, Tamara and Theresa. This leaves Tina as the only possibility for our killer.

162 Doris
Jake and Jasper say the same thing—namely that Jake is not the robber. There was only one lie, uttered by the robber, in the set of five statements. So, the two statements cannot be false. They are thus necessarily true. Diane and Debby say the same thing—Debby is not the robber. By the same reasoning, the two statements are true. So, to summarize so far: Jake, Jasper, Diane and Debby all told the truth. This means that Doris is the only liar in the group (by the process of elimination). She is the robber, despite what she says.

163 Vince
Van, Victor and Harriet say the same thing—namely that Van didn't do it. The three statements are therefore either all true or all false. They cannot be all false, since there were only two false statements in the set of five. Thus, the three statements must be all true. Since we are told that the robber lied, we can deduce that neither Van, Victor nor Harriet is the robber since they told the truth. This means that Helen and Vince are the two liars. Contrary to what they say—that Vince is innocent—Vince is, in fact, our robber.

164 Sid
Since everyone told the truth, Karen's statement eliminates Katy as our suspect, and Katy's statement simply confirms that she is innocent. With similar reasoning, Sam's statement eliminates Karen, Sal's statement eliminates Sam, and Sid's statement eliminates Sal. So far, we have eliminated Katy, Karen, Sam and Sal as our culprit. This leaves Sid as the embezzler by the process of elimination.

165 Andy
Since everyone lied, we can eliminate Sheila since she was accused by Arnie and we know that this is a lie. Sheila identifies Arnie in turn as the killer. We know that this is a lie, so we can also eliminate Arnie as the killer. Al accuses Sherrie. Using the same reasoning, we can eliminate Sherrie, as well. Sherrie accuses Al in return. Again, this means that Al is innocent because everyone, including Sherrie, lied. So, we have now eliminated four of the individuals as the killer—Sheila, Arnie, Sherrie and Al. This leaves Andy as the killer, who lied, of course, when he said that he didn't know who did it.

166 Ethan
We are told that the two women told the truth. Cara says that Eric is innocent and Cindy that Eddy is innocent. So, because their statements are true, we can eliminate both Eric and Eddy as the killer. Eddy accuses Eric as the killer. We know this is false. So, we have just identified Eddy as the one man who lied. The other two men thus told the truth. Eric says that neither woman is the killer. So we eliminate them, since this is true. By the process of elimination, this means that Ethan is the killer. His statement is irrelevant. He simply admits that he knows who did it, which is true (since he is the one who did it).

167 Mary
Mary is the only liar. She says that Frank did it. Since we know this is a lie, we can eliminate Frank as our culprit. Frank says that Flip didn't do it. As we know, this is true (all the men told the truth), and so we can also eliminate Flip from the suspect list. Francis claims innocence, and since we know he told the truth, we can also eliminate him from the list. Flip identifies either Mary or Flavius as the killer. Since Flavius claims innocence, and since we know he told the truth, we can eliminate him as our culprit. This leaves Mary as the killer.

168 Liz
Lana claims that she is innocent. If Lana is indeed the robber, then she lied. But her statement must be true because both Laura and Ben say that Lana is innocent. Since there is only one lie in set of statements, these three statements must of course be true. Thus, Lana is not the robber. This leaves either Lisa or Liz as the single liar (and robber). Lisa's statement is clearly true, since we have just cleared Laura of being a liar and thus the robber. This leaves Liz as the liar and the bank robber (despite claiming innocence).

169 Phil

Nora, Nina and Pat say the same thing—namely, that Paul is innocent. Their statements are thus all true or all false. There were only two lies in the set, not three, so they were all true. This means that Paul did not do it. It also means that the two liars were the other two, Paul and Phil. Paul's statement leads nowhere. It is a lie, but tells us nothing. On the other hand, Phil's statement, being false, indicates that he is the thief, contrary to what he says.

170 Roberta

We are told that both women told the truth. So, we can eliminate both Rosa, who truthfully says she didn't do it, and Jack, who is identified by Roberta as innocent. All three men lied. So, since Jack identifies Jason as the killer, and we know this is a lie, we can eliminate Jason. Jason identifies Jim as the killer. With the same reasoning, we can eliminate Jim, as well. That leaves Roberta as our killer. Jim's statement, which is false, is irrelevant for our purposes.

171 Bill

Bill (B) is older than Jane (J). We can show this as: B—J. Sarah (S) is younger than Jane. We can now insert S in the formula as follows: B—J—S. This shows Sarah as younger than Jane and that Jane is younger than Bill. It also shows that Bill is the oldest.

172 Dawn

Al (A) came in behind Bill (B). Let's show this as follows: B—A. Carrie (C) beat Bill. Let's add this in the formula to show that Carrie came in before Bill and thus before Al: C—B—A. Now, we are told that Carrie came in behind Dawn (D). This means that Dawn came in before Carrie: D—C—B—A. This now shows that Dawn came in first.

173 Wayne

Danny (D) scored higher than Shirley (S). We can represent this as follows: D—S. Shirley scored lower than Gina (G): G—S. Now, Gina scored lower than Danny but higher than Sheila: D—G—S. Wayne (W) scored lower than Sheila: D—G—S—W. Clearly, Wayne scored the lowest.

174 Darlene

Andy (A) is older than Ben (B): A—B. Darlene (D) is older than Carrie (C): D—C. Now, we are told that Carrie is younger than Ben: A—B—C. Andy is younger than Darlene: D—A—B—C. This shows that Darlene is the oldest.

175 Tara

There are four outcomes: first place, second place, third place and fourth (or last) place. If Sandy (S) did not win, but came in before two others, then we conclude that she came in second. If Wes (W) did not win and did not come in last, the only position left for him is third, since Sandy came in second: First—S—W—Last. Mitch (M) did not win since he was beaten by Tara (T), so he came in last, since second and third spots are already filled: First—S—W—M. The only position left for Tara is first place: T—S—W—M.

176 Carla

Robert (R) earns more than Carla (C), but less than Mohan (M). We can show this as follows: M—R—C. Now, Mohan earns less than Frieda (F), which means that she earns more than Mohan and, of course, Robert and Carla: F—M—R—C. Frieda earns less than Lucy (L). We can show this as follows: L—F—M—R—C. This formula now shows that Carla earns the least.

177 Jack

Phil (P) has a lower average than Sam (S) but a higher one than Bill (B). We can show this as follows: S—P—B. Now, we are told that Bill has a higher average than two others. This means that the other two—Jack (J) and Mack (M)—have a lower average than Bill. Jack has a lower average than Mack. All this can be shown as follows: S—P—B—M—J. This shows that Jack has the lowest overall average.

178 Helen

Bertha (B) was just in front of Martha (M). We can show this as B—M. Helen (H) was just in front of Norma (N): H—N. Now, Norma beat Bertha, so she also beat Martha: N—B—M. Helen beat all four (since she was in front of Norma): H—N—B—M. Jeannie (J) was in front of Sonya (S): H—N—B—M—J—S. This now shows that Helen came in first.

179 Lenny

There are six places: first place, second place, third place, fourth place, fifth place and sixth place. From the fact that Andrew (A) came in before four others but after Jake (J), we conclude that Andrew came in second and Jake first: J—A—four others. Among the four others, we are told that Earl (E) beat Kyle (K) and that Sid (S) beat Lenny (L) but not Kyle: E—K—S—L. We join this part of the formula to the other part above to get: J—A—E—K—S—L. It shows that Lenny came in last.

180 Karen

Dick (D) won more than Francesca (F): D—F. But he won less than Karen (K) and Laura (L). So, there are two possible arrangements of this outcome: K—L—D—F, which shows that Karen won more than Laura, or L—K—D—F, which shows instead that Laura won more than Karen. In both cases we can see that Dick won less than either Karen or Laura and that Francesca won less than all three. Now, Laura won less than Sally and Karen more than Sally. We can show this as follows: K—S—L—D—F. This shows that Karen won more than Sally, who won more than Laura, who won more than Dick, who won more than Francesca. Timothy (T) won more than Francesca but less that Dick: K—S—L—D—T—F. We show that Nicola (N) won less than Sally but more than Laura as follows: K—S—N—L—D—T—F. This shows that Karen is the person who won the most.

181

```
    3 2
+   8 1
─────────
  1 1 3
```

182

```
    4 5 8
+   6 0 2
─────────
  1 0 6 0
```

183

```
    8 9 0 1
+   8 9 1 0
───────────
1 7 8 1 1
```

184

```
  1 2 3 4 5
+ 9 0 3 4 5
─────────────
1 0 2 6 9 0
```

185

```
    4 3
−   2 8
─────────
    1 5
```

186

```
    9 3 1
−   4 1 2
─────────
    5 1 9
```

187

```
    7 6 3 4
−   7 5 1 2
───────────
      1 2 2
```

188

```
    6 5 9 8 3
−   1 7 9 2 0
─────────────
    4 8 0 6 3
```

189

```
    3 5 6
×       2
─────────
    7 1 2
```

190

```
    2 0 1 9
×         3
───────────
    6 0 5 7
```

191

```
    5 0
+   5 0
─────────
  1 0 0
```

192

```
    2 5 0
+   2 5 0
─────────
    5 0 0
```

193

```
    9 0 2 5
+   1 9 2 5
───────────
1 0 9 5 0
```

194

```
    5 1 1 0
+   5 1 0 1
───────────
1 0 2 1 1
```

195

```
    5 0 5 5 0
+   5 0 5 5 0
─────────────
1 0 1 1 0 0
```

196

```
    5 0 5
−   4 5 5
─────────
      5 0
```

197

```
    8 9 8 9
−     8 9 9
───────────
    8 0 9 0
```

198

```
  1 4 5 0 1
−   5 4 5 0
─────────────
    9 0 5 1
```

199

```
    2 5 0
×       2
─────────
    5 0 0
```

200

```
    1 0 5 5
×         5
───────────
    5 2 7 5
```

OR

200

```
    1 0 6 6
×         6
───────────
    6 3 9 6
```

201 Milo is a truth teller.
As in the illustrative example, Gila belongs to either the truth tellers or liars. So her answer to Dr. Shelley's question ("To which tribe do you belong?") would in either case be "I am a truth teller," no matter what the truth is. Let's go through the reasoning: (1) if she is a truth teller then she would simply say so, and thus "*Duba lo rooba*" translates as "I am a truth teller"; (2) if she is a liar, she would never admit to it, so she would say the opposite, namely, "I am a truth teller." Again, "*Duba lo rooba*" translates as "I am a truth teller." Now, Milo's answer is clearly the truth—Gila did say that she is a truth teller, even if we do not know if she really is. All Milo did was confirm that this was her statement. So, Milo is a truth teller.

202 Filo is a liar.
As we found out from the solution of puzzle 201, Milo is a truth teller. Filo, however, calls him a liar. This is a lie. So, the real liar is Filo.

203 Gila is a liar.
As we found out from the previous two puzzles, Milo is a truth teller and Filo is a liar. Clearly, Gila's statement is a lie.

204 The men are liars and the women are truth tellers.
The reasoning in this puzzle is the same as it was in the previous ones. Dilo is either a liar or a truth teller.

If he is a truth teller, then in answer to Dr. Shelley's question, he would say yes, of course. If he is a liar, he would lie and also say yes, never admitting that he and Filo are liars. Now, Nila clearly answered truthfully—Dilo did say yes, so she is a truth teller. The second part of her statement, which is thus also true, identifies Dilo as a liar. This means that the two men are liars and the two women, truth tellers.

205 The partners are: Filo and Nila, Dilo and Lila.
We found out from puzzle 204 that the men are liars. So, Filo's answer that Lila is his partner is false. So, his real partner is Nila. This leaves Dilo and Lila as the other couple.

206 Vilo is a liar, Zilo is a truth teller and Pila is a truth teller.
Once again, the key to the solution is the fact that Pila's answer to the question "Are you a truth teller?" is yes no matter to which tribe she actually belongs. The reasoning is the same as before. So Vilo's statement is obviously false because Pila had in fact answered yes, contrary to what he says. So Vilo is a liar. Now Zilo clearly told the truth since Pila did not say no. So being a truth teller, the rest of his statement—that Pila is a truth teller—is true.

207 Pila's partner is Zilo.
As we know, Vilo is a liar. With the same reasoning as above, his answer to Dr. Shelley's question would be yes, but it would a lie. Zilo, a truth teller, simply asserts this. So we conclude that Vilo cannot be Pila's partner, contrary to what he says. Thus, it is Zilo.

208 Dr. Shelley will not join Rilo's tribe.
Sila is either a liar or a truth teller. As above, her answer to Dr. Shelley's question would be yes no matter which tribe she actually belonged to. Now Chilo clearly answered truthfully—Sila did, indeed, say yes. He also points out that she is a liar. Since Rilo belongs to her tribe, he is also a liar. This means that Dr. Shelley will not join Rilo's tribe.

209 Rilo is a liar and Dr. Shelley will not join his tribe.
As we found out from puzzle 208, Sila is a liar and Chilo, a truth teller. So Sila's answer to Dr. Shelley's question is a lie. Dr. Shelley asks her if Rilo belongs to the truth tellers (whether he is part of the same tribe to which Chilo belongs). Sila answers yes but, as we know, this is a lie. So Rilo does not belong to the truth tellers. He is a liar after all and Dr. Shelley will not join his tribe.

210 Yes.
Rilo is a liar, so the only way he can tell Dr. Shelley that he loves her and wants to marry her is to deny it. So Dr. Shelley correctly interprets his statement in this way.

211 Mr. Smith has nine boys and one girl, for a total of ten. That one girl has, of course, nine brothers.

212 There is no difference in time, since 80 minutes = 1 hour (60 minutes) plus 20 minutes.

213 The other coin is the nickel.

214 Your name. Everyone calls you by name, but you use it mainly if asked "What's your name?" or for official reasons.

215 It is not legally relevant because any man who leaves a widow (his living wife) is a dead man.

216 The first ten digits include 0 (0, 1, 2, 3, 4, 5, 6, 7, 8, 9). As you know, multiply any number of digits by 0 and you will get 0 as the answer.

217 Sam's mother's daughter is his sister. His brother's sister is the same person—Sam's mother's daughter. That makes three: Sam, his sister and his brother. Sam and his brother have the same sister, of course.

218 The sister of Janet's mother is Janet's aunt. She is also her brother's aunt.

219 If the photo of Doris's mother's offspring is not Doris's brother, then it is Doris's sister.

220 Mark is looking at his father. Mark is an only child, so his mother's only offspring is Mark himself. Now his father has the same offspring, a son (named Mark). So, when Mark says, "That man's son," he is referring to himself (the son) and the man is, therefore, his father.

221 If the new email is true (The previous sentence is true), then the previous sentence (This sentence is false) was also true. But if this is so, then the previous sentence was false, since it says so. Again, the previous sentence cannot be both true and false. So, we must conclude that the new email is false. This means that the previous one was also false. But if this is so, then it says the truth (namely, that it is false). This makes it both true and false yet once again. So, despite the new email, we cannot decide if the previous sentence was true or false.

222 As argued in the solution for 221, it is clear that the truth value—if it is true or false—of the new sentence itself cannot be determined. If it is true, it produces circularity in the previous message; if it is false, it produces the same circularity.

223 The new email is accurate since we cannot determine if the previous ones were true or false. It is, therefore, true.

224 Recall from the previous puzzle that the email that read "Both previous sentences were neither true nor false" turned out to be true. So, this new one is false since it says that all the previous ones were false and we know that this is not true.

225 As we discovered, the previous email was actually false. So it is not correct to say that it was neither true nor false. So, the present email is itself false.

226 There is no paradox. The remaining two boxes both contain the penny because one box is inside the other.

227 Let us assume that inscription **A** is true. If so, then the ring is in **A**, as the inscription says. But then this would make inscription **B** also true, since, as it says, the ring is not in **B** (it is in **A**). Yet, there was (at least) only one true statement. This would imply instead that there were two true statements, and we know this is not the case. So, we discard the assumption that **A** is true. If it is not true, then logically it is false. Thus, contrary to what it says, the ring is not in **A**. Now, we can see that **C** is true, since it simply confirms that the ring is not in **A**. There can be no other true statements. So, **B** (like **A**) is false. Thus, contrary to what **B** says, the ring is inside **B**.

228 Note that **B** and **C** say the same thing, namely that the coin is not in **C**. Thus, the two are either both true or both false. They cannot both be false, since there was only one false inscription. So, they are both true. Thus, as they say, the coin in not in **C**. The only false inscription is **A**, of course. So, despite what it says, the coin is in **A**.

229 If the inscription is true, the box was in fact made by a truth teller, as the inscription informs us. But we do not know that this is so. If the box was made by a liar, he or she would still write the same inscription, not admitting that he is a liar. But we do not know that this is so, either. So, we cannot determine who made the box, a truth teller or a liar.

230 As we know, the box maker in puzzle 229 cannot be determined. So, we cannot logically determine who made this one, either.

231 You will need two weighings to be sure. Of course, if you are lucky only one weighing would work—leave two balls on the table and put one of the other two on the left pan of the scale and the other one on the right pan. If you are indeed fortunate, the culprit ball will be on one of the two pans—the one that goes up. But this outcome cannot be guaranteed because we

cannot be sure that the culprit ball is not in the pair on the table. So, here are the two weighings that will guarantee identification without needing luck. First, put two balls on the left pan and two on the right one. The pan that goes up contains the culprit ball, of course. Discard the other two balls that were heavier, since they are both good ones. Now weigh the pair that you have identified as containing the culprit ball by putting one ball on the left pan and one on the right pan. The pan that goes up will indicate which of the two is the culprit ball. Of course, all of this is hypothetical since you could get lucky, as discussed. But it's the hypothetical scenario that counts for this type of puzzle.

232 Again, you will need at least two weighings to be sure. First, leave one of the five balls on the table. Put two of the other four on the left pan and two on the right pan. Now, if you are lucky, the pans will balance and the culprit ball is, therefore, the one on the table. We must assume the worst-case scenario, namely that one of the pans goes up. We discard the two good balls and put them on the table with the other ball, which is also a good ball, of course. For the second weighing, put one of the two remaining balls on the left pan and the other on the right pan. The pan that goes up will identify the culprit ball. Again, if you are lucky, you will not need this second weighing. But you cannot assume this.

233 Once again, two weighings will do the trick. First, put three balls on the left pan and three on the right one. One of the pans will go up. The culprit ball is one of the three on that pan. Discard the three on the other pan. Now, take one of the three remaining balls and put it on the side, and weigh the other two, putting one on the left pan and one on the right pan. If a pan goes up, it will contain the culprit ball; if no pan goes up then the culprit ball is the one that you had put on the side. Either way, the second weighing will identify the culprit ball for sure.

234 Three weighings are required. Leave one of the balls on the table. Put six of the other balls on the left pan and six on the right pan. If the pans balance, then the culprit ball is the one you have left on the table. Lucky! But in a hypothetical scenario, you cannot assume luck, since you want to be sure that the weighing method will guarantee identification. So let's assume that one of the pans will go up. The culprit ball is in the set on that pan. Discard the other six balls. For your second weighing, put three of the balls in the culprit set on the left pan and three on the right pan. One of the pans will go up. The culprit ball is in this new set. Discard the other three balls. Now, for the third weighing, take one of the three remaining balls and put it on the side, and weigh the other two, putting one on the left pan and one on the right pan. If a pan goes up, it will contain the culprit ball; if no pan goes up then the culprit ball is the one that you had put on the side. Either way, the third weighing will identify the culprit ball for sure.

235 Six weighings

First weighing: Put fifty balls on the left pan and fifty on the right one. One of the pans will go up. The culprit ball is one of the fifty on that pan. Discard the balls on the other pan.

Second weighing: Put twenty-five of the remaining balls on the left pan and twenty-five on the right one. One of the pans will go up. The culprit ball is one of the twenty-five on that pan. Discard the balls on the other pan.

Now, put one of the remaining twenty-five balls on the side. This allows you to divide the remaining twenty-four into two equal sets of twelve balls.

Third weighing: Go ahead and weigh them as follows: Put twelve balls on the left pan and twelve on the right one. If you are lucky, the pans will balance. This means that the culprit ball is the one you put on the side. As usual, you cannot assume this. So, let's assume that one of the pans will go up. The culprit ball is one of the twelve on that pan. Discard the balls on the other pan.

Fourth weighing: Put six balls on the left pan and six on the right one. One of the pans will go up. The culprit ball is one of the six on that pan. Discard the balls on the other pan.

Fifth weighing: Put three balls on the left pan and three on the right one. One of the pans will go up. The culprit ball is one of the three on that pan. Discard the balls on the other pan.

Put one of the three balls on the side. This leaves two balls to weigh.

Sixth weighing: Put one ball on the left pan and one on the right one. If one of the pans goes up, it contains the culprit ball; if it does not, the culprit ball is the one you put on the side. At this point you have identified the culprit ball for sure.

236
Six weighings are needed again. If you put one of the balls on the side, you are left with 100. Since you cannot assume that the ball on the side is the culprit one, you should go ahead and weigh the 100 with the exact same method as the one used for puzzle 235. Strangely, as you can see, the addition of an extra ball changes nothing.

237
Put one of the balls on the side. Then, put one of the other two on the left pan and one on the right pan. If the pans balance, it means that the two balls weigh the same and are, thus, the two lighter balls. The one you had put on the side is the heavier ball. If one of the pans goes up, that pan contains the first lighter ball. The other one, therefore, is the one on the side. Either way, one

weighing will suffice. Of course, you could solve this by simply determining which of the balls is the heaviest. The reasoning is thus the same as in puzzle 231.

238 Three weighings

First weighing: Put two balls on the left pan and the other two on the right pan. If one goes up, then you are lucky, since you will have identified the two three-pound balls with this weighing. But, again, you cannot assume luck. So, we assume that the two pans balance. This means that the two balls on the left pan are the three-pound and the four-pound ones (for a total of seven pounds) and that the two balls on the right pan are the other three-pound and four-pound balls (for a total of seven pounds).

Second weighing: Put one of the pairs on the table. Then go ahead and weigh the other two balls on separate pans. One of the pans will go up, pinpointing the first three-pound ball.

Third weighing: Now weigh the two balls on the table on separate pans. Again, one of the pans will go up, pinpointing the second three-pound ball.

239 Three weighings

Scenario 1: Put one ball on the side. Weigh the remaining four by putting two on the left pan and two on the right pan. If the two pans balance, then you will know that there is one three-pound and one four-pound ball on each pan (creating the balance) and, thus, that the third three-pound ball is the one on the side. Let's continue with this outcome. For a second weighing, put two of the balls on the table and weigh the other two, one of which is, as we know, a three-pound ball and the other a four-pound ball. One of the pans will go up identifying the second three-pound ball. Finally, for the third weighing, put the final two balls—also three-pound and four-pound—on separate pans. This third weighing will identify the third three-pound ball, since it is the one on the pan that goes up.

Scenario 2: Put one ball on the side. Weigh the remaining four by putting two on the left pan and two on the right pan. If one of the pans goes up it will contain two three-pound balls. Take them off and label them as such. Now, on the other pan there might be two four-pound balls or a four-pound and a three-pound ball. Take one and put it on the left pan and the other on the right pan. If the two pans balance, then you have identified the two four-pound balls, and thus the third three-pound ball was the one you had put initially on the side. This means that you now have identified all three lighter balls. If one of the pans goes up, then you know that it contains the third three-pound ball. The ball on the other pan is a four-pound one and the other four-pound one is the one you had initially put on the side. Either way, two weighings will suffice.

Since we cannot assume scenario 2, which is luckier than the other one, we have to go with scenario 1, which consists of three weighings.

240 Nine weighings

First weighing: Put 500 balls on the left pan and 500 on the right one. One of the pans will go up. The culprit ball is one of the 500 on that pan. Discard the balls on the other pan.

Second weighing: Put 250 balls of the remaining balls on the left pan and 250 on the right one. One of the pans will go up. The culprit ball is one of the 250 on that pan. Discard the balls on the other pan.

Third weighing: Put 125 balls of the remaining 250 balls on the left pan and 125 on the right one. One of the pans will go up. The culprit ball is one of the 125 on that pan. Discard the other 125.

Now put one of the remaining 125 balls on the side. This allows you to divide the remaining 124 into two equal sets of sixty-two balls.

Fourth weighing: Go ahead and weigh them as follows: Put sixty-two balls on the left pan and sixty-two on the right one. If you are lucky, the pans will balance. This means that the culprit ball is the one you put on the side. As usual, you cannot assume this. So, let's assume that one of the pans will go up. The culprit ball is one of the sixty-two on that pan. Discard the balls on the other pan.

Fifth weighing: Put thirty-one balls on the left pan and thirty-one on the right one. One of the pans will go up. The culprit ball is one of the thirty-one on that pan. Discard the other thirty-one.

Now, put one of the remaining 31 balls on the side. This allows you to divide the remaining balls into two equal sets of 15 balls.

Sixth weighing: Put 15 balls on the left pan and 15 on the right one. If you are lucky, the pans will balance. This means that the culprit ball is the one you put on the side. As usual, you cannot assume this. So, let's assume that one of the pans will go up. The culprit ball is one of the 15 on that pan. Discard the balls on the other pan.

Put one of the balls on the side. This allows you to divide the remaining balls into two equal sets of seven.

Seventh weighing: Put seven balls on the left pan and seven on the right one. If you are lucky, the pans will balance. This means that the culprit ball is the one you put on the side. As usual, you cannot assume this. So, let's assume that one of the pans will go up. The culprit ball is one of the seven on that pan. Discard the balls on the other pan.

Put one of the seven balls on the side. This leaves six balls.

Eighth weighing: Put three balls on the left pan and three on the right one. If you are lucky, the pans will balance. This means that the culprit ball is the one you put on the side. As usual, you cannot assume this. So, let's assume that one of the pans will go up. The culprit ball is one of the three on that pan. Discard the balls on the other pan.

Put one of the three balls on the side. This leaves two balls to weigh.

Ninth weighing: Put one ball on the left pan and one on the right one. If one of the pans goes up, it contains the culprit ball; if it does not, the culprit ball is the one you put on the side. At this point you have identified the culprit ball for sure. You may have needed far fewer weighings with luck. But you cannot count on luck. The nine weighings guarantee, in principle, that you will locate the culprit ball for sure.

 Four draws

Again, we assume the worst-case scenario, drawing out three balls in a row of different color—one white, one black and one red. The fourth draw will produce a match: if you draw a white ball from inside with that draw, it will match the white one outside the box;

if you draw a black ball, it will match the black one outside the box; if you draw a red ball, it will match the red one outside the box. Whatever color the fourth draw produces, you will get a match.

 Five draws

Let's assume the worst-case scenario, drawing out four balls in a row of different color—one white, one black, one red and one green. The fifth draw will produce a match: if you draw one of the two white balls left inside the box, it will match the white one outside the box; if you draw one of the nine black balls left inside, it will match the black one outside the box; if you draw one of the seven red balls left inside, it will match the red one outside the box; if you draw one of the eleven green balls left inside, it will match the green one outside the box. Whatever color the fifth draw produces, it will be a match. Isn't it interesting that the different number of balls in each colored set does not affect the maximum number of draws needed?

 Six draws

Don't change the solution method! Start by assuming the worst-case scenario, not luck, drawing out five balls in a row of different color—one white, one black, one red, one green and one blue. That makes five draws in a row. Now, think of what's left in the box. The only white, the only black and the only red balls are now outside the box. This leaves one green and one blue ball inside the box, since the other green and the other blue are outside the box. So, the next draw (the sixth) will be either a green or blue ball. Whichever one it is, it will match the green or blue ball outside the box.

244 **Eleven draws**

Assuming the worst-case scenario, the following draws will be required:

First five draws: one white, one black, one red, one green, one blue (now outside the box)

Left inside the box: two white, three black, four red, five green, six blue

Next five draws: again—one white, one black, one red, one green, one blue

Now outside the box: two white, two black, two red, two green, two blue

Left inside the box: one white, two black, three red, four green, five blue

The next draw (the eleventh): This draw will produce a triplet match: if you draw the remaining white ball, it will match the two white ones outside the box (three white in total); if you draw one of the two remaining black balls, it will match the two black ones outside the box (three black in total); and so on.

245 **Yes**

The first five draws (under the worst-case scenario) will produce one of each color (one white, one black, one red, one green, one blue). The next five draws will produce pairs (two white, two black, two red, two green, two blue). The next draw, which is the eleventh, will produce a triplet match—either three white, three black, three red, three green or three blue, depending on which of these colors the eleventh ball is.

246 Ten draws
In this case, the worst-case scenario is different—it consists in drawing out all the white balls first, before a black one appears. Very unlucky, but those are the rules of the game. So, the first eight draws (being unlucky) will produce eight white balls outside the box, removing all the white balls from inside the box and leaving the two black ones. Now, the next two draws will clearly produce the two black balls. In total you will need ten draws.

247 Twenty draws
The solution method here is the same as it was for puzzle 246. In the worst-case scenario, all nine white and nine black balls will be drawn first, eighteen in total. The order doesn't matter. The end result is the same—all eighteen will be outside the box, leaving the two red ones inside. So, two more draws will produce a red pair. In total, twenty draws are required.

248 Three draws
The solution is similar to the solutions of the early puzzles in this section. In the worst-case scenario, you will draw a white and a black ball first (again the order is irrelevant). Now, there are only white balls in the box. So, the next draw (the third) will be a white ball that will match the one that is outside.

249 Seven draws
Assuming the worst-case scenario, the first five draws will produce the five black balls. This leaves only the white ones in the box. So, the next two draws will produce the required two white balls. That makes seven draws in total.

250 Nine draws
Assuming the worst-case scenario, the first six draws will produce the three white and three black balls (in any order), six in total. This leaves the two red and two green inside the box. Now, again under the worst-case scenario, the next two draws will produce two of different color—one red and one green. This leaves one red and one green inside the box. The next draw (the ninth) will produce a red or green ball and this guarantees a red or green pair outside the box.

251 Trip: (1) A trip is a journey taken for pleasure. (2) In the language of the hippies, the result of taking hallucinatory drugs.

252 Lead: (1) A lead is a clue, as in "The detective was following several new leads." (2) We follow someone who "takes the lead."

253 Ball: (1) When we tell someone that the "ball is in his or her court" it means that he or she must make the next move. (2) To "keep the ball rolling" means to preserve the momentum of an activity.

254 Feet: (1) To "get your feet wet" means to begin participating in some activity. (2) A person's "feet of clay" reveal his or her personality flaw.

255 Eye: (1) The "eye of the storm" is the calm zone at the center of a storm. (2) The "eye of the wind" is the direction from which the wind is blowing.

256 Pulse: (1) To "take someone's pulse" means to check someone's heart rate especially if we think he or she is not alive. (2) To "take the pulse of a situation" means to ascertain the general opinion about something.

257 Hat: (1) The expression "hat in hand" indicates an attitude of humility. (2) To "keep something under one's hat" means to keep something a secret.

258 Egg: (1) To have "egg on your face" means that you appear foolish. (2) To "lay an egg" is an expression meaning to fail badly.

259 Gloves: (1) Wearing gloves protects us from the cold. (2) To "take the gloves off" means that we are ready to engage someone in conflict.

260 Lips: (1) To "smack one's lips" conveys satisfaction. (2) To "curl one's lip" shows contempt.

261 Goose: To be on a "wild goose chase" means to be foolishly pursuing something unattainable.

262 Rainbow: "Chasing a rainbow," means pursuing an illusory goal.

263 Heart: To "break someone's heart" means to cause sadness in someone.

264 Ice: To "break the ice" is an expression that refers to doing or saying something to relieve tension, especially when people meet for the first time.

265 Iceberg: The "tip of the iceberg" refers to the small part of a much larger problem that remains hidden.

266 Bucket: To "kick the bucket" means to die.

267 Cake: A "piece of cake" refers to something that can be achieved easily.

268 Potato: A "hot potato" is a controversial issue or situation that is difficult to deal with.

269 Straw: The "last straw" is a further difficulty that makes a situation unbearable.

270 Cut: "Cut both ways" means that an action or utterance serves both sides of an argument and can have both good and bad effects.

271 Railroad: rail = steel bar; road = wide way

272 Lovesickness: love = intense feeling; sickness = illness

273 Football: foot = leg extremity; ball = sphere

274 Airplane: air = atmosphere; plane = level

275 Shipyard: ship = water vehicle; yard = enclosure

276 Ballpark: ball = sphere; park = public grounds

277 Peanut: pea = green spherical vegetable; nut = hard kernel

278 Keyboard: key = door opening device; board = rectangular plane

279 Blackboard: black = dark; board = rectangular plane

280 Notebook: note = memo; book = printed work

281 Dud: dud = ineffectual person; duds = clothes

282 Eve: period = as in the eve of destruction; woman = Eve, the mother of humanity

283 Civic: duty = as in civic duty; name = Vic

284 Hannah: biblical woman = mother of Samuel; nah = variant of no

285 Kayak: kayak = type of boat; yak = trivial talk

286 Level: device = level, as in carpenter's level; crossing = as in level crossing (= American railroad crossing)

287 Poop: something to scoop = as in dog poop; op. = as in op. cit. abbreviation for "work already cited"

288 Madam: Madam = a female title; mad = angry state; am = verb form of to be

289 Rotor: rotor = a machine part; rot = decay

290 Tenet: tenet = principle; ten = number

291 Temperature: temperature goes up and down inside (inside a house or inside the body) and outside (according to the weather).

292 Boomerang: a boomerang flies in the air and returns to the thrower.

293 Temper: to "keep your temper" means that you are remaining calm; to "lose your temper" means that you are getting angry.

294 Hat: "hat in hand" is an expression that is used to convey an attitude of humility as we saw in another riddle in this chapter; to "take your hat off" to someone indicates that you admire that person.

295 Gloves: to "take the gloves off" means that you are going to do something in an uncompromising way, without hesitation.

296 Table: to "lay something on the table" indicates that you are making something known openly; to put something "under the table" means that you are being secretive.

297 Cake: a "piece of cake" is an expression denoting that something can be easily achieved; if something "takes the cake," then it indicates that it exceeds all others ("Of all the greedy people, he takes the cake").

298 Bridge: bridge is both a card game and a structure for crossing over from one side to the other.

299 Red: to "see red" denotes to become very angry, and red is the color of blood (a vital body substance).

300 Breath: to "take someone's breath away" denotes to astonish someone; to "waste your breath" denotes giving advice without effect.

301 PIN

302 WED

303 NAME, AMEN, MANE

304 MEAT, MATE, TEAM, META

305 STEAL, SLATE, TALES, TEALS (species of ducks), LEAST, TESLA (magnetic unit)

306 LISTEN, ENLIST, TINSEL, INLETS

307 FINDER, REFIND

308 PRESENT, SERPENT

309 EARNEST, NEAREST

310 REPAINTS, PAINTERS, PANTRIES

311 HELP LESS, LESS HELP, HE SPELLS

312 CLOY RUT, CRY LOUT, CURL TOY, TO CURLY

313 HID LONG, HOLD GIN, HIND LOG, OLD NIGH

314 LAX USE, LAX SUE, AXLE US

315 CORN LOT (other possible anagrams do not make coherent phrases)

316 EVEN GIN

317 BED LUSH, BUS HELD, HUB SLED

318 RED SETS, REDS SET

319 I ENTER, NET IRE (other possible anagrams do not make coherent phrases)

320 MY RACE, A MERCY, MY ACRE, MY CARE, RACY ME (other possible anagrams do not make coherent phrases)

321 SLOPPY, POLYPS

322 AFRAID

323 DOUBLE

324 TRIPLED

325 PLENTIFUL

326 PARTIAL

327 BOREDOM, BEDROOM, BROOMED

328 WILDNESS, WINDLESS, SWINDLES

329 DUPLICITY

330 SPECIALTY

331 NEW ME

332 THEY SEE

333 OF DEBTS

334 FOR YOU

335 BAD LIGHT

336 VICE SQUAD

337 A GANG THUG

338 IT HURTS!

339 IT IS GOOD!

340 WISE OWL

341 DREW BARRYMORE (Barrymore does indeed always wear a merry wardrobe at the Oscars)

342 MADAME CURIE (She discovered radium)

343 JENNIFER ANISTON (No commentary needed)

344 HILLARY CLINTON (Again, no commentary needed)

345 DAVID LETTERMAN (Letterman is a late-night TV host)

346 CHRISTIAN SLATER (Slater is indeed a rich star who keeps away from the limelight and is thus silent)

347 OSCAR WILDE (Wilde was a great writer who did indeed "lace" his words)

348 FLORENCE NIGHTINGALE (Nightingale was a famous nurse who did a lot to help improve the treatment of the sick, or the "reclining")

349 GIOVANNI PERGOLESI (Pergolesi was a famous eighteenth century opera composer)

350 WILLIAM SHAKESPEARE (No commentary needed)

351

```
G E R A N I U M R E R C P
H Z T H E Z D F L I L Y R
Z S Z R O S E M O Z S P E
N R O T D R R T P M N N H
O R C H I D D W D A I S Y
E I S T O R G D W Q N C W
C R D S L L S U H S B C E
T W H E H T T U L I P D I
C A C S L L D H C C G S Y
P E T U N I A R H S H A Z
V Y W Z A X O Z W E W L Q
```

352

```
V R X N D I L M R E R C B
H G V E G E T A B L E S R
G S G H G U B M O U S P E
N K O T H R R T P M N N H
M E A T C E D H S I F R O
I I S T E R P O E R N C V
C R D S L B R E A D B P E
P A S T A Q L A T R N U I
C A F S L L D H C C G S Y
T I U R F T H R H S H L G
G Y W W A S W E E T S L S
```

353

```
S H I R T A H L O E R C B
C B T E M H R F S T N A P
A S N H L F B M O T N Q A
R R O G D R R T P M K N H
F K C D R E D P E L M R J
B I S S E V O L G R N I A
R R D S S L K U O S B A C
O F H Y S J L A T R N D K
M A C S L L D H C C G S E
S T O C K I N G S S H L T
E Y W I A M O C O E L L E
```

354

```
S R T S L I P P E R S Y T
E D T X E B H F B T H X R
O S X H X U B M O I S P E
H R O G A L O S H E S N D
S S C D C E O W E W L R Z
J I M T E R T O H R N C S
S L A D N A S U H S B S S
T S H Y H T S A T B N D I
C L O G S L D H C C G S L
S N D S N T H R H S H L S
L O A F E R S Q B E N L S
```

355

```
K R N A P K I N R F R N N
N P L H F O B O R T H T O
I T C U A P L M O X S P O
F R L O W B R T P M N N P
E S C D E E D B E P L R S
N P A T E R F O R K N C W
P U C T L L S W H S B O E
K K N Y E T A L P R N D P
R A C S L L D H C C G S O
K N D S T E A C U P H L B
N A L P N B O N A P L L W
```

356

D	R	E	N	I	N	C	R	R	E	C	L	E
G	R	G	O	O	D	G	R	E	I	N	D	W
W	C	R	N	D	U	E	M	R	X	F	P	O
U	L	E	D	D	R	E	A	M	Y	M	Y	N
C	L	A	N	E	H	A	G	R	E	L	R	D
E	I	T	T	E	R	G	O	W	R	N	C	E
I	N	C	S	Y	P	P	A	H	S	H	A	R
D	R	E	I	N	C	G	R	E	T	A	D	F
C	L	E	A	N	D	R	I	N	C	W	O	U
G	R	G	O	U	W	O	N	I	N	C	L	L
I	N	C	R	E	D	I	B	L	E	L	L	S

359

F	A	C	T	O	R	L	S	R	S	R	S	M	I	N
A	D	T	M	E	V	O	B	S	U	N	I	M		
A	D	M	U	L	D	I	V	O	L	F	A	C		
D	I	V	I	S	I	O	N	P	P	D	I	V		
M	T	C	D	C	E	D	W	E	I	L	R	T		
I	O	S	T	E	R	G	O	H	P	P	C	P		
R	N	D	S	L	L	S	U	H	L	B	R	L		
T	P	L	M	N	U	S	F	C	A	R	T	A		
S	U	B	T	R	A	C	T	I	O	N	S	Y		
S	U	B	A	B	D	I	V	M	U	L	F	A		
M	U	L	T	I	P	L	Y	C	E	N	L	G		

357

W	R	X	N	D	A	L	L	R	E	R	C	B
H	X	T	D	E	Z	O	G	N	I	S	X	R
X	S	X	I	X	U	B	M	O	X	S	P	E
N	R	O	S	H	R	R	T	P	L	A	Y	H
M	S	C	C	C	E	D	W	E	L	L	R	O
E	N	J	O	Y	R	T	H	R	I	V	E	W
C	R	D	V	L	L	S	U	H	S	B	A	E
T	W	P	E	R	F	O	R	M	R	N	D	I
C	A	C	R	L	L	D	H	C	C	G	S	Y
E	N	D	G	U	T	S	U	C	C	E	E	D
X	Y	W	X	A	X	O	X	W	E	L	L	S

360

P	L	P	L	S	H	O	V	E	L	S	W	A
I	W	R	E	C	N	H	S	H	R	L	O	H
C	H	M	A	R	P	L	R	E	I	S	V	I
K	S	C	R	E	D	R	I	S	H	V	E	L
W	R	N	C	W	R	E	N	C	H	C	K	P
S	I	S	T	D	H	M	A	R	A	E	S	W
R	S	C	R	R	D	R	V	E	M	R	I	A
E	H	M	A	I	M	R	E	S	M	H	V	S
I	C	K	P	V	L	H	M	A	E	R	E	M
L	N	D	S	E	S	H	R	O	R	V	E	L
P	L	R	E	R	S	C	R	W	R	I	V	R

358

B	O	K	N	D	M	A	G	A	B	O	O	S
T	B	L	D	O	A	I	D	P	O	S	S	T
F	L	R	E	I	G	N	S	E	L	A	P	A
N	E	W	S	P	A	P	E	R	T	N	A	B
M	A	G	Z	A	Z	N	E	I	S	I	R	L
P	O	S	N	S	I	G	N	B	K	O	O	O
S	G	N	S	L	N	T	V	A	L	I	O	I
T	B	A	Y	R	E	Y	L	F	R	N	D	D
P	S	T	O	K	O	B	N	E	S	W	A	P
Z	I	G	A	M	A	B	L	O	D	I	B	A
B	O	O	K	A	P	O	S	T	E	R	L	S

361 infatuation, heartache, embrace, date, flirting, kiss, fidelity

I	N	F	A	T	U	A	T	I	O	N	C	B
K	V	O	L	H	R	E	A	M	C	H	A	W
H	E	A	R	T	A	C	H	E	D	T	A	E
I	N	F	R	U	R	I	W	N	S	M	I	S
E	M	B	R	A	C	E	G	G	O	L	E	V
E	M	R	A	C	B	E	K	S	S	F	L	I
D	A	T	E	N	F	L	I	R	T	I	N	G
H	R	T	C	H	E	A	F	B	R	A	E	M
K	I	S	S	F	L	R	T	I	N	F	K	R
F	I	D	L	T	Y	I	H	H	E	R	A	T
L	V	E	F	I	D	E	L	I	T	Y	N	S

362 snow, rain, mild, cold, wind, hurricane, hot

W	O	N	S	D	W	N	S	O	E	R	N	A
H	U	R	C	S	R	E	H	U	N	I	A	R
M	I	L	D	T	C	B	K	L	P	S	P	E
N	J	I	T	H	R	R	T	P	M	N	N	H
M	S	C	O	L	D	D	W	I	D	N	R	O
T	I	S	L	P	R	G	B	W	R	N	C	Y
C	R	D	S	L	L	S	U	H	S	B	A	E
T	W	I	N	D	R	H	A	P	R	N	D	I
H	R	R	U	C	N	E	H	C	H	R	U	Y
S	N	W	O	H	U	R	R	I	C	A	N	E
H	O	T	M	L	D	S	N	W	R	N	S	S

363 hood, motor, wheel, trunk, brake, headlight, windshield

M	R	T	O	H	R	D	W	N	D	S	H	I
T	W	H	E	E	L	L	C	S	T	H	R	R
O	I	B	R	A	R	B	R	O	T	O	M	T
R	N	O	T	D	R	R	T	P	M	O	N	N
M	D	C	D	L	E	D	W	E	L	D	R	R
O	S	S	T	I	R	G	R	B	R	N	C	K
R	H	D	S	G	L	S	U	R	S	B	A	B
T	I	H	Y	H	T	H	A	A	R	N	C	R
H	E	C	S	T	R	U	N	K	C	G	S	K
D	L	D	S	U	T	H	R	E	S	H	D	E
O	D	W	H	E	L	E	T	R	U	K	M	S

364 sitcom, series, documentary, news, interview, reality, nature

S	T	C	O	M	S	D	O	M	C	U	M	I
H	R	S	E	R	I	E	S	N	W	V	E	N
N	T	I	R	E	U	B	W	R	B	B	L	T
N	A	T	U	R	E	R	E	P	M	R	B	E
M	S	C	D	C	E	D	N	E	L	E	R	R
E	I	O	T	E	R	G	O	W	R	A	S	V
C	R	M	S	L	L	S	U	H	S	L	T	I
T	R	L	E	I	T	Y	A	T	R	I	C	E
I	T	N	Y	V	R	I	E	W	S	T	O	W
D	O	C	U	M	E	N	T	A	R	Y	M	V
D	O	M	C	U	T	R	A	N	E	S	W	S

365 day, night, morning, noon, evening, twilight, dawn

M	R	N	N	I	N	G	N	G	G	H	T	S
T	W	I	L	I	G	H	T	B	N	D	Y	A
E	V	N	I	N	G	E	V	O	I	S	P	O
N	G	H	T	H	G	I	G	T	N	D	A	V
T	W	I	D	L	G	H	T	T	R	M	E	O
E	N	W	A	D	G	E	R	N	O	O	N	C
D	W	A	Y	N	M	R	N	O	M	I	I	N
T	W	I	G	H	T	L	V	E	N	N	G	I
M	R	N	I	N	G	N	O	O	T	G	H	B
E	V	E	N	I	N	G	R	M	S	H	T	X
E	V	M	O	R	N	G	H	T	L	G	H	T

366 Chicago, Detroit, Atlanta, Miami, Dallas, Boston, Hartford

C	H	C	G	O	B	R	T	N	D	E	T	H
A	T	L	N	T	A	B	D	L	L	A	S	A
C	H	I	C	A	G	O	M	I	C	H	P	R
N	W	I	S	C	N	S	N	M	M	I	A	T
M	I	C	H	I	C	T	G	O	A	T	L	F
H	O	D	E	T	R	O	I	T	I	P	C	O
C	R	A	S	L	L	N	U	H	I	O	A	R
T	W	L	M	N	N	E	S	T	A	H	R	D
A	T	L	A	N	T	A	H	A	R	T	F	O
B	N	A	S	S	C	A	R	O	B	H	L	K
D	Y	S	X	A	M	I	A	M	I	L	W	S

367 Paris, Rome, Berlin, Madrid, London, Geneva, Lisbon

P	R	I	S	R	O	L	E	A	T	H	N	S
L	N	D	P	A	R	I	S	L	N	D	O	N
B	R	L	I	N	U	S	L	S	B	O	N	A
G	N	E	V	E	A	B	D	T	R	O	I	T
R	M	O	D	R	E	O	P	R	I	S	M	A
A	M	S	N	O	D	N	O	L	A	E	A	R
D	A	M	S	M	L	S	U	H	S	B	D	E
L	I	S	B	E	R	L	I	N	R	N	R	I
G	N	E	E	V	A	P	R	I	S	G	I	T
G	N	D	R	I	D	H	L	I	S	H	D	X
M	G	E	N	E	V	A	B	R	E	L	I	N

368 China, France, Germany, Switzerland, Algeria, Italy, Argentina

A	R	G	E	N	T	I	N	A	A	L	C	E
F	R	N	C	E	Z	T	F	R	N	C	H	E
I	T	G	A	L	Y	A	L	G	E	R	I	A
L	R	E	M	N	Y	L	C	H	N	A	N	C
A	R	R	G	E	N	Y	T	I	N	A	A	A
A	L	M	G	E	R	I	A	B	R	T	A	N
M	R	A	N	A	C	O	P	O	R	G	A	L
E	C	N	A	R	F	F	R	N	E	C	D	H
C	A	Y	A	M	R	I	A	C	C	D	N	A
A	R	G	N	T	N	A	I	T	L	I	Y	S
S	W	I	T	Z	E	R	L	A	N	D	L	S

369 Wisconsin, Iowa, Texas, California, Alabama, Nebraska, Montana

W	I	S	C	T	E	X	M	I	C	H	I	G
H	A	W	A	S	S	I	M	N	T	A	N	A
W	I	W	I	S	C	O	N	S	I	N	O	H
C	A	L	I	F	R	W	N	I	A	E	N	M
T	X	A	T	E	X	A	S	E	L	B	R	O
A	L	A	B	M	A	A	L	A	B	R	M	N
V	C	A	L	I	F	O	R	N	I	A	C	T
O	R	G	O	N	I	L	N	O	I	S	A	A
N	B	R	A	S	K	A	N	E	B	K	S	N
W	S	C	O	N	T	A	M	A	B	A	L	A
W	A	S	N	G	T	O	N	S	T	T	A	S

370 mathematics, chemistry, history, English, geography, physics, biology

M	P	H	S	C	S	S	C	I	S	Y	H	P
A	C	H	H	M	I	S	T	R	Y	G	E	O
T	B	I	L	O	G	Y	M	C	A	T	H	G
H	E	N	G	B	L	I	S	H	M	A	T	E
E	N	G	L	I	S	H	H	E	S	T	R	O
M	I	S	T	O	R	I	O	M	G	E	O	G
A	W	R	I	L	L	S	I	I	N	G	A	R
T	C	H	E	O	M	T	I	S	T	R	Y	A
I	M	T	H	G	L	O	H	T	H	S	S	P
C	N	D	S	Y	T	R	R	R	S	H	L	H
S	T	R	Y	A	B	Y	T	Y	C	L	L	Y

371 (1) kitchen, (2) horoscope, (3) breath, (4) school, (5) sky, (6) broom, (7) tomorrow

K	K	I	T	C	H	E	N	I	T	C	H	N
H	R	O	M	A	K	T	M	O	V	H	R	E
H	O	R	O	S	C	O	P	E	K	S	Y	B
S	C	H	L	O	L	S	C	H	B	R	O	M
M	T	O	M	O	R	R	O	W	L	L	R	C
B	R	T	H	B	R	M	O	H	R	O	S	C
B	R	E	A	T	H	S	S	K	Y	S	Y	K
K	T	C	H	N	E	V	N	T	R	N	D	I
B	R	O	O	M	T	M	R	R	W	O	R	A
M	O	R	R	B	K	T	C	H	B	R	M	O
A	S	C	S	C	H	O	O	L	E	C	H	S

372 (1) bank, (2) mother, (3) father, (4) marriage, (5) job, (6) diploma, (7) gasoline

B	A	N	K	M	T	R	R	E	H	T	O	M
D	P	L	M	Y	M	V	R	A	J	N	Y	M
G	S	L	N	E	G	A	F	A	T	H	E	R
B	O	J	T	H	R	M	R	R	G	M	E	K
M	T	H	R	F	T	H	R	B	N	K	G	S
D	V	D	I	P	L	O	M	A	B	J	N	K
D	P	L	M	M	R	R	G	G	S	L	N	E
B	N	K	M	T	H	R	V	N	R	N	D	I
C	A	M	A	R	R	I	A	G	E	G	S	Y
E	G	S	S	L	N	N	M	M	D	N	J	K
G	A	S	O	L	I	N	E	M	F	T	H	S

373 (1) week, (2) son, (3) castle, (4) cinema, (5) teacher, (6) lawyer, (7) dentist

T	C	H	R	T	C	H	R	C	S	R	L	E
H	N	T	E	A	C	H	E	R	T	H	X	R
W	T	K	C	I	N	M	L	W	Y	R	P	E
N	S	K	T	H	R	R	T	P	M	N	N	H
M	C	C	S	C	T	W	E	E	K	L	E	B
T	E	A	C	I	H	R	C	S	T	L	E	S
N	S	S	O	N	L	W	R	E	Y	W	A	L
J	T	T	Y	E	C	S	T	L	T	L	W	Y
S	N	L	S	M	L	D	E	N	T	I	S	T
T	C	E	S	A	H	H	R	H	S	H	L	P
B	E	Y	N	M	B	R	M	W	K	E	E	M

374 (1) year, (2) daughter, (3) gallery, (4) sculpture, (5) judge, (6) doctor, (7) students

S	R	Y	N	D	S	C	U	L	M	R	C	B
C	X	E	H	E	Z	W	F	B	T	H	X	R
U	S	A	H	G	U	W	M	O	S	S	P	E
L	R	R	T	D	A	U	G	H	T	E	R	H
P	S	C	D	U	E	D	A	E	U	L	R	O
T	I	S	T	J	R	G	L	W	D	N	C	Y
U	R	D	S	L	L	S	L	H	E	B	A	E
R	D	G	H	H	T	R	E	V	N	N	F	I
E	A	C	S	L	L	D	R	O	T	C	O	D
S	T	D	N	T	T	H	Y	H	S	H	L	X
S	C	U	L	B	T	R	E	S	C	L	L	B

377 (1) minutes, (2) hand, (3) bed, (4) potatoes, (5) milk, (6) stadium, (7) skyscraper

S	K	S	C	R	A	H	P	R	S	K	S	C
P	T	T	S	M	L	A	S	D	D	K	K	S
S	S	N	D	M	I	N	U	T	E	S	P	E
T	C	S	H	R	D	T	P	B	P	T	T	
A	S	C	D	S	K	P	K	S	L	R	O	
D	S	C	R	E	R	G	N	H	N	N	H	K
I	R	P	O	T	A	T	O	E	S	S	K	L
U	P	T	T	T	L	K	M	S	C	R	P	I
M	A	C	S	K	Y	P	H	P	R	S	S	M
M	V	T	S	U	R	T	M	N	T	H	L	M
S	S	K	Y	S	C	R	A	P	E	R	K	Y

375 (1) months, (2) uncle, (3) museum, (4) athlete, (5) jury, (6) nurse, (7) husband

U	N	M	U	S	E	U	M	R	E	R	C	B
L	E	O	H	E	Z	O	F	B	T	H	X	R
C	U	N	C	L	E	B	M	O	X	S	P	E
N	M	T	T	H	R	R	T	V	Y	N	N	H
A	T	H	L	E	T	E	W	N	R	L	R	O
N	R	S	T	B	T	G	O	N	U	R	S	E
H	S	B	N	D	L	S	U	H	J	B	A	E
H	W	H	U	S	B	A	N	D	R	N	D	I
A	A	T	H	L	L	T	E	J	R	Y	J	R
L	S	E	M	U	M	N	T	H	S	H	S	B
M	S	R	R	T	H	A	L	N	R	S	E	S

378 (1) seconds, (2) leg, (3) radio, (4) beans, (5) coffee, (6) court, (7) truck

C	O	U	R	T	A	L	L	R	E	R	C	B
O	T	T	R	C	K	R	L	G	B	T	R	U
F	C	F	F	V	E	A	C	F	E	F	E	V
F	S	O	T	H	R	D	T	P	A	N	N	H
E	O	C	D	G	E	I	W	T	N	R	C	K
E	R	T	S	E	C	O	N	D	S	C	R	T
R	A	C	C	L	S	C	V	H	S	T	R	E
V	E	H	Y	H	T	H	A	T	R	N	D	I
V	E	C	S	C	R	T	T	R	K	C	S	Y
E	L	G	T	R	T	H	T	R	U	C	K	C
E	Y	W	X	A	V	R	C	S	R	D	D	O

376 (1) hours, (2) arm, (3) cane, (4) meat, (5) blueprint, (6) mall, (7) tent

B	L	P	R	N	A	C	B	L	P	R	N	T
H	O	U	R	S	T	A	Y	M	L	L	M	H
B	L	P	M	L	L	N	B	L	P	M	L	L
N	M	T	T	M	M	E	A	T	M	N	N	H
B	L	P	C	N	B	N	R	T	N	N	X	C
B	L	P	B	L	P	G	M	A	L	L	B	W
H	R	U	O	S	C	T	U	Q	S	B	L	A
T	B	L	U	E	P	R	I	N	T	M	P	I
B	L	P	R	N	T	B	L	C	E	G	S	Y
M	T	B	L	P	T	H	R	H	N	H	L	B
H	R	B	L	M	L	N	X	W	T	L	B	S

379 (1) roof, (2) chair, (3) ballet, (4) salad, (5) water, (6) hall, (7) beach

B	L	L	T	B	L	L	T	H	L	L	A	H
W	T	R	R	F	B	C	C	H	D	B	L	L
T	C	H	R	R	F	B	H	S	A	L	D	S
N	R	O	O	F	R	B	A	L	L	E	T	H
R	F	C	H	B	L	W	I	S	A	L	D	A
C	H	R	W	A	T	E	R	W	S	N	C	H
B	L	L	T	S	L	D	W	T	R	B	C	A
D	L	S	W	T	R	R	F	C	G	B	D	L
B	L	L	C	H	S	L	B	C	C	G	S	L
R	F	B	E	A	C	H	R	H	S	H	L	X
B	L	L	T	C	H	S	L	D	W	T	R	C

380 (1) window, (2) keyboard, (3) symphony, (4) hamburger, (5) joke, (6) classroom, (7) ears

W	I	N	D	O	W	W	N	D	W	R	C	B
K	Y	B	R	D	S	M	P	H	N	Y	J	K
C	L	S	S	R	M	K	H	M	B	R	G	R
K	Y	B	R	D	R	E	T	P	M	J	K	S
S	Y	M	P	H	S	Y	M	P	H	O	N	Y
S	Y	M	P	H	H	B	M	B	G	K	E	R
C	L	A	S	S	R	O	O	M	P	E	A	E
H	M	B	R	G	R	A	S	Y	M	P	H	A
C	H	A	M	B	U	R	G	E	R	K	Y	R
B	R	D	C	L	S	D	R	M	M	C	L	S
C	L	S	S	H	M	B	G	R	R	R	M	S

383 (1) attractive, (2) funny, (3) smart, (4) lucky, (5) valid, (6) nearly, (7) besides

A	T	T	R	A	C	T	I	V	E	C	T	V
C	T	V	B	S	D	S	N	R	L	Y	S	M
B	L	C	K	Y	U	B	V	L	D	V	L	T
E	F	N	N	L	F	N	N	Y	M	N	N	R
S	V	L	F	U	N	N	Y	E	L	E	R	A
I	I	S	T	C	R	G	T	W	R	A	O	M
D	R	D	S	K	B	S	F	H	S	R	A	S
E	A	R	Y	Y	V	L	A	T	R	L	D	I
S	A	C	Y	K	Y	D	H	C	C	Y	S	Y
T	T	R	C	T	V	V	L	D	N	R	Y	L
V	A	L	I	D	B	S	D	F	N	N	Y	S

381 (1) large, (2) happy, (3) faithful, (4) difficult, (5) wealthy, (6) feeble, (7) clever

H	A	P	P	Y	A	F	E	E	B	L	E	B
H	P	P	Y	F	B	L	H	P	P	Y	F	B
D	F	F	C	L	T	D	F	F	C	L	T	E
L	A	R	G	E	L	R	G	E	W	L	T	H
C	L	V	R	F	T	H	F	L	F	T	H	F
D	I	F	F	I	C	U	L	T	R	N	C	W
C	R	C	L	V	R	W	L	T	H	Y	A	S
W	E	A	L	T	H	Y	A	H	P	P	Y	T
D	F	F	C	L	T	D	C	L	E	V	E	R
L	R	G	C	L	V	R	W	L	U	H	D	F
F	A	I	T	H	F	U	L	F	B	B	L	E

384 (1) brave, (2) contrary, (3) destiny, (4) eager, (5) foolish, (6) gratuity, (7) handsome

G	R	G	G	R	A	H	N	D	S	M	C	E
D	S	T	R	B	R	O	F	L	S	H	X	A
L	F	H	A	H	U	B	B	R	V	S	P	G
C	O	N	T	R	A	R	Y	W	V	R	N	E
M	O	C	U	C	E	A	W	E	L	L	R	R
G	L	S	I	E	R	V	O	W	R	N	C	W
T	I	D	T	L	D	E	S	T	I	N	Y	E
R	S	H	Y	D	S	T	N	Y	R	N	D	U
A	H	C	N	T	R	Y	E	G	R	D	S	T
C	N	T	R	G	R	T	V	Y	F	L	S	H
U	Y	H	A	N	D	S	O	M	E	G	R	T

382 (1) normal, (2) courteous, (3) little, (4) scarce, (5) famous, (6) secure, (7) empty

N	R	M	L	S	C	R	E	N	R	M	L	L
N	O	R	M	A	L	V	S	E	C	U	R	E
C	R	T	C	R	T	L	T	L	L	E	S	C
N	C	O	U	R	T	E	O	U	S	N	N	H
F	M	S	C	P	T	Y	S	C	R	C	L	T
E	L	T	T	I	L	G	S	C	A	R	C	E
N	R	M	L	V	R	M	L	S	V	R	S	C
C	R	T	T	C	C	R	R	T	T	F	M	M
F	A	M	O	U	S	N	R	M	L	S	S	C
M	V	T	V	F	M	S	Y	T	P	M	E	N
C	R	T	C	R	T	L	T	T	L	L	S	C

385 (1) perhaps, (2) movie, (3) midday, (4) obsolete, (5) comment, (6) choose, (7) peak

P	K	P	K	P	A	L	C	H	O	O	S	E
M	O	V	I	E	V	M	M	V	P	K	P	K
V	R	H	H	R	M	B	C	O	B	S	O	P
O	B	S	L	H	M	V	O	C	H	S	A	E
M	I	D	D	A	Y	D	M	E	L	L	C	A
P	R	S	T	P	R	G	M	W	R	N	C	K
C	R	O	B	S	O	L	E	T	E	B	A	E
O	B	S	L	T	T	H	N	C	M	M	V	T
V	R	H	S	L	L	D	T	C	C	G	S	Y
O	B	S	L	T	O	B	P	L	T	G	T	R
P	H	R	P	S	P	R	H	P	S	P	R	H

386 (1) over, (2) cease, (3) leave, (4) present, (5) rabbit, (6) trash, (7) carpet

C	R	P	N	D	P	L	E	R	E	R	C	B
V	O	O	V	E	R	O	V	R	B	B	T	R
C	S	E	V	A	E	C	A	O	R	S	P	E
N	R	O	T	E	S	A	E	C	M	N	R	V
C	R	P	P	T	E	D	L	E	L	L	A	W
C	T	R	S	H	N	T	R	S	H	N	B	Z
C	T	D	S	L	T	S	Z	H	S	B	B	E
T	R	T	R	S	H	R	B	B	T	N	I	R
C	A	R	P	E	T	D	H	C	C	G	T	Y
E	S	P	R	S	N	T	L	V	B	B	R	R
R	H	B	B	T	P	R	S	N	T	L	L	S

387 (1) shut, (2) cook, (3) answer, (4) require, (5) arrive, (6) purchase, (7) comprehend

A	R	R	I	V	E	L	L	C	E	R	C	C
A	N	S	W	R	P	R	C	O	H	S	R	O
R	Q	R	H	C	M	P	R	O	H	N	D	M
P	R	A	C	H	R	R	T	K	M	N	N	P
M	S	N	R	Q	R	E	N	S	W	R	Q	R
R	Q	S	H	U	T	R	Q	R	R	N	C	E
C	K	W	R	R	V	C	K	C	M	P	A	H
P	R	E	C	H	S	C	K	T	R	N	D	E
P	R	R	E	Q	U	I	R	E	C	G	S	N
V	P	R	C	H	S	S	E	P	R	H	L	D
P	U	R	C	H	A	S	E	C	K	C	K	P

388 (1) excellent, (2) strange, (3) arrogant, (4) ruined, (5) proceed, (6) propose, (7) admit

P	R	A	D	M	I	T	C	D	E	R	R	P
R	R	G	N	T	R	N	D	S	Q	R	U	Q
E	S	X	C	L	L	N	T	P	E	R	I	E
P	P	O	T	H	A	R	R	O	G	A	N	T
R	R	P	S	E	E	X	C	E	N	L	E	O
E	O	R	R	G	N	T	R	W	A	N	D	X
D	C	R	R	V	N	L	L	E	R	N	T	V
T	E	X	C	E	L	L	E	N	T	N	D	V
R	E	P	R	P	S	D	H	C	S	G	S	P
E	D	X	C	L	L	N	T	S	T	R	N	G
S	D	R	P	R	O	P	O	S	E	N	G	E

389 (1) refute, (2) mislead, (3) disloyalty, (4) fondness, (5) vanity, (6) success, (7) popular

D	I	S	L	O	Y	A	L	T	Y	R	C	C
F	N	D	N	S	S	P	P	L	R	P	V	R
M	S	L	D	R	F	T	D	S	L	S	A	V
V	N	T	R	E	F	U	T	E	N	N	N	Y
M	S	C	A	C	E	D	G	E	L	L	I	O
M	I	S	L	E	A	D	O	W	R	N	T	G
S	C	D	U	S	C	C	S	S	S	L	Y	E
P	P	L	P	R	C	V	A	S	R	N	D	G
D	S	F	O	N	D	N	E	S	S	G	S	Y
E	S	D	P	U	C	H	R	H	S	H	L	X
V	S	L	Y	S	U	C	C	E	S	S	L	S

390 (1) construct, (2) abolish, (3) remark, (4) escape, (5) gather, (6) dispose, (7) evidence

G	T	R	N	G	A	T	H	E	R	R	C	R
H	C	T	H	P	Z	O	V	V	T	H	D	R
V	O	D	S	B	L	S	H	I	R	M	I	K
D	N	G	T	H	R	R	T	D	M	N	S	G
E	S	C	A	P	E	D	W	E	L	L	P	O
E	T	B	L	S	H	H	B	N	R	N	O	H
C	R	E	M	A	R	K	U	C	S	B	S	S
T	U	S	C	P	C	N	S	E	R	N	E	C
C	C	N	S	T	R	C	T	S	C	P	Q	P
E	T	V	D	N	C	D	S	P	S	D	L	H
R	M	R	K	A	B	O	L	I	S	H	L	D

391 (1) good, (2) safe, (3) common, (4) difficult, (5) begin, (6) give, (7) come

G	G	O	O	D	A	S	A	F	E	R	C	M
D	X	T	H	E	D	F	F	C	L	T	G	V
S	C	O	M	M	O	N	M	O	B	G	N	S
D	F	F	C	L	T	B	G	N	G	V	C	M
D	F	F	D	I	F	F	I	C	U	L	T	F
G	D	D	F	F	B	G	C	M	M	G	V	R
D	F	F	G	D	S	F	L	T	Y	G	V	M
N	B	B	E	G	I	N	G	N	G	V	C	M
B	G	N	G	V	D	G	S	G	I	V	E	Y
D	F	F	C	L	T	H	R	H	S	H	L	D
F	F	D	L	C	C	O	M	E	M	M	L	S

392 (1) disorganized, (2) late, (3) ordinary, (4) interesting, (5) decrease, (6) prohibit, (7) unite

```
D I S O R G A N I Z E D B
D S R G N Z D D S R G N R
L T U N I T E D D E T A L
P R H B T N T R S T I N G
O R D I N A R Y D R N R N
M C R S S R D S R G V Z D
Q I N T E R E S T I N G Q
D S R G N Z D P R H B T O
N T D E C R E A S E D S R
D C R S P R H B T N T R L
P R O H I B I T L A T L S
```

393 (1) clean, (2) short, (3) country, (4) strong, (5) under, (6) right, (7) never

```
C L N N D R R G H T N V R
C N C L E A N G R Y S T R
N G O F T L B M U N D E R
N R U T S R R T P E N O I
V S N D H E D V E V L R G
T S T R O N G V W E N C H
S H R S R L S B N R B R T
C W Y Y T G H A T R N D V
Q W R T P S F B N M M N B
T R R T P Y Y P M N N M V
S W V B A L O L P E Y L S
```

394 (1) soft, (2) below, (3) frown, (4) scarce, (5) ally, (6) artificial, (7) praise

```
P R A I S E L S R S R R S
S C R C E B L C W F R W N
R T F C S L B A L V S P E
N B E L O W R R P M N C U
P S C D F R D C B L L N Z
R T F T T R G E F C R W R
D R D S L L S V H S B O E
A R T I F I C I A L N R L
L P R R P F T T F F T F T
L P R S C R S R T T R L L
Y Y S C R C R T F C L L W
```

395 (1) brave, (2) bold, (3) narrow, (4) borrow, (5) expensive, (6) shallow, (7) contract

```
D L O B D B L D D L B D B
B R V R B R V V B R B C R
N R N A R R O W R W R O E
N R O V H R R O P M N N V
B S C E C E D R E L L T V
R I S T L R G R W R N R W
R R S H A L L O W N R A E
B W R P N S H B T R N C I
C N T R C T D H C C G T Y
E X P E N S I V E S H L X
E X P N S V E X P N S V S
```

396 (1) true, (2) enter, (3) seldom, (4) remember, (5) foolish, (6) found, (7) generous

```
R M B T F L S H R E R C V
R T T R E M E M B E R X R
G N E U R M B M B R S P V
N R G E N E R O U S N N H
G N R S C N D W E E L R O
R M B M B T R M E L B R V
G N R S L E H G N D R S E
R M M B R R H A F O U N D
S L D M G N R V S M V N S
G N R S E N T R R M B B R
F O O L I S H F N D S L D
```

397 (1) ignorance, (2) strict, (3) minimum, (4) minor, (5) freeze, (6) quiet, (7) drunk

```
M N I N F R Z L D F R Z B
H G G Q U T T F R E E Z E
M I N O R U B M U D R N K
I D O D R N K T N S T R C
N R R Q U E T W K L L R O
I N A T E Q S T R S T R Q
M K N S L U F R Z I G N O
U S C Y H I M I M M I M N
M T E S L E D H L C M S N
I G N S S T R I C T I G N
M N M M N R M N M M M N R
```

289

398 (1) sweet, (2) sunny, (3) vacant, (4) voluntary, (5) yang, (6) placid, (7) lethargic

S	S	S	U	N	N	Y	P	R	E	R	C	B
W	N	W	P	V	L	A	L	V	T	H	X	R
T	N	E	L	N	T	N	C	O	Y	N	A	G
S	Y	E	C	T	H	G	D	L	M	N	N	H
W	S	T	D	R	R	D	P	U	S	W	S	T
T	N	V	T	Y	G	G	L	N	Y	P	G	
S	N	C	V	A	C	A	N	T	V	C	L	T
W	Y	N	Y	H	T	H	A	A	Y	N	A	G
T	S	T	L	E	T	H	A	R	G	I	C	Y
S	N	N	S	T	T	H	R	Y	S	H	I	X
W	Y	G	D	S	C	O	D	S	W	W	D	S

399 (1) past, (2) apathy, (3) profound, (4) nice, (5) punishment, (6) receive, (7) provide

R	R	E	C	E	I	V	E	R	E	R	P	S
C	P	N	S	H	M	N	T	P	N	S	R	R
V	P	R	V	D	P	R	V	D	R	S	O	E
P	R	O	A	P	A	T	H	Y	M	N	V	H
T	S	C	D	A	P	N	S	H	M	N	I	T
P	P	R	O	F	O	U	N	D	R	N	D	T
H	R	D	S	T	L	S	I	H	S	B	E	E
Y	W	H	Y	T	H	C	T	R	N	D	K	
P	U	N	I	S	H	M	E	N	T	G	S	Y
R	N	D	P	R	V	D	P	N	S	M	N	T
V	Y	W	P	M	S	N	V	P	A	S	T	S

400 (1) genuine, (2) succumb, (3) grab, (4) phony, (5) advantage, (6) donate, (7) arrogance

G	E	N	A	R	R	D	N	D	V	A	C	P
S	G	E	N	U	I	N	E	G	R	B	S	H
U	R	D	V	V	V	A	E	P	H	Y	P	O
C	A	R	R	O	G	A	N	C	E	N	N	N
M	B	R	R	G	N	C	N	E	N	T	G	Y
B	I	S	D	O	N	A	T	E	R	N	C	W
A	R	D	S	L	L	S	T	H	S	B	A	N
A	D	V	A	N	T	A	G	E	R	N	D	I
C	S	U	C	M	B	G	P	H	N	Y	D	
N	N	D	S	T	B	C	C	O	M	B	G	G
S	U	C	C	U	M	B	G	R	N	R	B	B

401 KNIVES: Clockwise, each singular word is followed by its plural: LIFE—LIVES, KNIFE—KNIVES

402 LA (musical note) or AD (advertisement): Clockwise, a letter is removed to make a legitimate word each time: GLAND—GLAD—LAD—LA or AD

403 WRITE-OFF: Counterclockwise, "OFF" is added to the previous word to form a compound word: SPIN—SPIN-OFF, WRITE—WRITE-OFF

404 SLIVER: Clockwise, a letter is added on to the previous word to produce a new legitimate word (LIVE—LIVER—SLIVER—SLIVERS); vice versa, counterclockwise a letter is taken away (SLIVERS—SLIVER—LIVER—LIVE)

405 SAILS: Opposite each other, the pairs are noun with corresponding verb. So, if a DRIVER—DRIVES then a SAILOR—SAILS

406 TWILIGHT: Clockwise, each word is followed by its more poetic (figurative) synonym: MORNING—DAWN, EVENING—TWILIGHT

407 STRAW: Opposite each other, the pair of words can be read forward and backward: DEVIL—LIVED, WARTS—STRAW

408 BRAVE: Opposite each other, the pairs consist of an adjective and its corresponding noun form: HAPPY—HAPPINESS, BRAVE—BRAVERY

409 WORST: Clockwise, each pair consists of an adjective and its superlative form: GOOD—BEST, BAD—WORST

410 FLIP: Clockwise, the initial letter is changed to make a new word each time. These four words are the only possible ones: BLIP—SLIP—CLIP—FLIP

411 EVIL: These are all anagrams. Remember? They were discussed illustratively in the chapter on anagrams: LIVE—VEIL—VILE—EVIL

412 A: DES+PER+A+TION = DESPERATION

413 E: G+O+N+E = GONE

414 HEXAGON: The words refer to geometrical figures that are increasing in number of sides: TRIANGLE (three sides)—SQUARE (four sides)—PENTAGON (five sides)—HEXAGON (six sides)

415 HEARTS: The words refer to the four suits of cards

416 UN: The word in the top left box is broken up into its components in the remaining boxes: UNHAPPINESS = UN+HAPPY+NESS

417 EYES/FEET/KNEES/HANDS/and other possibilities: We have two of each of these: ARMS, LEGS, EARS, EYES

418 FRANCE: The four countries in the boxes border one another

419 EARTH: The boxes contain the words referring to the classical four elements

420 CE: SINCERELY = SIN+CE+RE+LY

421 COMPASSION belongs to the right side along with LOVE and VALOR, which are traits and emotions; CHARITY belongs to the left side, since it is one of the three theological virtues along with FAITH and HOPE.

422 PARALLELOGRAM belongs to the right side along with the other four-sided figures; ACUTE belongs to the left side along with the other types of triangles.

423 CHILDREN belongs to the right side along with the other words referring to groups of people of indefinite size; PAIRS belongs to the left side along with the other words referring to two people.

424 MAINE belongs to the right side along with the other states; DETROIT belongs to the left side along with the other cities.

425 GRANADA belongs to the right side along with the other cities that are not capitals; ROME belongs to the left side along with the other capital cities.

426 MOON belongs to the right side along with the other nonplanetary bodies; EARTH belongs to the left side along with the other planets.

427 WATER belongs to the right side along with the other drinks; SUGAR belongs to the left side along with the other condiments.

428 CAT belongs to the right side along with the other words that end in a consonant; ORCHESTRA belongs to the left side along with the other words that end in a vowel.

429 MEAN belongs to the right side along with the other four-letter words; TOP belongs to the left side along with the other three-letter words.

430 MATISSE belongs to the right side along with the other painters; PIRANDELLO belongs to the left side along with the other writers.

431 Top row: JACKET—SHORTS—PAJAMAS refer to clothing items

432 Left column: POPCORN—BREAD—ARTICHOKE refer to food items

433 Middle row: TENNIS—GOLF—SOCCER refer to sports

434 Middle column: FIND—MOVE—SEND are all verbs

435 Bottom row: TOO—FREE—TATTOO all end in a double vowel

436 Right column: BILL—OFF—PURR all end in a double consonant

437 Left diagonal: NEVER—NOBODY—NOTHING are negative words

438 Right diagonal: SILLY—ALLY—JELLY all end in -LLY

439 Top row: CRIME—SCENE—INVESTIGATION: the three words together refer to the title of a television crime story genre or to a procedure in crime detection: crime scene investigation

440 Left column: ROCK—AND—ROLL: the three words together refer to a musical genre: rock and roll

441 CUP. Category: table items; pattern from top to bottom: 6-letter word (NAPKIN)—5-letter word (SPOON)—4-letter word (FORK)—3-letter word (CUP)

442 SPECIAL. Category: adjectives; pattern from top to bottom: all adjectives end in -IAL

443 FIVE. Category: odd numbers in no particular order; pattern from top to bottom: the numbers end in a vowel (-E)

444 DECATHLON. Category: sports; pattern from top to bottom: the words start with the first four letters of the alphabet

445 SLUSH. Category: weather conditions; pattern from top to bottom: each word begins with S + consonant

446 DRIVEN. Category: words connected to driving; pattern from top to bottom: all verb forms, whereas DRIVER is a noun

447 BROOCH. Category: jewelry items; pattern from top to bottom: 3-letter word (PIN)—4-letter word (RING)—5-letter word (WATCH)—6-letter word (BROOCH)

448 POUND. Category: currencies; pattern from top to bottom: all words end in a consonant

449 FORTY. Category: cardinal numbers; pattern from top to bottom: each word consists of five letters

450 ITALIAN. Category: languages; pattern from top to bottom: all the words end in a consonant

451 GOOD
goad
GOAL

452 WINTER
winner
DINNER

453 BALL
balk
bark
PARK

454 LOVE
lave
have
HATE

455 SCARY
scare
stare
store
STORY

456 MALE
mile
milk
mink
pink
PUNK

457 FLIP
clip
clap
clay
play
pray
TRAY

458 LIVER
lived
loved
lover
lower
POWER

459 SPILL
still
stall
stale
scale
scape
SCOPE

460 BRAVE
crave
crane
crank
clank
plank
PLUNK

461 SMALL
malls (anagram)
mulls
PULLS

462 PLATES
staple (anagram)
stable
TABLES (anagram)

463 VEIL
live (anagram)
dive
dine
MINE

464 PLAN
clan
clap
clop
chop
shop
stop
POTS (anagram)

465 LOVE
move
more
mare
mart
part
TRAP (anagram)

466 TRAPS
strap (anagram)
straw
warts (anagram)
wards
WORDS

467 FRIEND
finder (anagram)
tinder
tender
rented (anagram)
rested
TESTED

468 SMART
trams (anagram)
traps
parts (anagram)
pants
wants
warts
STRAW (anagram)

469 DEVIL
lived (anagram)
lives
limes
miles (anagram)
mills
KILLS

470 PARTY
parts
strap (anagram)
scrap
scram
crams (anagram)
clams
CLAPS

471 Forget it!

472 A hole in one (golf expression)

473 Double life

474 Once again

475 A bird in the hand is worth two in the bush

476 A foot in both camps

477 Think twice!

478 Time after time **OR** double time

479 Ice cube

480 Too funny for words

481 Head over heels

482 Once upon a time

483 Temporary setback (Temporary is spelled backward)

484 Too good to be true

485 Too many times

486 Splitting hairs

487 Play around **OR** Foreplay

488 Appear before the judge

489 Go online

490 To be or not to be

491 Sam and Gina; Frank and Veronica
This is a simple one, isn't it? If Frank is playing with the other woman, not Gina, then he is paired with Veronica. This leaves Sam and Gina as the other pair.

492 Mark—machinist; Bill—foreman; Jack—accountant
Mark is not the accountant since he cannot stand the accountant (whoever he is). Bill is not the accountant, either, because Mark gets along very well with Bill. So, by the process of elimination, the accountant is Jack. Now, Bill is not the machinist because he and the machinist (whoever he is) earn the same, meaning that they are separate individuals. So, by the process of elimination, Bill is the foreman. This leaves Mark as the machinist.

493 Frank—father; Penny—mother
If Chantelle and Danielle are the youngest of the family, neither one can be the mother, of course. So, the mother is Penny. Similarly, since Will and Phil are not the oldest, they cannot be the father. This leaves Frank as the father.

494 Sunny—father; Funny—mother; Dreamy—daughter
Sunny is not the mother, and because Sunny is the oldest, then Sunny cannot be the daughter (who logically is the youngest). So, by elimination Sunny is the father. Funny is not the daughter. So, again by elimination, Funny is the mother. This leaves Dreamy as the daughter.

495 Wes—drummer; Robert—bassist; Marcel—pianist
We are told that Wes is not the pianist, and we can see that Robert is not the pianist, either, who is an only child, while Robert has a sister. So, the pianist is Marcel. Wes does not play the bass, so he plays the drums and, of course, Robert plays the bass.

496 Gillian
Anna played with someone, so she was not the referee. Bertha and Franca played, as well, so neither of them were the referee. Cathy and Debbie can also be ruled out because they obviously played (being the losers). This leaves Ella or Gillian as the referee. The referee was not an only child, which rules out Ella, who was. This leaves Gillian as the referee.

497 Mr. Red—Ms. Blue; Mr. Green—Ms. Red; Mr. Blue—Ms. Green
No one danced with a partner who wore the same color. Also, Mr. Red did not dance with Ms. Green because, as he himself pointed out, she was dancing with another partner. And Mr. Red did not dance with Ms. Red, because they both wore the color red. So, by elimination, Mr. Red danced with Ms. Blue. Mr. Green did not dance with Ms. Green, of course. So, by process of elimination, he danced with Ms. Red. This leaves Mr. Blue and Ms. Green as the third couple.

498 Nick—publicist; Joe—manager; Gill—technician; Mary—marketer; Shirley—comptroller; Dina—programmer
We are told that Gill is the technician, and that takes care of Gill. Nick, Mary and Dina, being only children, cannot be the comptroller because the comptroller has two sisters. Joe is not the comptroller, either, because he has a brother, not two sisters (like the comptroller). We know that Gill is not the comptroller. So, by process of elimination, the comptroller is Shirley. Of course, Shirley and Gill could be only children, but we have already discovered what their positions are. The only children left to consider are Nick, Mary and Dina. One of them is the programmer. So, Joe, who has a brother, cannot be the programmer. We are told that he is neither the marketer nor the publicist. So, Joe is not the programmer, not the marketer, not the publicist, not the technician (Gill is) and not the comptroller (Shirley is). By elimination, he is the manager. Nick, the male only child, is neither the programmer nor the marketer. This means that he is the publicist (the only position left for him). The positions left for Mary and Dina are programmer and marketer. Dina cannot be the marketer because she works next to her. So, she is the programmer and Mary is the marketer.

499 Paul and Lola; Rob and Barb; Lou and Hillary
Lou and Paul lost, so the male winner was Rob. Rob, therefore, is Barb's husband because she points out that her husband was in the winning couple. Hillary won (meaning that she was paired with Rob). Hillary is not married to Paul (who lost) and, of course, she's not married to Rob, either. So she is married to Lou. This leaves Paul and Lola as the third married couple.

500 Dora—Cam—Nick—Cora—Dick—Nora
Nick is older than Cora. This means that Cora is not the oldest sibling (who is a female). So, either Nora or Dora is the oldest. We are told that Nora is younger than Dick. So, she cannot be the oldest. This leaves Dora as the oldest. Dick is younger than Cora. So, Cora is not the youngest. This leaves Nora as the youngest. We are told that Cam is the second oldest. With knowledge that Nick is older than Cora and Dick is younger than Cora, we can now set up the order easily (shown above): It shows that Dora is the oldest, Nora the youngest, Cam the second oldest, Nick older than Cora, and Dick younger than Cora.